Telling the Truth, Taking Sides

Essays for N. Ram

TELLING THE TRUTH, TAKING SIDES

Essays for N. Ram

Edited by
V.K. Ramachandran
with Madhura Swaminathan

Tulika Books

Published by
Tulika Books
44 (first floor), Shahpur Jat, New Delhi 110 049, India
www.tulikabooks.in

© 2018 Valeria Chomsky, essay by Noam Chomsky titled "Shaping the Post-War World"

© Individual essays, respective authors, 2018

© This collection, the editors of the volume, 2018

First edition (hardback) 2018

ISBN: 978-81-937329-2-2

Printed in India at Chaman Offset, Delhi 110 002

Contents

Preface *V.K. Ramachandran and Madhura Swaminathan* — vii

1. Notes on the Political Economy of Indian Development
   Venkatesh Athreya — 1

2. The Transformation of Mike Bloomberg
   Wayne Barrett — 21

3. The Resilience of Neoliberal Ideology
   C.P. Chandrasekhar — 32

4. Shaping the Post-War World
   Noam Chomsky — 45

5. Promises to Keep: Science and Scientific Temper in India
   T. Jayaraman — 59

6. The Story of Kamala Ratnaveli: Caste in Sri Lanka and Left Intervention
   Kumari Jayawardena — 86

7. The Rise of the Bharatiya Janata Party: Two Essays and an Introduction
   Prakash Karat — 110

8. The Market Economy: Ideology and Reality
   C.T. Kurien — 141

9. A Critique of Economics as a Discipline
   Prabhat Patnaik — 156

10. Gabriel Selvam: A Biography of Work
    V.K. Ramachandran — 171

11. After Snowden
    Alan Rusbridger — 178

12. The Zero Hunger Challenge
    M.S. Swaminathan — 188

13. How the Present Reads the Past
    Romila Thapar — 208

14 Working with N. Ram

    Ram at 70
    John Cherian   225

    The Thinking Intellectual as Editor
    P. Jacob and Suresh Nambath   228

    Working with N. Ram
    Parvathi Menon   231

    Freedom to Function
    Prabhakara S. Motnahalli   235

    There Is No Other Ram
    Nirmal Shekar   240

Contributors   246

Preface

This volume is for N. Ram, journalist, writer, social scientist, researcher in politics and international affairs, cricketer, and public figure and activist of the Left in India.

Ram, now Chairperson of Kasturi and Sons Limited and Publisher of *The Hindu*, was Editor in Chief of *The Hindu* group of publications, including *The Hindu*, *Frontline*, *Sportstar* and *BusinessLine*, whose credo, content and design he revolutionized.

The idea for this festschrift came in 2015, when Ram turned 70. The contributors to this book were given the title of the book and requested to write a piece for Ram. The response was prompt and diverse (although the arrival of articles, in some cases, took time).

We who have lived in Chennai have seen the many worlds that Ram inhabits: the worlds, for example, of the Left in India, of journalism and journalism education, of politics and political personalities more generally, of academia, of science, medicine, music and the arts, sports, and social activism. This book does not – could not – do justice to Ram's scope, but the list of contributors and their distinguished contributions to this volume themselves speak for Ram's unique friendships and career.

We thank Susmita Vinod for help with keying in articles. We are grateful to Mariam Ram for her help and support, to Indira Chandrasekhar of Tulika Books for her editorial encouragement and leadership, to M.V. Bhaskar of TNQ Books and Journals – as always – for his incomparable design ideas and work, and to Samson Duraisamy and V. Shankar for their contributions to the preparation of the final manuscript.

Thiruvananthapuram V.K. RAMACHANDRAN
April 2018 MADHURA SWAMINATHAN

Notes on the Political Economy of Indian Development

Venkatesh Athreya

Introduction

Over the decades that I have been privileged to know and to interact with N. Ram, I have noted that a consistent concern of his has been the nature of the political economy of development in India. This article speaks to that concern.

The growth and development of the Indian economy since Independence can be broadly divided into four phases:

Phase I: The period from 1947 to the crisis of 1965–66
Phase II: The period of relative industrial stagnation, 1966–80
Phase III: The period of growth driven by government expenditure, 1980–90
Phase IV: The period of neoliberal reforms, 1991 till today.

During the first two phases, growth was driven primarily by public investment and import substitution, with limited land reforms also playing a role in expanding the domestic market, though the monopoly of landed property remained pretty much intact. The 1980s marked a turning point, with important changes in the international economy and in national economic policies. The phase of neoliberal reforms since 1991 followed from both the crisis of the path of development broadly pursued since Independence and the emergence of a unipolar world dominated by international finance capital.

In this article, I shall provide an overview of India's economic development since Independence, with particular focus on the current period, from the perspective of Marxist political economy.

Phases of Development

Phase I: 1950–66

Three major developments that took place around the time of India's Independence played a key role in determining the strategy of development pursued by the ruling classes in this phase. First, following the thirty-year crisis of world capitalism beginning with the First World War (1914–18), through the Russian Revolution (1917), the Great Depression (1929–39) and the Second World War (1939–45), traditional imperial powers such as Great Britain, France, Germany, Italy, Holland and Japan were greatly weakened. Second, from a situation of virtual isolation from 1917 to 1945, the USSR emerged stronger despite the losses it sustained in the Second World War, and was soon joined by several countries of Eastern Europe, the People's Republic of China, North Vietnam and North Korea (and a few years later, Cuba), resulting in the emergence of a powerful socialist camp. Against the background of these positive developments, national liberation movements across the colonized countries soon began to overthrow colonial rule, leading to massive global decolonization between 1945 and 1960. This set of circumstances made it possible for at least the ruling classes of the larger and more populous newly independent countries to initiate relatively autonomous capitalist development, using the presence of the socialist camp as a bargaining counter vis-à-vis imperialism.[1] India was a classic case of such a country.

While international circumstances provided some space for development, domestic circumstances made development an urgent political task. From 1944 onwards, as the Second World War drew to a close, there were militant movements of working people all over the Indian subcontinent against imperialist rule and on basic demands. There were strikes in the railways, strikes and struggles of government employees, the heroic mutiny by sailors of the Royal Indian Navy, and other working class struggles. A wave of peasant unrest swept the country from Punjab in the north to Assam and Bengal in the east, to Maharashtra in the west, to Punnapra Vayalar and east Thanjavur in the south. All of this was capped by the armed struggle of the peasants of Telangana under the leadership of the communists.

While the development agenda thus became both possible and urgently necessary for the ruling classes, the challenge was huge. The Indian economy at Independence was extremely backward. Colonial rule had done little to develop the productive forces. Between 1900 and 1950, India's gross domestic product (GDP) grew at less than 1 per cent per annum, while agricultural as well as foodgrain output grew at just 0.5 per cent per annum. In 1950, agriculture accounted for 49 per cent of GDP, large-scale industry for 7 per cent, small and medium industry for 10 per cent, and the remaining 34 per cent came from services and construction. Nearly 72 per cent of the work force was in agriculture, and only 2.5 per cent was employed in factories and mines. Another 7 per cent was employed in small industry, and the remaining 18.5 per cent in services and construction. There was very poor development of both physical–industrial and human resource infrastructure. As per the 1951 Census, only 16 per cent of the population was literate, the percentage among females being even less, 8 per cent. The infant mortality rate was 150. That is to say, of every 1,000 live-born infants, 150 would die before reaching the age of one. The average length of life of an Indian born in 1947 was only thirty-two years. The country's power generation capacity was a mere 3,000 megawatts, and its financial infrastructure was very poorly developed.

It was clear to the Indian ruling classes that economic development of such a backward economy would be impossible unless the state played a leading role. Also, the remarkable achievements of the USSR under a regime of central planning, the leading role of the state between 1928 and 1940, and its ability to withstand the brutal Nazi onslaught when many western powers withered and surrendered, had caught the imagination of nationalist leaders across the colonized world.[2]

It was widely accepted at that time that the state had to play a leading role in newly independent countries, that central planning was imperative and that things could not be left to the market. This was the background to the efforts of the Indian state at planning, with a leading role for the public sector. Of course, neither the public sector nor central planning in the Indian context of the 1950s and 1960s should be confused with any notion of socialism or of building socialism. The goal was to build a capitalist economy. Given the fact that the Indian bourgeoisie at Independence was not in a position to undertake large and long-gestation investment projects to create the infrastructure that they needed for their growth, the state was to do it for them. This was pretty much the refrain of the Bombay Plan, commissioned by captains of industry in 1946.[3] The public sector was to invest in those infrastructure industries requiring large amounts of capital and taking a long time to generate output/revenue. It was then to supply these products at subsidized prices to private players to enable them to make handsome profits and grow, both by reinvesting a part of their profits and by availing development finance from public sector financial institutions.

Driven by public investment, import substitution and limited land reforms, the Indian economy grew at nearly 4 per cent per annum between 1950 and 1965. The impact of these policies can be seen from Table 1.

However, this growth process ran into serious difficulties by the middle of the 1960s, towards the end of the Third Five Year Plan, landing the economy in a three-fold crisis in 1965–66. First, there was the crisis of resource mobilization. Since public investment was a key driver of growth,

Table 1 *Rates of growth of the Indian economy* in per cent per annum

Sector	1900–47	1950–65
Primary	0.4	2.6
Secondary	1.5	6.8
Tertiary	1.7	4.5
Gross Domestic Product (GDP)	0.9	4.0

Note: The primary sector includes crop agriculture, animal husbandry, forestry and fisheries. The secondary sector refers to industry, while the rest constitutes the tertiary sector.
Source: Figures for 1900–47 are taken from Jean Dreze and Amartya Sen, *An Uncertain Glory: India and Its Contradictions* (London: Penguin, 2014). Figures for 1950–65 are calculated using data from various issues of the *Economic Survey* of the Government of India.

the government had to sustain such investment. Resources for doing so could come from taxation, the profits of government-owned enterprises and charges levied for services provided by the government. They could also come from government borrowings inside and outside the country. But since the government represented and protected the interests of the bourgeoisie and the landlords, it did not impose direct taxes on the rural landed gentry and taxed the capitalists lightly.[4] Moreover, since the purpose of the public sector was seen as that of facilitating the growth of industry, it had to make available its products at modest prices to the private sector. Therefore, public sector profits could not be a major source of resource mobilization. There were severe limits to charging for services, given the prevalence of mass poverty and the limited provision of services by government. The government did rely on anti-poor, regressive indirect taxes to a great extent, but the scope of using these to mobilize resources for undertaking public investment was limited. Borrowing was resorted to, but this too was not an unlimited option. In view of the fact that large government deficits were seen as inflationary, and the political impact of inflation when the working class was concentrated in major cities following the rapid growth of industry between 1950 and 1965 was seen as dangerous, the government was not willing to take the route of greater deficit financing or borrowing.

Second, there was the crisis of foreign exchange. Though the policy of import substitution had helped protect the Indian market for Indian big business, the fact that imports grew as the economy grew made it necessary to enhance exports to meet the foreign exchange requirements for imports. But India's exports were largely stagnant in the face of competition from numerous other developing countries and the emergence of synthetic substitutes for many of the agro-based exports from poor countries. There was not much flow of private capital to the developing countries in the 1950s and 1960s (as there was in the 1980s and later). Nor were many Indian nationals living and working abroad, and sending home dollars! Additional foreign exchange could only be got by grants or loans from other country governments, or from the International Monetary Fund (IMF) and World Bank. The scope for such grants or loans was limited, and they had implications for national sovereignty.

Third, there was the foodgrain crisis. Though limited land reforms in terms of some degree of abolition of zamindari and absentee landlordism had taken place in many parts of the country, and some tenancy reforms had also been carried out, there was no serious weakening of land monopoly, though there was some change in the social composition of the big landowning sections in some parts of India. The persistence of land monopoly and of semi-feudal relations in large parts of India meant that the incentive to invest in increasing agricultural productivity was not very strong. Large landlords could appropriate considerable surplus by rack-renting, moneylending, and monopolizing trade. Given insecure tenancy conditions, tenants could not be expected to invest substantially. Credit infrastructure for agriculture was also very poor prior to the nationalization of banks. Together with the presumed resource constraints on public investment that limited investments in irrigation and rural infrastructure by the government, all this meant that the marketed output of agriculture would be at the mercy of the monsoons, and would also grow slowly in relation to the requirement of rapidly expanding urban industry for raw material and of the urban work force for foodgrain. With two successive poor monsoons, this was precisely what happened. In 1965–66, the country faced a very severe shortage of foodgrain.

Phase II: 1966–80
How did the ruling classes respond to the three-fold crisis? They responded to the fiscal crisis by cutting back public investment and putting planning on hold. For three successive years, 1966 to 1969, there were only "annual plans," which were no more than budgets. Five-year planning was put on hold, and the period is often referred to as the "plan holiday" years. Finally, when the Fourth Five Year Plan was announced, to run from 1969 to 1974, the draft plan document did not even arrive until some time in 1970. By 1972, in a mid-term review, most plan targets were slashed, but even the reduced targets were not met at the end of the plan term in 1974.

The response to the balance of payments crisis was to buckle under IMF pressure and devalue the rupee. Following the death of Lal Bahadur Shastri in January 1966, Indira Gandhi had become the prime minister. On 6 June 1966, she devalued the rupee from 4 rupees 80 paise to the US dollar, to 7 rupees 50 paise: a decline in value of more than 50 per cent. The result was an acceleration of inflation already under way because of successive monsoon failures and the resultant rise in foodgrain prices.

The response to the foodgrain crisis was somewhat more purposeful and effective. This was to hasten the introduction of the so-called new agricultural strategy, which later came to be called the "green revolution." Putting land reform firmly on the back burner, the government sought to modernize agriculture and increase productivity by bringing in new technology with high-yielding varieties (HYV), first of wheat and then of rice. The new technology package involved biological (HYV seeds), chemical (fertilizers and pesticides) and mechanical (tractors, motor pumps, etc.) inputs. But the green revolution was much more than mere technology. It was made possible by the major role the state played by way of procurement, provision of institutional credit, input subsidies, strengthening of the national agricultural research systems, and setting up and consolidating the extension system. While agricultural output had grown at about 2.6 per cent per annum in 1950–66, this had happened mainly through expansion of the area cultivated, made possible by limited land reform and some expansion in irrigation. There was, however, no technological breakthrough. It was the "green revolution" that made possible, through technological change and state policy, agricultural growth at about 3 per cent per annum between 1966 and 1980.[5]

The consequences of the crisis of the mid-1960s and the response of the ruling classes to it led to a slowing down of industrial growth. Apart from the weakening and gradual abandonment of serious planning, the government response to the fiscal crisis of cutting back public investment led to a long recession in industry. Industrial output, which had grown at nearly 7 per cent per annum during the first three five year plans, from 1950–51 to 1965–66, grew only at 4 per cent per annum between 1966 and 1980. Even this was only because of an improvement in the second half of the 1970s.

The crisis of 1965–66 had serious political consequences. The Congress Party, which had been in power at the centre and in practically all the states from the time of Independence, was defeated in several states in the general elections of 1967.[6] Its majority in Parliament was also considerably reduced. The severe inflation caused by monsoon failures and made much worse by devaluation, and the severe recession and rise in unemployment caused by cutbacks in public investment, were important factors in this outcome.

These political developments soon led to a split within the Congress, with Indira Gandhi striking an ostensibly radical posture that culminated in the nationalization of fourteen commercial banks and the abolition of privy purses. The support extended by the Left to the government was crucial in getting these measures passed. Soon, however, as the crisis intensified, the Congress under Indira Gandhi returned to its authoritarian ways. It unleashed semi-fascist terror in West Bengal from 1970 onwards. It sought to impose a wage freeze, against which the Centre of Indian Trade Unions (CITU), formed in 1970, mobilized workers and other trade unions – leading to the formation of the United Council of Trade Unions (UCTU) in 1972. Though the events in the then East Pakistan, leading to the emergence of Bangladesh, raised Indira Gandhi's popularity and enabled her to win a majority in the parliamentary elections in late 1971, called ahead of the end of term, this did not bring political stability. The worsening of inflation on account of the oil price increases in 1973, and the severe industrial recession and rising unemployment led to countrywide unrest in 1974. One stream of the opposition to the Congress government came from Jayaprakash Narayan and his followers in Bihar, while the Jana Sangh took the lead in Gujarat. With the Communist Party of India (CPI) aligned with the Congress, the Communist Party of India (Marxist) (CPI[M]) made efforts to forge united fronts against the government's economic policies among the working people. The culmination of the working class struggles of the early 1970s was the all-India railway strike of 1974, which was crushed by the central government. In 1975, Emergency was declared on grounds of internal disturbances. Following the end of the Emergency, the Congress lost the general elections of 1977, but the Janata Party dispensation that formed the government in 1977 did not last a full term. Its collapse in late 1979 led to the general elections of 1980, which saw the Congress led by Indira Gandhi come back to power.

During this entire period from 1966 to 1980, the economy was in one crisis or another. Certain international developments in the 1970s worsened the economic crisis. There was a four-fold rise in the price of crude petroleum in 1973, imposed by the Organization of Petroleum Exporting Countries (OPEC), which functioned as a cartel. Again, in 1978, there was a further near-doubling of oil prices. Oil price hikes hit India hard, especially since the adoption of the new agricultural strategy had made agriculture more import-intensive and more energy-intensive. Ruling class policies that involved cutbacks in expenditure, more borrowing, and a continued reluctance to tax the landlords and capitalists essentially fuelled inflation, worsened unemployment and increased rural distress. With the new agricultural strategy, land reform had been taken off the government's agenda. The profitability of cultivation in the wake of the green revolution had led to the eviction of tenants by landlords in the late 1960s and early 1970s, fuelling the rise of peasant movements in eastern India, and in parts of Andhra Pradesh and Tamil Nadu. On balance, the economy suffered relative stagnation in the second phase, and ended with a crisis similar to that of 1965–66. In 1979–80, foodgrain output fell by 18 per cent, inflation reached high levels with the consumer price index rising by more than 20 per cent and the foreign exchange situation worsened sharply. This crisis played an important role in helping the Congress to win the elections.

Phase III: 1980–91
The world capitalist economy had undergone important changes between 1945 and the end of the 1970s. Between 1945 and 1973, the world capitalist economy grew at a compound annual rate of 5 per cent. There was no simultaneous recession across the major capitalist economies until 1974–75. There was only a short recession in the US in 1958. Such relatively rapid, uninterrupted growth over a period of more than two decades was unprecedented in the history of capitalism.[7] An important consequence of such a long boom was the accumulation of enormous profits in the hands of big transnational corporations of the advanced capitalist world. Also, the sharp rise in petroleum prices in the 1970s had added to the funds in the international financial system. Further, the savings of the working people in the rich countries entered the financial system. Taken together, there was a huge increase in liquidity in the international financial system. One consequence of this was that private capital, through international commercial banks and other sources, began to flow into the developing countries. This was seen as an opportunity by the ruling classes in several developing countries to augment domestic savings through external borrowing and achieve higher rates of economic growth.

Faced with an inherited balance of payments crisis in 1980 and weighing the developments in the international economy, the Congress government went in for a large loan of 5.4 billion dollars from the IMF. This entailed severe conditionalities and pushed the economy towards an externally oriented path. In comparison with growth rates in countries such as South Korea and Taiwan, the 3 to 3.5 per cent annual growth rate of the Indian economy between 1950 and 1980 was seen as inadequate. Under the pressure of the IMF loan, emphasis shifted from import substitution to export orientation accompanied by import liberalization. Growth of the economy was sought to be accelerated through government spending, financed by both domestic and external borrowing, with the IMF loan playing a catalytic role.

These policies were intensified from 1985, when Rajiv Gandhi became the prime minister. Several "new" policies were announced for various sectors, but the main thrust was on reducing government regulation of industry. Import liberalization was also a key feature of the new policies. The growth model was based on promoting elite consumption, with government spending providing the main stimulus. The economy did indeed grow faster in the 1980s than earlier. Agriculture did well, growing at nearly 4 per cent per annum compound between 1980–81 and 1990–91 (wheat at 4.38 per cent and rice at 3.84 per cent). The Index of Industrial Production grew at 7.8 per cent per annum between 1980–81 and 1989–90. The service sector grew even faster than agriculture and industry, with the share of the tertiary sector in GDP rising from 36 per cent in 1980–81 to 39 per cent in 1990–91.

However, while the economy grew much faster in the 1980s than earlier, the fact that it was driven by government spending based on domestic and external borrowing, and accompanied by import liberalization, had serious consequences. India's external debt rose from US$ 20 billion in 1980 to US$ 82 billion in 1990. Debt owed to private banks and individuals rose much faster, from US$ 2 billion in 1980 to US$ 22 billion in 1990.

While India's exports did grow at 8.3 per cent per annum between 1981 and 1990, the balance of payments deficit became quite severe by 1990, especially since much of the borrowing was short-term and commercial, bearing high rates of interest. Political instability in the period 1989–91 and adverse international developments in the Persian Gulf region also played a role in worsening the balance of payments situation. A World Bank assessment in late 1990 that the Indian rupee was "overvalued" contributed to capital flight in early 1991.

Government deficits also rose sharply through the 1980s, since the government did not finance expenditure through taxation but indulged in borrowing instead. The simultaneous existence of high fiscal deficits and severe balance of payment deficits with foreign exchange reserves being hardly sufficient to finance six weeks worth of imports was seen as a crisis, requiring India to go in for huge loans from the IMF and the World Bank.

The rise to hegemony of international finance capital in the capitalist world, the collapse of the USSR, and the restoration of capitalism in Eastern Europe and the former USSR also led to changes in the perception of the ruling classes on the prospects of self-reliant development. Major policy changes followed. The ruling classes in India, which had already begun deregulating and privatizing the economy in the 1980s, abandoned the effort at relatively autonomous and self-reliant capitalist development under the leadership of the state. Under pressure from the IMF and the World Bank, as well as the US and other western powers, the minority Congress government with P.V. Narasimha Rao as prime minister and Manmohan Singh as finance minister embarked on the path of liberalization, privatization and globalization (LPG), even though these policies were not part of the electoral agenda of the Congress Party in the 1991 general elections.

Phase IV: 1991–2015
It is now more than two decades since these LPG policies have been in place, pursued vigorously by both Congress-led governments and Bharatiya Janata Party (BJP)-led coalitions at the centre and in most of the states. The regional parties, of whom several had earlier opposed LPG policies, gradually came around to accepting and implementing these policies as they sought to retain power in their respective states through a process of political collaboration with either the Congress or the BJP.[8] The Left-ruled states and Left parties have been more or less alone in opposing LPG policies both theoretically and on the ground.

LPG policies involve deregulation of the economy, opening up the economy as widely as possible to private capital and opening up the nation as widely as possible to foreign capital. Specifically, deregulation (also called liberalization) means the removal of regulations governing the operations of private companies, especially large ones. In other words, it frees these companies from the constraints of social accountability. They are to be left free to make profits in any manner they wish and to any extent possible. This naturally implies that the state will no longer defend even the minimal rights of the working people. It also implies that large companies are free to gobble up smaller companies and become powerful monopolies, in the name, ironically, of promoting competition!

Privatization relates not only to government selling some of its shares in state-owned companies to private capital and gradually dismantling the public sector, but also opening up all economic and social activity, including those related to education, health, infrastructure and so on, to private players, and allowing them to convert all these activities into profit-making opportunities rather than activities governed by the need to promote social well-being. This has obvious implications in terms of denying the poor access to education and health beyond minimal levels, and to raising the costs to the people of infrastructure services, including those relating to energy and power, water, and transport.

Globalization, the third element of LPG, means liberalizing imports, lowering import tariffs and removing all quantitative restrictions on imports. Even more importantly, it means removing all restrictions on the free movement of capital as finance into and out of India as a strategy to attract foreign capital flows into the country. This is the single most important aspect of LPG reforms, and the one with the most far-reaching consequences. The moment restrictions on bringing money into India and taking money out of India in foreign currency are removed, the government can no longer be independent in its economic policy-making. It will have to worry about whether foreign finance capital brought into India may be taken out if any government measure is not to the liking of foreign finance capitalists.

Finance capital always demands minimal government regulation and minimal government expenditure. It does not like to be taxed and it wants complete freedom to speculate, in the name of "financial innovation." This has serious consequences for the government's welfare and investment policies. Since 1991, successive governments in India have, in general, cut back welfare programmes and public investment to keep foreign finance capital happy, in violation of democratic verdicts against the consequences of these policies in successive elections to the Parliament.

The Impact of Neoliberal Reforms

How have India and Indians fared during the period of neoliberal reforms? First, the annual rate of growth of GDP of the economy was already close to 6 per cent per year from the mid-1980s. Between 1991, when the reforms were accelerated, widened and deepened, and 2003, the average annual growth rate of GDP was no higher than in the period from 1985 to 1990. However, from 2003–04 to 2007–08, the GDP grew more rapidly, at between 7 and 9 per cent. Following the global economic crisis that erupted in 2008, the annual GDP growth rate fell to 6.7 per cent in 2008–09. The government responded to the global economic crisis and its potential impact on the Indian economy by announcing considerable concessions to capitalists and the well-to-do in respect of excise duties, customs duties, and corporate and personal income taxes. The growth rate of GDP rose to 8.4 per cent between 2009 and 2011. But with the stimulus wearing off, the GDP growth rate in 2011–12 was 6.2 per cent, that in 2012–13 just 5 per cent and that for 2013–14 did not even reach 5 per cent.[9]

One can argue that even an average of 6 to 7 per cent growth rate of GDP is impressive when many countries, including the developed capitalist countries, are growing at much lower rates, and only China grew at between

9 and 10 per cent per year for over three decades from the late 1970s.[10] The issue, however, is not just the rate of growth, but the nature and composition of growth and its implications for different socio-economic classes. There are major concerns in this regard.

First, it is the service sector that is growing most rapidly. The share of the service sector in India's GDP is now close to 60 per cent. The secondary sector – which includes manufacturing, gas, electricity and water supply – has grown at much lower rates than the service sector, and has also shown instability. Its share in GDP is only around 25 per cent, much lower than in China. The share of the manufacturing sector in GDP has been stagnant, at about 16 per cent.[11] The share of the primary sector – agriculture and allied activities, forestry and fishing, and mining and quarrying – has declined to somewhere around 17 per cent.

Secondly, while the decline in the share of the primary sector in GDP is to be expected as an economy modernizes and industrializes, the point to be noted with concern is that the share of the labour force in the primary sector, at nearly 50 per cent, is much higher than its share in GDP. By contrast, the services sector contributes 58 per cent of GDP but its share of employment is less than 30 per cent.

Thirdly, the last two decades have seen a huge and continuing agrarian crisis with more than 250,000 farmers committing suicide from 1997 to late 2012. Growth in agriculture and in foodgrain has been the lowest since Independence during this reform period, with the annual growth rate having been just 0.6 per cent between 1994–95 and 2004–05. Agriculture and the rural economy have been devastated by neoliberal policies that have:[12]

1. Slashed subsidies to agricultural inputs, including fertilizers, pesticides, credit, energy and transport, leading to sharp increases in input costs
2. Removed restrictions on imports of agricultural produce, causing both a collapse of prices for farm produce at certain times and greatly increased price fluctuations throughout
3. Reduced the supply and increased the costs of bank and cooperative credit to agriculture and allied activities
4. Cut back on development expenditure to meet the demands of foreign finance capital for low budget deficits, in the process weakening rural infrastructure, farm extension and farm research, and halting the expansion of irrigation critical to agricultural growth
5. Weakened food security by imposing a targeted public distribution system, excluding millions of the poor from access to food at affordable costs.

Fourthly, the growth in employment during the reform period has been less than in the decade preceding the reforms. Moreover, practically all the increase in employment over the last two decades has been in informal jobs that are not only often at very low wages but carry no welfare benefits, are completely insecure with no protection for workers, involve long working hours, and deny workers the right to form unions and fight for better wages and working conditions. Between the mid-1980s and mid-2000s, the share of profit in net value added in manufacturing, for instance, has gone up from around 40 per cent to around 80 per cent.

With global economic growth rates remaining persistently low and no significant revival of the global economy anticipated for some years to come, the Indian economy is in for rough weather. Neoliberal policies of the last two decades and more have made the economy more vulnerable to the global crisis than earlier. On top of the rural and agrarian crisis, and the crisis of massive and increasing unemployment, we have had very high rates of inflation, especially in food articles and in some other essential commodities until well into 2013–14. While inflation rates have moderated in recent months, the rates of retail price increase for food articles remain significantly higher than the overall inflation rates, causing acute distress to the poorer sections.

Fifthly, the reforms have led to a much greater integration of the Indian economy with the world capitalist economy. For instance, the combined share of exports and imports in the Indian economy in India's GDP was only one-seventh in 1991. It is now around one-half of GDP. In addition, because the reforms allowed free entry and exit of foreign finance capital, there is a much greater degree of instability in the economy, with foreign institutional investors bringing money into the country to make quick profits in Indian stock markets and taking them out quickly. While foreign capital makes sizeable profits in this manner, there is no benefit to the Indian economy as no wealth is created by trading in already existing shares. But the unregulated entry and exit of foreign finance capital only cause great instability in the financial and currency markets, and the integration of India's economy through trade and capital flows makes India far more vulnerable than before to external shocks emanating from any part of the world capitalist economy.

All evidence – from the National Sample Survey (NSS), the National Family Health Survey (NFHS) and various other surveys done across the country – shows that the reforms have not made a significant impact on the depth and severity as well as the spread of poverty, even though the government often claims the contrary. Recent research shows that per capita income in fact decreased between 1993–94 and 2004–05 in regions located more than 5 kilometres from urban settlements, and these regions account for over half the population of India. With the global economic crisis impacting the Indian economy, decline in growth, little increase in employment between 2004–05 and 2011–12, and sharp cuts in subsidies, the extent of poverty is likely to have gone up in recent years. There has been no significant reduction in malnutrition, and the indicators even show a worsening in some parts of the country, and among socially and economically vulnerable sections. Food insecurity is a widely prevalent condition in India.

The Class Nature of Economic Policies

We have given an analytical-historical account of the different phases of Indian economic development above. What emerges from this account is that ruling-class policies have largely served the interests of the capitalist and landlord classes. The big bourgeoisie has been the biggest beneficiary. A brief elaboration of the class nature of economic policies, focusing on the current neoliberal regime, is provided below.

Class Nature of the Agrarian Regime

The fact that land monopoly has not been seriously eroded, despite a great deal of rhetoric on land reforms and a large number of legislations, reflects the exercise of state power by the landlord class. While Professor Mahalanobis estimated in 1960 that roughly 63 million acres of land would be surplus under prevailing ceiling norms, hardly one-tenth of this figure has even been identified as surplus and even less has been distributed.[13] Likewise, while the green revolution had enabled a significant increase in agricultural output through increase in yields per acre, the agrarian policies of the Indian state, including the green revolution, have largely benefited the landlords and the big capitalist farmers as well as sections of the rich peasantry. Even in the neoliberal reforms period, which has seen a deep and persistent agrarian crisis, the process of peasant differentiation has continued, and a small section of rural exploiters consisting of landlords and big capitalist farmers have benefited from the neoliberal reforms, and strengthened their control of land and other productive assets. On the other hand, data from the census and from National Sample Surveys show that landlessness has been increasing rapidly in the reform period. The penetration of foreign capital into Indian agriculture is an important aspect of the consequences of neoliberal reforms. But this has not negated the continued hold over the countryside of landlords and of big capitalist farmers who have emerged in the post-Independence period, taking advantage of agrarian policies favouring the richer sections of the cultivating population.

One may sum up the agrarian crisis under the current neoliberal regime in the following terms:

1. There has been a significant slowing down of the growth of output and yield of most major crops.
2. Crop agriculture and animal husbandry have become unviable for a large majority of the peasantry.
3. Agrarian distress has been responsible, in the main, for more than a quarter million farmers ending their lives between 1997 and 2012.
4. Rural employment has grown more slowly during the period of reforms than earlier. Nearly all the increase in employment has been of poor quality, characterized by informality and low earnings.
5. At the same time, the crisis is not uniform across space and time. The period 1997–2003 saw stagnation, while the period since then has seen some revival of agricultural growth. However, even with some recovery in growth, the crisis remains severe in its impact on the majority of the agrarian population.
6. While the crisis continues, there has also been some degree of capital accumulation. This is reflected in rising yields of most crops, though at rates much slower than before the acceleration of neoliberal reforms. It is also reflected in a considerable rise in the sale and use of agricultural machinery.
7. While there has been dispossession, operations of the land and real estate mafia, corporate land grab and so on, not all the accumulation is through dispossession alone. There has been growth of productive forces and enrichment of a small section of the agrarian population as well.
8. While the role of international capital and its penetration of India's agrarian and rural economy have increased rapidly during the period of neoliberal reforms, the basic contradiction in the Indian countryside between landlordism and the mass of the peasantry and agricultural labourers is intact, and is very far from being resolved. Land monopoly and concentration of productive assets in the hands of landlords and big capitalist farmers as well sections of the rich peasantry continue to define the countryside in large measure. Land ceilings laws have been diluted and even reversed in many states. Oppression of Dalits, Adivasis and women remains an important and persistent feature of the rural economy and society.[14]

9. Finally, the permanent structural crisis of the Indian economy – that of landlordism, and the pursuit of a path of capitalist development under a capitalist–landlord state structure and under the leadership of monopoly capital, must not be lost sight of.

The Role of the Big Bourgeoisie

The class which has had the greatest power over the state, and is the leader of the ruling-class alliance of capitalists and landlords, is clearly the big bourgeoisie. This has been the case both before and after neoliberal reforms. For instance, even prior to the reforms, the assets of the Tatas rose from just Rs 369 crores in 1964 to Rs 7,546 crores in 1990. The assets of the Birlas grew from Rs 290 crores to Rs 7,235 crores.[15] Liberalization policies led to an even more rapid growth of the big business houses.[16] Thus, in 2011–12, the Tatas had a market capitalization of Rs 4.46 lakh crores, while that of the Aditya Birla group was Rs 1.28 lakh crores. The Reliance group, which had come into the top twenty later than many other well-known business houses, has grown phenomenally. In 2011–12, the market capitalization of the Mukesh Ambani group was Rs 2.43 lakh crores, next only to the Tatas, while the Anil Ambani group had a market capitalization of Rs 82,859 crores. Others in the top ten business groups by market capitalization included such well-known names as Vedanta, Bajaj and Jindal. From relatively more modest beginnings, the Adani business group catapulted into the top ten with a market capitalization of nearly Rs 60,000 crores in 2011–12. Through the many twists and turns of policy, big business has prospered all the time, and under all governments. While some old traditional business houses have declined, new ones have emerged – several of them in the period of neoliberal reforms. The big business houses have continued to grow rapidly during the recent period of crisis as well. Thus, between 2008–09 and 2011–12, the market capitalization of the Tatas grew at 13.6 per cent per annum and that of the Birlas by 8.1 per cent. The Bajaj group has been growing at a spectacular rate of 24.4 per cent per year.

The period of neoliberal reforms has seen increasing collaboration of Indian big capital with foreign finance capital. Moreover, Indian big business houses have also expanded overseas, and contributed significantly to the outflow of foreign direct investment in recent years. However, while the period of neoliberalism has seen a growing collaboration between Indian big capital and foreign finance capital, we must not lose sight of the fact that the Indian big bourgeoisie still enjoys some measure of autonomy. The trend of growing multi-polarity in the international political arena helps widen the relative autonomous space of Indian big capital, though of course within limits.

Overall, in class terms, the big bourgeoisie has benefited the most in the political economy of Indian development. Landlords, big capitalist farmers and a section of the rich peasantry have also substantially benefited from neoliberal policies, though they are also facing increased volatility on account of opening up and exposure to international economic shocks. A section of the middle class – professionals, for instance – has also benefited to some extent. But the rural poor, consisting of rural manual workers, poor peasants and traditional artisans, as well as sections of the middle peasantry, have largely been victims of neoliberal policies and have seen a worsening of their livelihood prospects.

Conclusion

The world has changed remarkably since India gained Independence. The relatively greater autonomy that India had in implementing its strategy of development at that time has been eroded both by dramatic global developments and by the logic of the capitalist path of development itself, which has entailed increasing collaboration with foreign finance capital.

Three major developments of the period since 1990 have to be noted. One is the economic crisis of 1991, which resulted from the path of capitalist development pursued since Independence. The second is the changed balance of class forces in the international arena following the collapse of socialist regimes in the USSR and Eastern Europe, in the period 1989 to 1991. The third is the rise of *Hindutva* forces and the resultant rightward shift in Indian politics as well as in economic policies. It is remarkable that despite these adverse developments, progressive movements and forces in India have been able to slow the juggernaut of neoliberal reforms with mass action on both the political and the economic planes. For a short period from 2004 to 2007, it even proved possible to get important progressive legislation passed. These include the Forest Rights Act (FRA), the Right to Information (RTI) Act and the Mahatma Gandhi National Rural Employment Guarantee Act (MGNREGA). However, the balance of forces in the country has remained strongly in favour of the parties of the ruling classes, and the decade from 2005 to 2015 has seen an intensification of neoliberal economic policies as well as a revival of the communal politics of *Hindutva*.

The economic policies of the *Hindutva*-led government have been possibly even more neoliberal than those of the regime it replaced. The budgets of the BJP government have imposed substantial burdens on the working people and unleashed a savage agenda of privatization as well as fresh concessions to foreign capital. Fresh indirect taxes have been levied even while concessions in direct taxes are being handed out to the super rich, a striking instance being the abolition of the wealth tax. There is little increase in overall government expenditure and the budget thus fails to provide any stimulus to growth. The schemes under the MGNREGA have been pruned drastically and the National Food Security Act (NFSA) remains unimplemented two years after its passage. The mid-year economic review of the Ministry of Finance noted with ill-concealed glee, in November 2014, that its policies of "moderating" minimum support prices (MSPs) for farmers and cutting down expenditure on MGNREGA schemes, both had helped curb inflation (evidently by reducing the purchasing power of peasants and rural workers, a majority of the rural population). Though the government, on account of massive opposition of the peasantry and progressive political forces, has for now been forced to abandon its attempt to get the Land Acquisition Bill passed, it is more than likely that attempts will be made again to bring the issue to the fore and to get pro-big business legislation passed in this regard.[17]

It is clear that a huge challenge lies ahead for progressive forces in India who wish to see pro-people economic policies implemented. While the task may seem daunting in the short term, development across the world of resistance to neoliberalism, including in Latin America and Europe, suggest that the challenge can be met over the long term. The struggle for a progressive political economy in the Indian context would, however, also involve a struggle against the forces of obscurantism that seek to use religion to capture political power.

Notes

1 The "autonomy" was, of course, limited and relative, since the western imperialist monopoly of technology, international markets and finance remained largely intact.

2 It was only in 1928 that the Russian region of the USSR was able to regain the levels of output reached in 1913, before the onset of the First World War. But within the next twelve years, the USSR, with central planning under a socialist regime, became the second largest industrial power in the world after the USA. This was achieved without exploiting colonies, without plundering workers and peasants, and while facing the economic, technological and diplomatic boycott imposed by imperialism, and ensuring defence-preparedness against western militarism.

3 The best reference on this is E.M.S. Namboodiripad's classic, *Indian Planning in Crisis* (1982). Also useful are his earlier books: *Economics and Politics of India's Socialist Pattern* (1966) and *Political India: Crisis into Chaos* (1981).

4 On paper, the tax rates on corporate profits and personal income might even have appeared prohibitive to some, but this was nullified by numerous exemptions and very lax collection.

5 Though the green revolution had a number of negative consequences, we would not have been able to increase foodgrain output at a rate higher than population growth without it.

6 In the 1952 elections, the Congress did not secure a majority only in PEPSU (Patiala and East Punjab States Union). But it manufactured a majority soon by organizing defections. In 1957, the undivided Communist Party of India won the Kerala Assembly elections with a one-seat majority. The Congress was unable to organize the defection of even a single legislator. It therefore chose to dismiss the elected state government undemocratically. It is worth noting that Jawaharlal Nehru was the prime minister of the country and Indira Gandhi the president of the Congress Party when this occurred.

7 While we cannot go into the reasons for this long boom, the reconstruction of war-devastated Europe, the growth of newly independent countries and militarism were important factors in sustaining demand. Keynesian demand management policies also played a role, as did rapid technological change. The political and economic dominance of the US within the capitalist world was also a key factor.

8 The rightward shift in economic policies of central and state governments from the early 1990s was also accompanied by a rightward shift in the Indian polity marked by the rise of *Hindutva* forces represented by the Bharatiya Janata Party (BJP). The demolition of the Babri Masjid following a huge, all-India "Hindu"-communal mobilization around the theme of *Ram Janmabhoomi* was a key marker of this shift.

9 More recently, the GDP series has been revised. The GDP is now being reckoned in terms of market prices as opposed to factor cost, which was the case earlier. The numbers are now based on 2011–12 prices as opposed to 2004–05 prices. There have also been some changes in the methods of evaluation of output. All these have resulted in rather different numbers for growth rates of GDP from those reported earlier, but this need not detain us here. The consensus is that there has been no dramatic turnaround in GDP growth rates since 2012–13, as these lines are being written in late 2015.

10 The rate of growth of GDP in China has come down in the last year or two, but is still high at about 7 per cent.

11 By contrast, the share of manufacturing in China's GDP is 34 per cent. While India accounts for 1.8 per cent of global manufacturing, China accounts for 13.7 per cent, up from just 2.9 per cent in 1991.

12 See Ramachandran and Swaminathan, eds (2002).

13 It is noteworthy that West Bengal, which has just 3 per cent of net sown area in the country, accounts for 23 per cent of ceiling-surplus lands taken over and

distributed. A large part of this redistribution took place under the Left Front government.

14 The meticulous village surveys carried out by the Foundation for Agrarian Studies since 2005 in several villages spread across many states of India bring out the strong presence of landlordism as well as the emergence of a class of capitalist farmers and continuing differentiation in the countryside. Some of the studies have been reported in various issues of the journal *Review of Agrarian Studies*, available online at www.ras.org.in

15 Para 3.12 of the Programme of the Communist Party of India (Marxist) notes: "The assets of the top 22 monopoly houses shot up from Rs 312.63 crores in 1957 to Rs 1,58,004.72 crores in 1997, which is a five hundred-fold increase."

16 The assets of the top ten corporate houses in the private sector tripled from Rs 3.54 lakh crores in 2003–04 to Rs 10.34 lakh crores in 2007–08.

17 This article was written in late 2015. The Land Acquisition Act has since been passed. – *Editor*

References

Namboodiripad, E.M.S. (1966), *Economics and Politics of India's Socialist Pattern*, New Delhi: People's Publishing House.

Namboodiripad, E.M.S. (1981), *Crisis into Chaos: Political India 1981*, Delhi: Orient Longman.

Namboodiripad, E.M.S. (1982), *Indian Planning in Crisis*, New Delhi: National Book Centre.

Ramachandran, V.K. and Madhura Swaminathan, eds (2002), *Agrarian Studies: Essays on Agrarian Relations in Less-Developed Countries*, New Delhi: Tulika Books.

The Transformation of Mike Bloomberg

Wayne Barrett

When I wrote to Wayne Barrett in early 2015 about this volume, he wrote back: "It is an honour to be asked to contribute to this volume for Ram. I remember so well our nights out in 1968 at a Broadway bar where he schooled me as if I was his intern on so much of the world, his eyes afire. Although we have rarely seen each other since, I continue to feel him in my bloodstream. We will share a bond until death. Most of my career has involved coverage of New York City and State politics and government, and so I send this piece on Mike Bloomberg." Wayne Barrett died of lung cancer and complications of interstitial lung disease on 19 January 2017. N. Ram's book, Why Scams Are Here to Stay: Understanding Political Corruption in India *(2017), is dedicated to him. This article was first published in the* Village Voice *on 19 November 2008. – Editor*

Mike Bloomberg is the best mayor – in fact, the best state or city chief executive – I've covered in thirty-one years at the *Voice*. He is also the worst.

In his first term, he was able to close a gaping budget chasm without crippling city services by imposing the largest and bravest property tax hike in history – and it sent his approval ratings plunging. When the city boomed again, this Nixon-to-China boldness by a businessman/mayor had forever refuted the knee-jerk right-wing orthodoxy that higher taxes invariably kill growth. His smoking ban proved that a mayor can literally change the air we breathe, and was part of a life-saving public health commitment that pumped resources into city hospitals that his predecessor had stripped of city funding. While mayors before him had hidden behind the independent Board of Education to diffuse responsibility for the seemingly intractable dysfunction of the schools, Mike Bloomberg put himself in charge and staked his mayoralty on the slow but steady improvement that has occurred with him at the helm. The continuing decline in the murder rate under Bloomberg was a rebuke of the Giuliani years, when New Yorkers were led to believe that a polarized city was the price we had to pay to reduce crime.

As thankful as the city is for all Mayor Mike accomplished after 9/11, that was nearly a full term ago. Now he has decided he wants a third term, even though he still owes us a second.

Even his strongest allies have a hard time naming a memorable achievement from Bloomberg's second term – beyond his sparking a national gun control campaign. Instead, he was fixated for most of the last two years by an always-improbable yet ballyhooed pursuit of the presidency, followed by a largely unnoticed, two-month-long audition for the consolation prize of vice president.

In one of the most sordid performances by a city executive in modern history, Deputy Mayor Kevin Sheekey appeared on NY1 in May to declare that "the person who picks Mayor Bloomberg as their vice-presidential candidate wins the election," partly because Bloomberg would "help finance a campaign" with "between zero and a billion" dollars. This televised and indiscriminate bribe offer generated no takers and, more remarkably, drew not one word of fire from the city media.

Two weeks later, Bloomberg acknowledged that he had asked a pollster to see what voters thought about extending term limits so he could run again. The day before Joe Biden's selection was formally announced in late August, *The New York Times* revealed that the mayor had been reaching out to fellow media titans – including Arthur Sulzberger of the *Times*, Rupert Murdoch of the *Post* and Mort Zuckerman of *Daily News* – to see if they would support a City Council bill to reverse the two-term limits that voters had approved in two overwhelmingly popular referendums. Two of the newspapers had to distance themselves from their own prior opposition to altering term limits by legislation, as did Bloomberg (he called a previous attempt "an absolute disgrace") and his council consigliere, Christine Quinn (in December, she nixed the possibility of a bill, saying that "the voters have made their will very, very clear").

Last month's 29-to-22 council vote to do Bloomberg's bidding was the most tawdry moment in city politics I've ever seen. More camera crews and reporters attended the vote than any other session in City Council history – some said the passage of the bill was as close as we would get to a mayoral election in 2009.

The mayor justified the bill by saying that it gave voters an additional choice – namely, himself. But unnamed sources had already told the *Times* that Bloomberg would spend $80 million on his re-election (at least $20 million of it on attacks on anyone daring to oppose him). The $80 million, roughly what Bloomberg spent in a non-competitive race in 2005, is cheap compared to what Sheekey claimed Bloomberg was willing to pay for a vice-presidential run. If Comptroller Bill Thompson or Congressman Anthony Weiner runs against Bloomberg with the support of Barack Obama, Hillary Clinton and a respectable slice of the party's New York establishment, the mayor might have to double that number.

Bloomberg's threat of using attack advertisements, coupled with the possibility that Thompson could settle for a safe re-election and the 44-year-old Weiner might decide to wait, could leave us next November with no real choice.

The Bloomberg who came into office as the anti-politician, promising to transform city government, has been transformed himself. Some of us liked him precisely because his wealth insulated him from the kind of horsetrading that diminished his predecessors. But seven years later, Bloomberg has not only proved himself to be a master politician, as hungry for power as anyone we've ever seen, but he has also ended up putting nearly everyone who deals with the city deep into his political debt.

Bloomberg is not, obviously, the first mayor to try to undo term limits as his days dwindle. After 9/11, Rudy Giuliani cajoled the council to re-introduce a bill that the previous January had been bottled up by a 5-to-4 vote in committee, but councilman Stan Michels, who had introduced the bill, refused. Giuliani then pressed to have his term extended for three months, but he needed the agreement of the three candidates then in the race to replace him – and when one, Democrat Fernando Ferrer, said no, he dropped it. Giuliani's excuse was the 9/11 attacks; Bloomberg and his billionaire backers apparently believe that the end of the credit swap and subprime orgies at Lehman and elsewhere are an even greater cause for emergency mayoral retention than the slaughter of three thousand.

The *Times* called it "a terrible idea" when Giuliani tried to prolong his stay, noting that neither the city nor the nation had "ever postponed the transfer of power" in the belief that it "could not get along without the current incumbent." But seven years later it decided, after the next mayor and Sulzberger had reconnoitred, that term limits "would deny New Yorkers – at a time when the city's economy is under great stress – the right to decide for themselves whether an effective and popular mayor should stay in office." Conveniently, the paper saluted Bloomberg, *before* the mayor publicly announced his new third-term pursuit (as did the *Post* and *Daily News*).

We are all used to editorial boards making endorsements determined by their owners, but this was the first time in memory that these three proud institutions had marched in such lockstep on a policy matter after meetings between a political figure and their three owners. But the editorial pages were hardly the only compromised voices. The New York City Campaign

Finance Board (CFB), which the *Times* has called the "crown jewel of city political life," was compelled by the mayor and Quinn – who together appoint its members – to issue the "draft" of an advisory opinion designed to push undecided council members into the "yes" column. The board assured the council that if the extension passed and a member decided to run for re-election, the thousands of dollars that some term-limited members had already spent in seeking higher office would not count against their cap in a new council race. But it wasn't the substance of the ruling that was dismaying – it was the timing of it. According to sources close to the CFB, Bloomberg and Quinn staffers demanded that the board act before the council vote, with Quinn threatening to pass a similar bill – but with detrimental consequences – if the CFB failed to act. Asked twice if Bloomberg aides had lobbied the board to issue this unprecedented opinion in anticipation of a legislative vote, executive director Amy Loprest dodged the question and finally said: "I can't comment on that." Bloomberg even sullied his own charitable generosity, summoning non-profits he funds to council hearings to pay homage despite their tax-exempt status, as if there is now a turnstile at his supposedly "anonymous" foundation.

Mario Cuomo trudged down to testify for the extension without revealing that the managing partner at his law firm is a director of Bloomberg L.P. (Limited Partner) and that the company is the law firm's top client. Ed Koch went from hosting his weekly show on Bloomberg Radio to celebrating the prospect of a third Bloomberg administration. Peter Vallone, who insisted when he was speaker that the only way to undo term limits was by referendum, switched sides without mentioning the $1.8 million in fees his family firm collected last year for lobbying City Hall (to say nothing about his son keeping the family seat). Five unions with fresh new contracts, thanks to Mike Bloomberg, rushed to the witness table, some closing their deals right before and some right after their appearance. Time Warner's Richard Parsons did a stint at the hearing and on his own channel (NY1), even while the Bloomberg administration was extending the company's lucrative cable franchise for six months and considering a ten-year renewal.

No one is suggesting that these giants didn't actually believe their arguments for a third term, but the large number of Bloomberg fans who are also Bloomberg beneficiaries makes it harder and harder to distinguish enthusiasm from interest. His control over a vast city budget, hundreds of millions in private donations and billions in undisclosed personal investments cloud the authenticity of every nice thing said about him. And a day-after-Christmas decision last year by the Bloomberg-appointed Conflicts of Interest Board (COIB) has made his money trail both more expansive and more elusive. At his request, the board decided that he would no longer be restricted to salting away his money in "large, professionally managed mutual and exchange-traded funds." The COIB now allows Bloomberg's influential investment advisor Steve Rattner, another big third-term booster, to put Bloomberg's estimated $20 billion fortune to work in a wide variety of investments, so long as he and the rest of us never find out precisely what they are.

Supposedly, Bloomberg is only consulted about the broad categories of his investments, and Rattner, whose other top job is advising his lifelong friend Sulzberger, makes the rest of the decisions. Perhaps that's why there was so much press speculation prior to Bloomberg's third-term decision that he might buy the troubled *Times*, a deal that could have put Rattner at the negotiating table with himself (Bloomberg told *Newsweek* that Rattner "couldn't represent either" because he is a friend of both). Even Sheekey, who appears to spend much of his fantasy life speculating about what to do with Mike Bloomberg's money, was telling his friends until shortly before the term-limits decision that he thought Bloomberg would go ahead with the *Times* purchase.

Sulzberger insists that the paper isn't for sale, but with the value of the family's controlling stock plummeting, a generous offer from a white knight like Bloomberg might be too much for some members of the Sulzberger clan to resist, making a third term for Mayor Mike a potential firewall protecting Arthur Sulzberger's ability to continue controlling it.

If Bloomberg is mayor again, it is certainly less likely that he would bid for the *Times*, whose total market capitalization is a meagre $1 billion. With the obvious cost-saving synergy between Bloomberg's information company and the *Times*, this acquisition has a business logic that transcends politics, even while it might be already influencing it.

There is just as unnerving and confounding a tangle of interests between Bloomberg and Murdoch. In 2007, Bloomberg L.P. decided, apparently after some consideration, not to compete with Murdoch for *The Wall Street Journal*. Murdoch similarly decided this July not to compete with Bloomberg when he paid $4.5 billion to buy Merrill Lynch's 20 per cent interest in Bloomberg L.P. In this walled-off billionaire playground, it is impossible to tell if any of these third-term mogul endorsements spring in part from a business motive.

The colossus we know the most about is Zuckerman. When Bloomberg ran for mayor in 2001 and the *Daily News* was the only paper to endorse him, he held more than a half million dollars of stock in Boston Properties, the publicly traded real estate company that Zuckerman controls

(Bloomberg may have actually owned more, but by law he was required only to disclose dollar amounts up to that ceiling). Bloomberg had to give up those holdings when he took office, prompted by an earlier COIB ruling, and the Bloomberg administration ended up doing its share of deals with Zuckerman's company – like air rights and other approvals on the company's thirty-nine-storey tower at 250 West 55th Street. At an 8 October investors' conference, Boston's senior vice president Robert Selsam boasted of the company's success with City Planning, recounting how the firm had secured three complicated variances across five zoning districts that allowed it to maximize floors and footage. "The key," said Selsam, "is knowing how to effectively navigate the review and approval processes" of the city. He did not, however, mention that he might have a bit of an edge at that game.

Zuckerman served as a prime promoter of Bloomberg's presidential candidacy ("He is the most gifted public servant I've ever encountered") before he moved on to become the editorial hammer against anyone who dared oppose a third term (blasting some as "Term Limit Hypocrites" on the same page that called supporters of a similar 2006 bill "shameless"). And the warm embrace between these two raises questions about everything the city does when Zuckerman's interests are involved. Zuckerman tells the *Voice* that he doesn't think "anything other than the normal process" was done by the city on West 55th Street.

At least Zuckerman doesn't need Bloomberg's cash. Many New Yorkers have an eerie feeling now that Mike's money is literally everywhere, and that a city, said to be for sale in the era of the big-time bosses, has actually been bought by a mayor so much bigger than they ever boasted of being. The richest man in New York is also, for the first time, the mayor of the city and one of its grandest philanthropists, making it almost impossible for the rest of us to talk to him without wondering at some level of consciousness: "Can I get a slice of this guy?" His personal and public outlays have flooded the city's bloodstream for years now, and few are so uninterested in a possible transfusion of their own that they will take him on.

The claim that all this was done because of Bloomberg's sudden discovery, apparently in late September, that the city faced a daunting financial crisis is a joke. Had the mayor decided to seek a third term sooner, a referendum could have been put on the ballot to allow voters to have a say about term limits for a third time.

Bloomberg would have us believe that the city requires his mastery of market and municipal economics, though he was one of the few people in town who, by his own account, did not recognize that the crisis was so severe that the city needed him – until Lehman collapsed, which is when he ostensibly made up his mind to run again. Zuckerman is at a loss to explain why Bloomberg didn't see the crash coming sooner. "I don't know," he says, "I never talk to him about stuff like that." The mayor is such a financial seer that he is still awarding new 8 per cent salary increases to supportive unions even while Governor David Paterson is publicly asking the state's unions to reopen their contracts for cost savings that could prevent mass lay-offs. The police union, which used to picket Bloomberg's townhouse and drive him nuts, got such a rich deal recently that the mayor restored four paid days off that state arbitrators had just taken away. Their leader then put in some overtime for the third-term bill.

No one played a larger role in making the term-limit extension happen than public relations giant Howard Rubenstein, who, usually only an agent for the town's invisible heavy lifters, became a "principal" this time, according to those in the know. Rubenstein, who represents Bloomberg L.P., insists he did his term-limits work as a "volunteer." He got client Murdoch in on the deal, and sat Bloomberg and Deputy Mayor Ed Skyler down with Ron Lauder, another client and the billionaire who got the term-limits law passed in the first place, way back in 1993. Lauder, who was already doing advertisements opposing an extension, agreed to muzzle himself. Rubenstein also reached out to Zuckerman and Sulzberger, appeared as an unnamed source in the *Times* story that launched the build-up to the bill, served as the spoon that fed the *Post* the Lauder story, and put together the press conference that twelve supportive unions held at City Hall. Yet, as intimately involved as he was every step of the way, Rubenstein's chronology of how the mayor made his decision demolishes the notion that the market crash was the cause.

Rubenstein, registered as a city lobbyist with nineteen clients, acknowledges that he has been talking to the mayor about a third term for at least many months. "I've been asking again and again, and he never said, 'Absolutely no'," says Rubenstein, contrasting that with the flat rejection he got from Bloomberg about any possible run for governor. "He'd say, 'Let's see.' He was thinking about it. He was publicly saying he wasn't interested, but I always felt he'd really like to do it." Asked about a paragraph at the bottom of a *Times* story that claimed that Rubenstein's client and close, personal friend, developer Jerry Speyer, and financier Henry Kravis, who jointly co-chaired the omnipotent Partnership for New York City, had approached Lauder about supporting a one-time extension of term limits for Bloomberg and the council *two years ago*, Rubenstein says: "It's all true." Not even Rubenstein argues that the pitch Speyer and Kravis made in 2006 was prompted by a prophetic sense of municipal doom.

What kicked the third-term campaign into high gear, Rubenstein concedes, was a shrinking of Bloomberg's options. Asked if the mayor started seriously weighing the idea of another term after the presidential and vice-presidential dreams died, Rubenstein says: "I think you're accurate. He really enjoys the action." Rubenstein says there's "no doubt" that the mayor then began "searching" for a way to stay in play. His friend Zuckerman offered the *Times* a similar explanation. Most jobs, Zuckerman said, "would never fully engage him." He would "waste away if he were in a state of semi-activity." Asked by the *Voice* if this psychic need contributed to Bloomberg's decision to run again, Zuckerman seemed at loggerheads with himself, at first saying, "It's not as if he's totally bored" with his other life, and then adding that "he's addicted to the public life of politics." Since Bloomberg did not want to be governor, where there is actually a constitutionally proscribed vacancy in 2010, the only available therapy for his strobe-light addiction became another stint at a familiar and friendly hall, particularly one where he would not also be responsible for the plight of Buffalo. It mattered little that he, more than any mayor, has repeatedly made the case that the state dictates everything the city can or cannot do, down to how many cameras it can post at stoplights. The only way he could save the city, his supporters bizarrely argued, was from City Hall, forcing them to toss out the will of 1,173,558 voters in two referendums.

The recorded sequence of events, some of it abetted by Rubenstein, unmistakeably shows how Bloomberg's moods and personal needs, rather than Wall Street's spiral, were setting the agenda. The *Post*, the paper Rubenstein prefers to leak to, reported in April that the mayor was considering another term, sparking adamant denials from City Hall. On 4 June, the *Post*, citing a secret source, reported that Bloomberg had already done a private poll about changing term limits. On 6 June, Bloomberg confirmed that a poll had been done and said that there was "still plenty of time" to put an initiative on the 2008 ballot extending term limits, promising reporters to "get back to you in the next few weeks." Instead, he dallied until it was too late to do a referendum this year and got Quinn to defeat a motion for an early 2009 referendum and ram an extension, without a referendum at all, through the council in record two-weeks time.

Quinn was in such a Bloomberg-induced rush to back the bill that she did it three days before the council hearings began, then skipped the hearings she had called, only to cite their mere occurrence during the council vote a few days later as proof of how democratic the process had been. It was not the economic panic that prompted the term-limits bill; it was the bill that prompted a *legislative* panic. Never before was the moribund council so apoplectic.

Kathy Wylde, the president of the Partnership, says she learned "in July" that the mayor was "seriously thinking about it," after making inquiries for at least a year. Wylde's board of directors includes virtually everyone whose name has appeared in stories detailing the early lobbying for another term – Speyer, Rattner, Kravis, Rubenstein, Parsons, Murdoch and even Lauder's nephew, William, who actually runs the cosmetics company (Speyer went to William Lauder's father, Leonard, to put pressure on brother Ron). Bloomberg was once on the Partnership board himself, and its twenty-member executive committee voted unanimously to support the extension legislation.

Wylde also lobbied Quinn, who has been a friend since the two worked together in housing organizations more than a decade ago. Wylde introduced Quinn to the Partnership honchos at a luncheon at the Speyer-owned Rockefeller Centre shortly after she became speaker in 2006. "The universal opinion of the CEO is that she has a bright political future," Wylde declared from the onset. Wylde got thirty bigwigs to sign a letter backing the bill, twenty-five of whom are on her board, and an advertisement featuring it soon appeared in the *Times*. The fact is that under Wylde and Speyer's leadership, the Partnership is the closest thing we now have in New York to a political club with the clout to make a mayor.

Of course, the Partnership sees itself as a civic association acting on behalf of us all, but Bloomberg has not just been good for business in the broadest sense – he has been especially good for particular businesses, like Jerry Speyer's. Speyer is both an owner of the Yankees and the developer of its new stadium, which is steeped in so many layers of suspect Bloomberg subsidy that both a state assembly and a house subcommittee are investigating alleged violations of bonding laws. Speyer was also designated by the city as the developer for the Gotham Centre in Queens five years ago and is only now beginning to build a twenty-one-storey tower, tenanted entirely by the city health department under a twenty-year lease. Speyer started out seeking a city lease for less than half of the building's 600,000 square feet, but when he failed to locate any other tenants, the Bloomberg administration decided to take it all, moving 2,700 employees from fifteen different sites to Speyer's building. The city will also spend another $50 million on streetscape and other improvements near the new tower, making it a monument to Bloomberg subsidies, with city-owned land and a $29.6 million starting annual rental stream emanating from City Hall.

In 2006, Speyer also bought Stuyvesant Town and Peter Cooper Village, an 11,000-apartment heaven for middle-class families for decades. The largest and most controversial real estate deal in American history with a price tag of $5.4 billion, the Speyer purchase was fiercely opposed by tenant organizations, who submitted their own $4.5 billion offer and were seeking tax breaks and other support from the Bloomberg administration. The mayor refused to intervene, calling Speyer a "great landlord" and declaring, "I think the tenants will be well protected." News accounts later contrasted his hands-off policy on the Speyer deal with actions he had taken in two other similar tenant fights, with the *Times* even suggesting that Speyer's unique role in the Manhattan elite may have insulated him.

In fact, hundreds of rent-stabilized tenants have been denied renewal, and Speyer is losing most of the legal cases that have been filed challenging the company's manoeuvres. A recently uncovered financial document for Speyer states that the company expects to convert 6,397 units to market rents by 2011, yet Bloomberg insisted earlier this year that he stood by his earlier claim that tenants would be protected. What no one seemed to notice was that just days before the acquisition was completed, Merrill Lynch bought 49 per cent of Speyer's partner in the deal, money manager BlackRock. The COIB had ruled when Bloomberg took office that he had to recuse himself on Merrill Lynch matters because of its partial ownership of Bloomberg L.P., suggesting that the mayor should have allowed others in his administration to determine the city's role in the sale.

I remember in the early Bloomberg days – seizing any opportunity to observe, with pleasure – that his money had bought us a leader that was finally free of the circle of donors, lobbyists and powerbrokers that consumed earlier mayors and confounded the public good.

His message, and it once was true, was that he owed nothing to anybody. He began parcelling himself out in the 2005 campaign, when he did five contracts with unions that endorsed him and spent more of our money to re-elect himself than his own. And since his re-election was never in doubt, he dipped into his money and ours, it turned out, for vanity: it merely increased his margin of victory. Imagine how many own a piece of him now.

If you believe it is worth all of this to get a savvy hand at the tiller in turbulent times, think back to what the *Times* wrote in 2001 when they endorsed his opponent:

> Even within the annals of businessmen-candidates, he is ill-matched to the job he covets. His company has no stockholders and no unions. It is a brand-new business, its corporate culture and decision-making structure devised to

suit his character. . . . Many of Mr. Bloomberg's greatest talents would turn out to be utterly beside the point.

When the bursting collective bargaining, pension and debt costs of the recent Bloomberg boom years are considered, the *Times* of old might have had a point. As it also had as recently as 9 June, when it warned against a term-limits gambit and urged Bloomberg to seek another office: "We are wary of changing the rules just to suit the ambition of a particular politician."

Bloomberg is so set on writing his own story that he decided to produce a memoir, set for release just as he left City Hall. He asked Margaret Carlson, who is on Bloomberg L.P.'s payroll, to collaborate on it. But he recently put it off, the *Times* said, because he was worried about its "boastful tone" possibly turning off voters. The book might have had other, related problems: A tell-all is fine for someone walking away from the game, but not for someone about to begin a new campaign. The claimed successes might have been an irresistible target for reporters, and the petty side of Mike may have led him to dish on people he now needs to seduce one more time. Obviously, most candidates would think that a bestseller in a campaign year, with a 300,000 initial printing, would be an asset. But not Mike, who isn't ready yet to buy his own history. He is determined, regardless of the moral costs, to make history instead.[1]

Note

1 A year later, in 2009, Mike Bloomberg won a third term as mayor of New York.
– Editor

The Resilience of Neoliberal Ideology
C.P. Chandrasekhar

On 16 October 1981, readers of *The Hindu* in India woke up to a major investigative newsbreak from N. Ram, then Washington correspondent of the newspaper. Ram had not only discovered that the Indian government had been negotiating a large International Monetary Fund (IMF) Extended Fund Facility loan, but also that it had submitted a letter of intent accepting conditions that implied a shift away from India's strategy of promoting growth behind protective barriers and capital controls with substantial state regulation of domestic economic activity (Ram 1981). India's government had, in Ram's words, committed itself to "a shift, in some instances a sharp shift, in the "pragmatic,' conservative direction, and in boosting the private sector, Indian and foreign, in the economy at large." This involved freeing trade, liberalizing foreign investment and collaboration rules, deregulating policies affecting domestic investment, reducing subsidies, and adopting conservative fiscal and monetary policies to manage demand, besides accepting IMF surveillance of adherence to time-specific performance clauses and other requirements.

That was a time when, in the opinion of a significant section of the Indian intelligentsia and media, such open door strategies, adopted for example in Chile by the military dictatorship that overthrew Salvador Allende's elected government in 1973, were inimical to national development and the welfare of the people. The IMF-dictated "neoliberal" turn to economic policy was seen as a neocolonial ploy to prise open third world markets to goods marketed by a developed world faced with stagnation, and to open third world economies to the predatory operations of foreign industrial and finance capital.

Not surprisingly, Ram's investigative reports led to a heated debate that embarrassed the government and subjected its policies to a scrutiny that assessed and exposed the degree to which these policies took the country down the neoliberal path. There seemed to be little strength in the justification that the loan was needed in order to ensure that India could face up to the changed situation following two oil shocks, restructure its economy, expand exports, and earn the additional foreign exchange needed to finance a larger oil import bill. This argument seemed to be an excuse to push through a neoliberal turn in economic policy-making that a section of the ruling elite wanted.

The government held out and took the loan, but, influenced perhaps by the debate, it chose to go slow on the reforms it had promised the IMF, and it did not take the last instalment of the loan because of pressure from the IMF to "perform" in ways that could hurt the elite as well.

Along with domestic deregulation, some "external" reforms, focused principally on liberalising import policy, were introduced. The latter contributed to a rise in imports, widened the current account deficit and increased external borrowing, finally precipitating the balance of payments crisis of 1991 (see Chandrasekhar and Ghosh 2002). Nevertheless, growth was driven mainly by debt-financed public expenditure and the reforms were nowhere as dramatic as the advocates of a neoliberal strategy wanted.

Those advocates had to wait till the policy-generated balance of payments crisis of 1991 provided them another opportunity to make the transition to full-blown neoliberalism. They exploited this opportunity by exaggerating the magnitude of the crisis and pushing the government to negotiate another IMF loan. This ability to turn a crisis generated by hesitant liberalization into an opportunity to accelerate neoliberal reforms indicated that India's vocal elite had decided that a strategy of liberalization using access to international liquidity (which had been ensured by the global rise to dominance of finance capital) was the one to endorse.

Prabhat Patnaik and I have argued that despite the collapse of foreign exchange reserves in 1990–91, "India could have managed her payments and restored confidence in her currency with a relatively low-conditionality IMF loan without going in for the whole gamut of structural adjustment measures" (Patnaik and Chandrasekhar 1995). The choice of the IMF-dictated structural adjustment route was not because it was the only option available, but largely because the pro-liberalization lobby saw this as an opportunity to force policy down that path rather than address the institutional constraints underlying the failure of the interventionist strategy pursued since India's Independence. The result was an accelerated process of policy revision that jettisoned the interventionist regime.

There had always been differences of opinion on the value and efficacy of interventionist, import-substituting regimes. But the critique of this strategy was never strong enough because domestic deregulation and trade liberalization with the intent of pursuing an export-oriented strategy was not an option in the two decades and a half that followed the Second World War. During that period, almost all the developing countries (with one or two exceptions) were dependent on foreign direct investment and the development aid network for foreign capital that could finance a current account deficit. Access to foreign capital through these routes was determined by decisions taken on the supply side by investors and governments of the developed industrial nations. So, to the extent that trade liberalization widened trade and current account deficits, countries faced a real prospect that access to capital to finance these deficits may not be available. This was because while an immediate increase in imports was inevitable, exports would not necessarily rise (and even if they did, the rise would come after a lag – after special efforts were made and goodwill created).

It was only in the 1970s, when increased liquidity in the international financial system allowed the more developed among the less developed countries to (mistakenly) believe that they could gain access to foreign finance on demand, that a deregulation and liberalization-based export-oriented strategy became feasible. Interestingly, it was at that time also that intellectual advocates of such strategies began espousing their views.

N. Ram had captured the first attempt in India to push through a neoliberal strategy based on those views with the aid of IMF finance. The country and its intelligentsia, let alone Indian big business, were not fully prepared for the transition at that time. But they were a decade later, and the balance of payments crisis of 1991 somehow persuaded them that now the moment was opportune.

In the twenty-five years since then, much evidence has accumulated that whatever growth has been achieved in India's neoliberal era has been volatile and has increased its external vulnerability. Yet the opposition to neoliberalism has not gained strength to the extent that it did in many Latin American countries over the last fifteen years or so. Even in 2016, by which time liberalization had gone a long way, the Indian government voluntarily committed to fiscal consolidation, reduction of direct taxes, privatization and embrace of foreign capital. And it not only received support for this from big business, the media, and a large section of the social and political elite, but was also exhorted to stay on the neoliberal path despite evidence that the social and development outcomes have been adverse, and that even the growth achieved is unsustainable.

In Latin America, crises resulting from the transition to neoliberalism led to three lost decades in terms of growth, and had consequences for welfare that could not be defended within the framework of democratic politics. By contrast in India, after the decade of the 1990s when the neoliberal, marketist regime was consolidated, the country benefited from a liquidity surge in international capital markets driven by the easy monetary and low interest policies adopted by central banks in the United States and other developed countries. This substantially enhanced cross-border flows of capital to the so-called emerging markets, which ensured a period of high growth led by debt-financed private expenditure in some of these countries. India, as one of the beneficiaries, experienced high, debt-financed, private spending-led growth for a longish period beginning 2003–04 – with the exception of one year of global crisis, 2008–09. This growth spurt, however, started tapering off and lost momentum after 2011–12. It damaged the balance sheets of banks because of defaults on a rising proportion of the large volumes of credit that had been advanced, raising questions about the sustainability of the government's neoliberal trajectory. But India has still to experience the equivalent of one or more lost decades that triggered Latin America's disillusionment with neoliberalism.

That the trajectory in India which began with a balance of payments crisis has not yet run into another deep crisis is not the sole explanation for the relative resilience of the neoliberal thrust. The global evidence is that the period since the 1980s, when a shift in policy occurred across both developed and developing countries, has been marked by periodic crises that have been far more in number and intensity than in the immediate post-Second World War years (including one that almost matched the Great Depression). It is also the period when the top 1 per cent of the income spectrum captured most of the income gains, unemployment among the youth ruled high, and improvements in the most basic of human development indicators was disappointingly slow across the world. What is noteworthy, then, is that the global record notwithstanding, the governments of India and other developing countries (barring a few) have stayed with the neoliberal strategy. This points to a kind of "resilience" of the neoliberal ideology, which calls for an explanation.

Neoliberalism is of course an ambiguous and loosely defined term even when it is restricted to the economic sphere. So it would be useful to clarify the sense in which it is being used in this context. In what follows, neoliberal theory and practice are taken as referring to: (i) the use of the rhetoric of market fundamentalism, in which the market or, ostensibly, "free economic exchange" is presented as the most efficient mechanism to make the economic system work, and to pave the way for increasingly unfettered functioning of private capital, both domestic and foreign; (ii) the use of the notion of a minimalist state, to be realized by dismantling its developmentalist version, in order to legitimize the shift of various terms of trade and mechanisms of distribution in favour of the owners of capital and their functionaries, and to conceal the conversion of segments of the state apparatus into sites for forms of primitive accumulation of capital; and

(iii) the pursuit of a regime of accumulation in which the home market and deficit-financed state expenditure are replaced by exports and debt-financed private expenditure as the principal stimuli to growth.

As has often been noted, the rise of neoliberalism has been coterminous with the rise to dominance of finance in the developed industrial world and the global economy. Neoliberalism and financial globalization feed on each other. Since the liberalization of trade and of the rules governing cross-border flows of capital result, in the first instance, in a widening of the trade and current account deficits in the balance of payments of the liberalizing economy, access to foreign capital to finance that deficit is a prerequisite for "successful" liberalization that is not aborted by a balance of payments crisis. Thus, the pursuit of a neoliberal economic strategy is not feasible in a world in which access to international finance to developing countries is severely limited.

While this explains the link between the global rise to dominance of finance and neoliberalism, the rise to dominance of finance was itself the result of a sharp increase in liquidity in the international financial system in the years after the 1960s. This increase was triggered by a host of developments: the accumulation of large surpluses by the oil exporting countries after the two oil shocks (much of these surpluses were invested in assets created by the international financial system); reckless spending abroad by the government of the United States, exploiting the status of the dollar as the world's reserve currency; the accumulation of large resources with pension funds as the post-war, baby boomer generation entered the work force and had to save for retirement; and the decision of developed country governments (influenced by finance) to rely on monetary as opposed to fiscal policy for macroeconomic management, with an emphasis on infusing liquidity to drive credit and growth and keeping interest rates low when inflation was not the immediate problem. Prompted by the need to profitably invest the resulting large financial surpluses, it became clear to the managers of these funds that they could not restrict themselves to developed country markets but needed to move into developing countries as well. This resulted in a change in perception among developing country governments, which now began to believe that international finance was available "on demand," providing room for ambitious export-oriented strategies led by deregulation and liberalization.

The problem, however, was that capital flows were actually still determined from the supply side. All that these countries could do was to adopt policies that could make them attractive destinations for foreign direct and portfolio investors. Foreign investors favour environments in which markets and private capital are allowed a free rein. Once trade and investment rules are liberalized to attract foreign capital, domestic controls on the operations of institutions that bring that capital need to be diluted or dismantled. This inevitably leads them down the neoliberal path.

However, this does require a decision on the part of governments to open their borders in the first place. Given the failure to successfully pursue import-substituting strategies of industrialization and development, and the fascination with the export-oriented, mercantilist strategies generated by South Korea's and Taiwan's successes, most governments did open their borders. In contexts where the political system was authoritarian, such as in Chile, this was easy to implement. In other environments, there was resistance to the first step. But everywhere the shift occurred over time.

What is evident now is that no country that embraced a neoliberal strategy has succeeded the way South Korea and Taiwan did. The success of Chinese growth, even if associated with a greater role for markets, is by no means an instance of a typical neoliberal strategy (though with an increasing shift in that direction, it too is facing new difficulties). And even South Korea, which opted for liberalization after its successful use of interventionist measures, was badly hit during the Southeast Asian crisis of 1997. Whenever neoliberalism has achieved success, such as in the second-tier industrializing countries of Southeast Asia, such success has inevitably proved to be temporary, with the neoliberal frontier shifting continuously. It moved from Latin America to Asia, and within Asia is moving from the second-tier, newly industrializing countries to countries like Vietnam and India. Although the success may be striking, it has thus far been temporary – and the subsequent decline can be sudden and traumatic.

In terms of human development advance, the outcomes of neoliberal trajectories have been extremely adverse. There have been periodic crises of varying intensity triggered by developments in the capital, credit and currency markets, resulting in slow growth, rising unemployment and increased economic deprivation.

The livelihoods of those dependent on agriculture, which is home to much of the labouring poor, have deteriorated and are even endangered. The free rein given to private capital has resulted in predatory practices, as in forestry and the mining industry, for example, which have had devastating effects on the poor and the marginalized, and have been identified as a process of development through "encroachment" or "dispossession." These trajectories have also altered the form and curtailed the volume of state spending, adversely affecting the degree to which welfare expenditures of the state can redress the negative outcomes of growth for a large section of the population.

Overall, neoliberal trajectories have involved extracting surpluses from productive sectors and damaging the livelihoods of working people engaged in these sectors. The fact that even in countries that are successfully pursuing a neoliberal trajectory decent jobs are scarce, and inequality and poverty are on the rise, discredits this path of capitalist development even more.

POSSIBLE EXPLANATIONS

Despite this record, as noted earlier, the popular legitimacy of the neoliberal trajectory in India (and much of Asia) has not been undermined although it has been challenged. One obvious reason for this is that the actually existing alternatives to the neoliberal trajectory offered by the centrally planned, socialist economies have collapsed. That collapse was partly a result of the rise of globalized finance and its influence even outside the capitalist world order. But a host of internal contradictions and developments paved the way for an increase in dependence on foreign capital and the weakening of the planning principle in the centrally planned economies. These included structural constraints on ensuring adequate access to the information needed for designing and implementing an *a priori* plan and bureaucratization, which distorts the decisions taken by agents involved in plan design and implementation on behalf of the society and the people. In the words of Irfan Habib:

> Who controls the socialist state (and how) is the crucial question determining the destiny of socialism. When socialism is established there is no blind economic "law" which would take socialist society in one particular direction, that of advance. There are policy alternatives at every step; and the choice can always be coloured by group, sectional, and (ultimately) the choice-makers' own interest as distinct from, and therefore, possibly opposed to, the interest of the people at large. (Habib 1994)

This experience with actually existing planned economies has made the task of delineating an appropriate "planning principle" which can be counterposed to the market mechanism, and of defending a substantial role for the state, that much more difficult. And since the state must play a role in shaping and sustaining more egalitarian systems, this does delay the fruition of the socialist project, since it not only postpones the dates at which the milestones on the road to egalitarianism may be crossed, but leaves unfinished the task of defining the contours of an alternative society.

The delegitimization of the socialist project has isolated those engaged in a critical discourse, with sections of the so-called Centre, including those in the judiciary and the media, now adopting the discourse of the Right rather than of the Left. As time goes by, much of the intelligentsia begins to see not just the path but also the objectives of development differently. Despite the lack of supporting evidence, a view has gained ground that if the neoliberal project can be appropriately tweaked to suit country characteristics and if high growth can be ensured for, say, a decade, then, an exit from underdevelopment is ensured. Inequality may increase, but poverty can be dealt with through public action. This perspective has been strengthened by the fact that in its phases of success, neoliberalism is able to expand (and even relies on an expansion of) consumption among the upper middle classes. Even when offered contractual employment with self-funded social security, leading sections of the middle class are bought off with the promise of high salaries and opportunities for credit-financed consumption. That promise is not a result of largesse to the middle class but part of the change in the regime of accumulation of neoliberal strategies, which coopt a section of the erstwhile middle class. This deprives the opposition of the support of some of its most vocal and articulate voices of dissent and protest. The lethargy in protest induced by the middle class crossing over to a defence of neoliberalism is another cause for the ascendancy of neoliberal ideology.

This cross-over affects practitioners of the media as well. The defence of neoliberalism by the media is intensified by the financialization of the media at an institutional and individual level. The media in India, especially television but also sections of the print media, are now directly or through the activities of subsidiaries or sister firms of media enterprises, exposed to the stockmarket. As a consequence of investments and stock options, well-paid senior personnel of the media are also exposed to the stockmarket. The media therefore has a stake in a strategy that privileges finance, makes the performance of financial markets an indicator of economic health, and is designed to ensure high returns to rentiers and financial investors.

In February 2008, the then outgoing chairman of the Securities Exchange Board of India (SEBI), M. Damodaran, warned of the media's role in "talking up" or "talking down" stocks, and called for strict disclosure norms. In an interview on television, Damodaran said:

> When we heard the term anchor investors first, I thought anchor investor is the guy that brings in a lot of money initially into a project around whose reputation others invest. I am beginning to believe at the end of my three-year tenure that an anchor investor is one who is an anchor and an investor put together. I am worried that (they are) those who are responsible . . .

who take the message to a billion plus people who will hopefully, one day be interested in the market. If that message gets distorted, what happens? (*Indian Express* 2008)

A critical analyst of the media writes: "The media themselves have become more and more self-conscious, with little going for those below a set purchasing power threshold. The lower you are in the social and economic scale, seems the moral and the model, the less relevant you are to the media, either as subject or consumer" (Sashi Kumar 2011).

As N. Ram (2011) notes, the phenomenon goes beyond those who are directly compromised. In Ram's view, while "the propaganda of state-controlled television and radio is widely recognized and ridiculed in the Indian public arena," it is true that "the press too can be seen to manufacture consent from time to time in relation to sensitive, contentious issues." Among the instances he quotes is "the propaganda role played by much of the press on issues and controversies raised by the post-1991 experience of economic liberalization." Elaborating on this, Ram writes:

> As for post-1991 economic liberalization, press and broadcasting media coverage to date has tended to adopt a laudatory tone, keep out or underplay the criticisms and objections, censor the negative political and socio-economic effects, especially among the poor, and provide little space to the voices of robust criticism and opposition, including those raised from the ranks of professional economists. (Ibid.)

In such a situation, it often happens that professional journalists who consciously carry forward the critical-investigative function do not have the impact or influence they deserve. One explanation for this is offered by Prabhat Patnaik, who writes of the effects of the hegemony of finance over the media. "As a result, where the media are on the same side as international finance capital, they appear powerful; but in fields where they strike out on their own, upholding humane values and expressing concern for the poor and the suffering, they appear powerless" (Patnaik 2002).

The net result is a propagandist promotion of neoliberalism in large parts of the media and visceral attacks on those who oppose it. This turns an important instrument of dissemination of information and critical engagement (as illustrated by Ram's exposé discussed earlier) into an instrument to promote the neoliberal agenda. The dominant opinion purveyed by the media, barring a few exceptions, is supportive of neoliberalism. Opinion to the contrary is noticeable, if at all, because of its near-absence and the conscious effort to underplay its relevance.

The media merely echo a larger tendency, nurtured by the establishment and internalized by the elite, to argue that there is a "consensus" regarding the lack of any alternative to neoliberal capitalism, not just capitalism per se. To some in the media and outside, this position is opportunistic, since it serves their own narrow interests. Corporate and finance capital have entered the media as owners of equity, dependence on advertising revenues is large, and some members of the media have their eyes trained on the stockmarket where their savings are invested. But there are many who have accepted the propaganda of neoliberal advocates uncritically, either because of the promise it holds out or because they believe there is no alternative to neoliberalism, despite its blemishes.

The relationship between the rise of finance capital and the rise of neoliberalism has a further implication. This relationship inevitably results in the increased presence of and dependence on foreign capital in countries pursuing neoliberal strategies. Any effort to challenge or reverse neoliberal economic policies inevitably leads to the exit of portfolio and footloose productive capital, and to a crisis of sorts that must be endured if an alternative strategy is to be experimented with. Such a crisis not only worsens the conditions of the poor, but also gives rise to the view that any attempt at a transition to some form of an alternative to neoliberalism would lead to capital flight and precipitate a crisis, making the alternative impracticable in the new world dominated by finance.

The Turn to Welfarism

One consequence of all this has been a change in the nature of "radical" discourse. If neoliberalism is worsening the living conditions of the poor and the working people, and the egalitarian alternative system is both difficult to define and clearly not imminent, then the immediate tactics and practice of opponents of neoliberalism must incorporate elements of welfarism, or actions aimed at providing some succour to the poor. Thus, as opposed to focusing on the unequalizing, unsustainable and unstable nature of neoliberal growth, demands for access to employment, food and nutrition, and education and health services, for example, have become important planks of the opposition's programme. In response, neoliberalism seeks to legitimize itself by packaging its ideology with new views of justice, new ways to define development and new policies to give development a human face. Neoliberal policies are presented as unavoidable if growth that generates surpluses to distribute is to be achieved; but deprivation itself, it is argued, must be dealt with independently of growth. If this is the form that neoliberal rhetoric takes, then the immediate task placed before the opposition, of fighting to deliver welfare benefits to the working people and the poor, gives it the external image of saying much the same.

The result is that the last decade and a half have been characterized by a kind of ideological convergence in mainstream economic and social thinking. On the one hand, the defeat of actually existing socialism and the spread of many hybrid forms of capitalism, including in China, for example, have led to an almost cynical acceptance of actually existing capitalism as inevitable from the point of view of productivity increase, growth and the delivery of an ever-widening set of goods to satisfy an increasingly consumerist society. On the other hand, there is a growing consensus that actually existing market economies are based on and accentuate extreme forms of social and economic inequality, and are associated with externalities in the forms of environmental destruction, displacement and (some would argue) persistent war. That the top 1 per cent, besides a few around the middle of the income distribution, gain most from capitalist growth is increasingly accepted by many. The uneven development that capitalism delivers is also seen as having resulted in distorted distribution of a carbon budget defined by scientific assessments of the relationship between carbon emissions resulting from the pattern of growth, global warming and climate change. Yet market economies *as we know them*, often implicitly and on occasion explicitly, are seen as the only viable systems from the point of view of reproduction and expansion of the economy, and, therefore, of economic welfare.

Part of the explanation for this is the "evidence" offered by the historical success of actually existing capitalism in the developed capitalist countries today. But what is ignored by that interpretation of the historical evidence is that the success in part has been built on the destruction of economic activity in and deindustrialization of the periphery in the search for markets for capitalist growth; in part on the ability of the metropolitan centres to reduce unemployment at home by encouraging migration to the regions of recent settlement; and in part on the drain of surpluses from what has become today's periphery to finance accumulation and growth in the metropolitan centres and regions of recent settlement. This did indeed help sustain growth and improve welfare in what has come to be known as the North, but it simultaneously not only held back development in the South, but also generated and strengthened structural features that limited the growth potential of the South.

The neglect of this history has created a special problem that has plagued the discourse on making growth less unequalizing and, more importantly, capable of offering a solution to the problems of the absence of adequate sources of decent livelihood for all global citizens and of the persistence of extreme forms of social deprivation. The result has been a tendency to dissociate the two objectives: of ensuring growth, on the one hand, and of fairly distributing the benefits of growth, on the other. The claim seems to be that growth-inducing factors (such as technological change, globalization and "reform" that allows for the unbridled operation of market forces) tend, unfortunately, to be unequalizing, given the unequal initial conditions on which they are based. So what is needed to make growth "inclusive" is: (i) to address, through direct public action, the worst forms of social and economic deprivation, captured till now in the campaign to realize the Millennium Development Goals and embodied in the campaign to realize the recently formulated Sustainable Development Goals; and (ii) to increase the capabilities of those at the deprived end of the social spectrum through better education, health and much else, to participate fruitfully in the market process, and help them better their social and economic status. The thrust now is not intervention to regulate the functioning of a market economy but intervention to neutralize the effects of its most destabilizing consequences.

The presumption here, of course, is that the features and mechanisms that render capitalist growth – especially increasingly unregulated capitalist growth – socially unequalizing and environmentally destructive will not also limit the ability of the state to directly address those outcomes adequately to deliver the welfare "goals" and "indicators" that would be reasonable at any stage of overall development. In practice, in market-friendly and reformed capitalist regimes, policies such as low taxation to incentivize the private sector and restraints on public borrowing to ensure "fiscal consolidation" have resulted in governments cutting back on social sector expenditures and expenditures on poverty alleviation. The solution, then, is to set less ambitious goals and celebrate their achievement. The stronger the adherence of the state to neoliberal policies, the weaker is its ability to counter their adverse effects on human development through public action.

Despite the fact that neoliberal growth and welfare advance are incompatible, the separation of the two goals helps legitimize neoliberalism in so far as the persistence of deprivation is seen as a result of inadequate public action rather than as a consequence of neoliberal growth. To separate the goals of growth and welfare is to reduce the force of the progressive claim that realizing a welfarist and egalitarian order requires the pursuit of an alternative rather than a neoliberal strategy. The weakening of that progressive claim further strengthens neoliberal ideology and makes it more resilient.

REFERENCES

Balassa, Bela *et al.* (1971), *The Structure of Protection in Developing Countries*, Baltimore: Johns Hopkins Press.

Bhagwati, Jagdish N. and Padma Desai (1970), *India: Planning for Industrialization*, London: Oxford University Press, for OECD, Paris.

Boughton James M. (2001), *Silent Revolution: The International Monetary Fund, 1870–90*, IMF.

Chandrasekhar, C.P. and Jayati Ghosh (2002), *The Market that Failed: A Decade of Neo-Liberal Economic Reforms in India*, New Delhi: Leftword Books.

Habib, Irfan (1993), "The Marxian Theory of Socialism and the Experience of the Socialist Societies," *Social Scientist*, Vol. 21, Nos. 5–6, May–June. Revised and published as an appendix in Irfan Habib, ed. (2009), *On Socialism: Selections from the Writings of Karl Marx, Frederick Engels, V.I. Lenin, J.V. Stalin, Mao Zedong*, New Delhi: Tulika Books and Aligarh: Aligarh Historians Society.

Indian Express (2008), "TV anchors, media talking up, talking down stocks, need clean-up: outgoing SEBI chief," 16 February.

Little, Ian, Tibor Scitovsky and Maurice Scott (1970), *Industry and Trade in Some Developing Countries*, London: Oxford University Press.

Patnaik, Prabhat (2002), "Markets, Morals and the Media," Convocation Address, Asian College of Journalism, Chennai.

Patnaik, Prabhat and C.P. Chandrasekhar (1995), "Structural Adjustment and India," *Economic and Political Weekly*, 25 November.

Ram, N. (1981), "Conditions which IMF will impose for loan," *The Hindu*, 16 October, available at http://www.interestingreads.org/wp-content/uploads/2012/08/19811016_01-Conditions-which-IMF-will-impose-for-loan.pdf

Ram, N. (2011), "The Changing Role of the News Media in Contemporary India," Presidential Address, Indian History Congress, 72nd session, Patiala, December.

Sashi Kumar (2011), "The exercise of hegemony in contemporary culture and media and the need for a counter-hegemony initiative," *Social Scientist*, Vol. 39, Nos. 11–12, November–December.

Shaping the Post-War World
Noam Chomsky

Seventy years have passed since the end of the most horrific war in human history. I would like to review some of the developments that have taken place during this period and what they suggest about the future.[1]

In 1945, the United States (US) was in a position of overwhelming power with no historical precedent. Long before the war it had been the world's richest society with unparalleled advantages. During the war other industrial powers were severely damaged or virtually destroyed, while the American economy boomed. Industrial production quadrupled, and wartime technological developments laid the basis for the rapid growth that followed. The US had literally half of the world's wealth, along with overwhelming military predominance and a position of security that had no parallel. It controlled the hemisphere, both oceans and the opposite sides of both oceans. And it alone possessed the ultimate weapon, the atomic bomb.

It was no surprise that under those circumstances, US planners prepared to organize as much of the world as possible in ways that would satisfy the needs of the American economy – the standard formulation, which means, in reality, primarily the needs of dominant elements within US society, the powerful corporate sector.

The New World Order that was to be established is sometimes described with admirable candour in mainstream scholarship. Diplomatic historian Gerald Haines, senior historian of the Central Intelligence Agency (CIA), writes in a highly-regarded study, "Following World War II the United States assumed, out of self-interest, responsibility for the welfare of the world capitalist system. . . . American leaders tried to reshape the world to fit US needs and standards." That required dismantling imperial preference systems and creating an "open world," but with exceptions: the US desired a "closed hemispheric system in an open world," Haines observes. As explained by Secretary of War Henry Stimson in May 1945, other regional groupings were to be dismantled, but the US would control "our little region over here which has never bothered anybody" – Latin America and the Caribbean.

These ideas capture very well the operative principle of the famous Open Door principle: what we have, if it is of some importance, we keep; elsewhere, open access to all. The principle was articulated by the State Department in 1944 in a memorandum called "Petroleum Policy of the

United States." The US then dominated western hemisphere production, which was to remain the largest in the world for another quarter-century. That system must remain closed, the memorandum declared, while the rest of the world must be open. US policy "would involve the preservation of the absolute position presently obtaining, and therefore vigilant protection of existing concessions in United States hands coupled with insistence upon the Open Door principle of equal opportunity for United States companies in new areas."

That Latin America would be ours is an expectation that goes back to the earliest days of the Republic, given an early form in the Monroe Doctrine of 1823. The intentions were articulated plainly and illustrated consistently in action, and generally well-understood by political leadership. In the 1890s, Secretary of State Richard Olney, citing the Monroe Doctrine as his authority, sternly admonished Britain that its day in the sun was waning: "today," he informed his British students, "the United States is practically sovereign on this continent, and its fiat is law upon the subjects to which it confines its interposition." Britain must therefore bend to Washington's will in a dispute over Latin American borders, recognizing, as Olney explained, that "its infinite resources combined with its isolated position render [the US] master of the situation and practically invulnerable as against any or all other power." It is hard to improve upon the formulation by Woodrow Wilson's Secretary of State, Robert Lansing, which the President – the great advocate of self-determination (in some places) – found "unanswerable" though "impolitic" to state openly: "In its advocacy of the Monroe Doctrine the United States considers its own interests. The integrity of other American nations is an incident, not an end. While this may seem based on selfishness alone, the author of the Doctrine had no higher or more generous motive in its declaration."

Fair enough. And worth bearing in mind as we turn to how the world has been changing, particularly in this millennium.

Returning to the early days of the contemporary era, even before the US entered the Second World War, high-level meetings were taking place to consider the shape of the post-war world. Planners determined that the US should seek "to hold unquestioned power," acting to ensure the "limitation of any exercise of sovereignty" by states that might interfere with US global designs. They called for "a programme of complete rearmament" as the core part of "an integrated policy to achieve military and economic supremacy for the United States" in what they called a "Grand Area," which would include at least the western hemisphere, the former British empire and the far east. As Russia began to beat back the Nazi armies and it became fairly clear that Germany would be defeated, the plans were extended to include as much of Eurasia as possible, certainly its West European industrial and financial heartland.

At the war's end, these plans were spelled out in detail and then implemented. Much of the work was done by the State Department Policy Planning Staff, directed by George Kennan, a leading architect of the post-war world.

The first and most important task had already begun during the final years of the war, as US and British armies advanced into southern Europe. A primary concern was to restore much of the traditional order, including fascist collaborators, and to destroy the anti-fascist resistance with its dangerous commitment to radical democracy. Europe was to be reconstructed in ways that would integrate it into the US-run system of global state capitalism with a prime role for the US-based multinational corporations that were by then coming to assume their modern form.

Other regions were assigned their "functions" within the overall system. Thus a primary function of Southeast Asia was to provide raw materials for the recovery of the former imperial powers, to enable them to import the US manufacturing surplus. One region, Africa, was given a special status. Kennan regarded Africa as of little importance for the US – a conception that has changed in recent years – so that its function was to be "exploited" by Europe for its reconstruction (in Kennan's words).

Official policy continued to articulate the leading concerns. For example, National Security Council memorandum 5432 in 1954 perceived US interests to be threatened by "radical and nationalistic regimes" that are responsive to popular pressures for "immediate improvement in the low living standards of the masses" and development for domestic needs, tendencies that conflict with the need for "a political and economic climate conducive to private investment," with adequate repatriation of profits.

Naturally, there have been many changes over the years. One very instructive case is "our little region over here." In very recent years it has undergone quite a remarkable development. For the first time in five hundred years, Latin America has taken significant steps towards freeing itself from imperial domination, in the recent period of US domination. These include steps towards meaningful integration, a prerequisite for independence; and towards confronting extremely serious internal problems that have impeded the healthy growth of what should be one of the most dynamic and prosperous regions in the world, and a leader in the global struggle for emancipation and justice. These are developments of truly historic significance with considerable import for the future.

The character of these historic changes is well illustrated by two western hemispheric conferences. The first, in Chapultepec Mexico, was called by the United States in February 1945, in the final days of the Second World War. The second was in Cartagena Colombia, the Sixth Summit of the Americas, in April 2012. The conferences were radically different in ways that tell us a good deal about the recent evolution of world affairs.

The Chapultepec Conference was called by the US to lay down the rules to the countries of Latin America. It imposed an Economic Charter for the Americas, which determined that economic nationalism must be barred "in all its forms" – with the unspoken exception of the United States, where it was even more vigorously pursued than in earlier years with large-scale state expenditures, commonly through the Pentagon funnel, which laid the basis for the modern high-tech economy: computers, the internet, microelectronics, etc., largely created within the dynamic state sector for decades by various devices (research, funding, procurement, etc.) before the technology is handed over to private enterprise for marketing and profit – a policy of public subsidy, private profit, conventionally called "the free market."

Washington's primary concerns in 1945 were explained by the State Department. What was particularly troubling was "the philosophy of the New Nationalism" in Latin America, which seeks "a broader distribution of wealth and to raise the standard of living of the masses," and which holds that "the first beneficiaries of the development of a country's resources should be the people of that country." That is quite unacceptable. As Kennan observed, we must ensure the "protection of our raw materials" – ours, though they happen to be located elsewhere. And the "first beneficiaries" must be US investors, not the people of the country – who are "an incident, not an end," in Lansing's perceptive words.

Kennan was a respected realist, and therefore understood that such measures might not be welcome. Therefore, he explained, "the final answer might be an unpleasant one: police repression by the local government." "Harsh government measures of repression" are no problem as long as "the results are on balance favourable to our purposes." In general, "it is better to have a strong regime in power than a liberal government if it is indulgent and relaxed and penetrated by Communists." The term "Communist" refers very broadly to anyone infected by such heresies as the philosophy of the New Nationalism.

Under the circumstances of 1945, the Economic Charter was accepted. There is no need to review how the policies were implemented in the years that followed.

Let us turn now to the second of the two hemispheric conferences, the Summit in Cartagena in 2012. Its outcome was well summarized by a headline in the Jamaican press: "Summit shows how much Yanqui influence had waned." The conference could reach no consensus decisions because the US and Canada were isolated on the major issues: admission of Cuba to the organization and steps to reverse the US drug war, which has been an utter disaster for Latin America.

The summit was hosted by the closest US ally in South America, President Juan Manuel Santos of Colombia. He forcefully condemned the unilateral US policy of barring Cuba, and he called for rethinking the destructive US "war on drugs." He was strongly supported by others, including the Guatemalan president Perez Molina, one of the country's most brutal military offices and another US ally. On both of these key issues, the US and Canada rejected the demands of the hemisphere.

There was also a third issue: Argentina's call for support on the Falklands–Malvinas conflict. Again, the US and Canada were isolated in opposition.

The isolation of the US and Canada is revealed further by the formation of new regional groupings, such as UNASUR, the Union of South American Nations, and CELAC, the Community of Latin American and Caribbean States, which includes all the Americas apart from the US and Canada. Obama's partial steps towards normalization of relations with Cuba were doubtless impelled by an effort to prevent total isolation in what used to be "our little region over here," which did as it was told in the old days but no longer.

The comparison of the two conferences is one manifestation of the theme of America's decline that has become a leading topic of debate and discussion in the past few years. To give one illustration, the journal of the Academy of Political Science opened an issue by declaring, "It is a common theme" that the United States, which "only a few years ago was hailed to stride the world as a colossus with unparalleled power and unmatched appeal – is in decline, ominously facing the prospect of its final decay." In the major establishment journal, *Foreign Affairs*, the headline blaring on the cover of the December 2011 issue read in bold face: "**Is America Over?**" A commonly drawn corollary is that power will shift to China, and perhaps India, in the next century.

There is some truth to these laments, as the developments in Latin America in recent years illustrate, but qualifications are in order. Despite their economic development and increasing international role, China and India remain very poor countries. In the 2016 *Human Development Report* of the United Nations, China is ranked 91st and India 131st, right below

Tajikistan and Honduras. Both face very serious problems, unknown in the rich developed states. The world is surely becoming more diverse, but despite America's decline, in the foreseeable future there is no competitor for global hegemonic power.

Furthermore, the decline is not a recent phenomenon. It has been under way ever since the high point of US power was reached in 1945.

Within a few years, the Grand Area seriously eroded with China's Independence in 1949, an event routinely called "the loss of China." The "loss" quickly became a major issue in US domestic politics, including the rise of McCarthyist repression, inspired in large part by the search for those who were responsible for the loss of China. At once there was concern about the possible loss of Southeast Asia, impelling Washington to support France's war to regain control of its Vietnamese colony, then on to the Indochina wars, the worst crime of the post-war era.

The conventional term "loss" is interesting: one can only "lose" what one possesses. The tacit assumption is that the US owns most of the world by right, not an unreasonable assumption under the early post-war circumstances. Decline was, however, inevitable, as the industrial world reconstructed and decolonization pursued its agonizing course. By 1970, US share of world wealth had declined to about 25 per cent, still colossal but sharply reduced. The industrial world was becoming "tripolar," with major centres in the US, Europe and Asia, then Japan-centered, already becoming the most dynamic region.

Another major change occurred when the Soviet Union collapsed, ending the Cold War. One of the best ways to understand the reality of the Cold War is to look at what happened when it ended.

The Bush I administration, then in office, immediately made it clear that policies would remain pretty much unchanged, but with different pretexts. A huge military establishment would be maintained, but not for defence against the Russians; rather, to confront the "technological sophistication" of third world powers. Similarly, it would be necessary to maintain "the defence industrial base," a euphemism for advanced industry, highly reliant on government subsidy and initiative. Intervention forces still had to be aimed at the Middle East, where the serious problems "could not be laid at the Kremlin's door," contrary to half a century of deceit. It was quietly conceded that the problems had always been "radical nationalism," that is, attempts by countries to pursue an independent course in violation of Grand Area principles.

The principles themselves were not modified. The Clinton administration declared that the US has the right to use military force unilaterally to ensure "uninhibited access to key markets, energy supplies, and strategic resources," and must have military forces "forward deployed" in Europe and Asia, "in order to shape people's opinions about us" and "to shape events that will affect our livelihood and our security." Bush II went on to establish the principle of pre-emptive war. Obama's main innovation has been a global drone assassination campaign targeting individuals suspected of perhaps intending to harm the United States, along with other unfortunates who happen to be nearby – terrorism on a scale never before contemplated.

It is of some interest that Washington's dramatic cancellation of the principle of "presumption of innocence" is taking place on the 800th anniversary of the Magna Carta, which articulated the principle in a limited form that was subsequently greatly expanded and that is generally understood to be the foundation of Anglo–American law, or, as Winston Churchill put it, "the charter of every self-respecting man at any time in any land."

The fate of NATO (the North Atlantic Treay Organization) is revealing as well. Instead of being reduced or eliminated, as propaganda of earlier years would have led one to expect, NATO was expanded to the east – in violation of verbal pledges to Mikhail Gorbachev when he agreed to allow a unified Germany to join NATO, no slight concession in the light of history. By now NATO has become a global intervention force under US command with the official task of controlling the international energy system. NATO Secretary-General Jaap de Hoop Scheffer instructed a NATO conference that "NATO troops have to guard pipelines that transport oil and gas that is directed for the West," and more generally, to protect sea-routes used by tankers and other "crucial infrastructure" of the energy system.

There was a period of euphoria after the collapse of the superpower enemy with excited tales about "the end of history" and awed acclaim for Clinton's foreign policy, which had entered a "noble phase" with a "saintly glow" as for the first time in history a nation is guided by "altruism" and dedicated to "principles and values"; and nothing stood in the way of the "idealistic New World bent on ending inhumanity," which could at last carry forward, unhindered, the emerging international norm of "humanitarian intervention" – to sample just a few of the impassioned accolades by prominent intellectuals.

Not all were so enraptured. The traditional victims, the global South, bitterly condemned "the so-called 'right' of humanitarian intervention" at the South Summit in April 2000 – clearly with NATO's attack on Serbia in mind – recognizing it to be just the old "right" of imperial domination. The stand was reiterated in the summit of non-aligned countries in Malaysia in February 2003. And more sober voices at home among the policy elite could perceive that for much of the world the US was "becoming the rogue superpower," considered "the single greatest external threat to their societies," and that "the prime rogue state today is the United States" (Samuel Huntington, Harvard Professor of the Science of Government; Robert Jervis, President of the American Political Science Association).

The stand of the global South was reiterated by a December 2004, high-level UN Panel that included such prominent figures as Brent Scowcroft, National Security Adviser for George Bush I. The Panel reaffirmed the basic principle of the UN Charter, banning the use of force, with two exceptions: when authorized by the UN Security Council; or under Article 51, in defence against armed attack until the Security Council acts.

With "humanitarian intervention" having lost its lustre, something new was needed, and just in time, a new doctrine was created: Responsibility to Protect (R2P). The patron-saint greatly lauded for this contribution to liberal internationalism is Australian diplomat Gareth Evans, who had a shocking record of support for murderous aggression, indeed virtual genocide, as Australia's Foreign Minister. The doctrine has two versions. The first, adopted by the UN General Assembly in 2005, breaks little new ground, basically reaffirming the stand of the high-level UN Panel a year earlier. The second, authored by Evans, is the same with one change: it authorizes regional groupings (which in effect means NATO) to intervene by force in violation of the UN Charter. The second version is the operative one; the first is invoked to demonstrate the universal endorsement of the right of NATO to intervene.

Meanwhile decline continued, as South America was "lost," not to other states but to its own people – a contingency that Olney and others like him did not contemplate. That was serious enough. When the Nixon administration was planning the destruction of Chilean democracy, the National Security Council warned that if the US could not control Latin America, it could not expect "to achieve a successful order elsewhere in the world." But even more serious would be moves towards independence in the Middle East. Post-war planning recognized that control of the incomparable energy reserves of the Middle East would yield "substantial control of the world," in the words of the influential Roosevelt advisor A.A. Berle; and, correspondingly, that loss of control would threaten the project of global dominance that was clearly articulated during the Second World War and has been sustained since in the face of major changes in world order.

It seemed for a time that the Arab Spring might lead to a greatly feared upsurge of independent nationalism. Every effort was made to prevent it, first by France in its Tunisian dependency, then by the US and England in their traditional domains. In Egypt, Washington followed the usual guidelines when some favoured dictator is losing control: support him as long as possible, and if that can no longer be done, send him off somewhere and try to restore the old system to the extent possible. Cases include Somoza, Marcos, Duvalier, Suharto, Mobutu and many others, and the same was done with Egyptian dictator Mubarak. The US is now supporting the brutal dictatorship of General Sisi, which is heading Egypt into some of its darkest ages. In the oil dictatorships, mild reformist efforts were quickly crushed. The rest of the region has since fallen into disaster, but the most important states are still well in hand.

I mentioned earlier that the driving theme of US policy throughout the period, inherited from precursors in global management, was concern for radical nationalism, meaning independent nationalism which succumbs to the fallacy that "the first beneficiaries of the development of a country's resources should be the people of that country" rather than US investors. Those concerns apply domestically as well, leading to a constant war by the highly class-conscious business classes against their domestic enemy, the general population.

The wave of radical democracy that swept through much of the world during the Second World War reached US shores as well, and called for a harsh response to restore obedience and undermine the reformist measures of the New Deal, which did improve conditions for the general population. Those efforts began as soon as the war ended, relying on the anti-communist hysteria of the early Cold War years, invoking the "loss of China" and Russia's control over its Eastern European domains, a grim counterpart to what the US and its clients were doing elsewhere.

The Taft–Hartley Act of 1947 began the rollback of labour gains. It was followed by an enormous corporate-propaganda offensive seeking to impose "the American way" of subordination of labour to capital – disguised as all working together to protect ourselves from the commies and union bosses who want to undermine our harmonious existence.

Another target was the media. A battle was waged in the late 1940s between advocates of corporate control of the media – under the guise of libertarianism – and a social democratic alternative that understood freedom of speech to include the right of the population to have access to a wide range of information and opinion, and to means of popular expression – as articulated in the Universal Declaration of Human Rights, which includes the right "to seek, receive and impart information and ideas through any media and regardless of frontiers." The broader conception, including the right to receive and impart information, had prevailed to a considerable extent in earlier years, and was in fact encouraged by explicit government policies. But freedom of press in this broader sense succumbed to capital concentration and advertiser reliance. The option of corporate tyranny won a resounding victory, leaving the US with virtually no media outside of business control.

The onslaught against the population was slowed by the commitment to New Deal reformism and by the economic boom of the first few post-war decades. By the late 1970s the neoliberal assault began to take shape, accelerated in the Reagan–Thatcher years, and becoming a worldwide attack on basic human rights and democracy.

With the collapse of regulation, financial crises began for the first time since the war. For the perpetrators the crises are not a very serious problem because of a tacit government insurance policy that protects the major financial institutions. This goes far beyond the publicized bail-outs, and has a huge impact. The International Monetary Fund (IMF) estimates that virtually all the profit of the major US banks depends on the government insurance policy, which provides access to cheap credit, inflated credit ratings, incentive to carry out risky and in the short term profitable transactions, and much else. The business press estimates the subsidy at over $80 billion a year. There is a counterpart in Europe, where the European Union bail-outs for the southern countries end up being payments to the German and other northern banks that made risky and profitable loans, but naturally want the costs transferred to the public.

While business and the wealthy are doing fine, for the public it is a different matter. They suffer. Through the neoliberal period the majority in the US have suffered stagnation or decline. One indication is that real wages for male workers in the US are at the level of the late 1960s. A major factor contributing to this outcome is that labour unions have been practically destroyed. The rest of the picture is familiar in much of the world, in one or other form.

Some of the fundamental reasons are sometimes discussed in mainstream economics. In his standard history of the international monetary system, Barry Eichengreen explains that in the late nineteenth century, the severe costs of the "sound economics" imposed by the dominant business classes could be transferred to the general population. But that changed when government became "politicized by universal male suffrage and the rise of trade unionism and parliamentary labour parties," and it changed still more after further radicalization of the public during the Great Depression and the anti-fascist war. The luxury of transferring costs to the public was no longer readily available to private power and wealth. Hence, in the post-war

Bretton Woods system, "limits on capital mobility substituted for limits on democracy as a source of insulation from market pressures."

We can then add the obvious corollary. With the dismantling of the Bretton Woods system regulating capital from the 1970s, it becomes necessary to reduce substantive democracy so that the costs of financial rectitude can again be imposed on the public, who must be diverted and managed in some fashion – tasks undertaken through the neoliberal period.

The latest crisis, the most severe since the Great Depression, provided new tools to undermine the social democratic measures that had somewhat reduced the dominance of private capital – increasingly financial capital since the breakdown of the Bretton Woods system. These weapons have been used with great effect in Europe under the lash of the German and French banks, and the Brussels bureaucracy, a brutal form of naked class war. On economic grounds the policies of austerity during recession make little sense, as even the IMF economists recognize; and they have been generally disastrous. But in terms of class war, the policies are succeeding in eroding the much disliked welfare state and popular democracy.

A particularly ugly example is Greece, which has suffered brutally under the savage measures imposed by the Troika. Self-righteous German rejection of debt restructuring is particularly sadistic in the light of the fact that Germany is the one country to have benefited enormously from a bail-out in 1953, cancelling half of its debt and laying the basis for its economic growth. By rights, Germany should be providing massive reparations to Greece in partial compensation for Nazi crimes in Greece. But class war dictates otherwise.

Latin America has taken the lead in countering the neoliberal assault, now joined by new movements arising in southern Europe, Syriza in Greece and Podemos in Spain, where the population also suffered severely from the policies of austerity for the public and bail-out of the banks that were responsible for the crisis.

The global state capitalist system is in one of its periodic periods of crisis. Outcomes, as always, will depend on how an aroused public will respond.

I do not want to conclude without at least mentioning the fact that the crisis is far more ominous even than what I have been discussing. Everyone with eyes open understands that the human species is standing on the edge of a precipice, perilously close to virtual suicide. There are two dark shadows that loom over everything that we discuss: nuclear war and environmental catastrophe. In January 2015, the famous Doomsday Clock of the Bulletin of Atomic Scientists was moved two minutes closer to midnight, the closest it has been for thirty years, when there was a major war scare.[2] The reason, as they explain, is that each of these threats is growing.

The statement accompanying the move of the clock to three minutes to midnight warns that:

> Unchecked climate change, global nuclear weapons modernizations, and outsized nuclear weapons arsenals pose extraordinary and undeniable threats to the continued existence of humanity, and world leaders have failed to act with the speed or on the scale required to protect citizens from potential catastrophe. These failures of political leadership endanger every person on Earth. The clock ticks now at just three minutes to midnight because international leaders are failing to perform their most important duty – ensuring and preserving the health and vitality of human civilization.

The regular, five-year review conference of the Nuclear Non-Proliferation Treaty (NPT) ended in May 2015 without agreement on a final document. A primary reason was the refusal of the US, along with Canada and Britain, to accept language calling for a conference on establishing a zone free of weapons of mass destruction in the Middle East, a sticking point for twenty years since Egypt introduced this proposal, backed by most of the world. There are flimsy excuses, but the real reason is not hard to discern. The US and its allies support Israel's refusal even to publicly reveal its nuclear weapons programmes, let alone to have them inspected. Instead western doctrine demands that all must focus on what high officials and commentators call "the gravest threat to world peace," Iran's nuclear programmes. The world, incidentally, has a rather different perspective. In an international poll run by the leading US polling agency, Gallup, the winner of the prize for the greatest threat to world peace was the United States; no one else was even close. Fortunately, Americans were spared the unpleasant news by the Free Press.

The Iranian threat has been explained by US intelligence in its regular review of global security: if Iran were to develop nuclear weapons, it would be part of its deterrent strategy. It is clear why deterrence is a threat to rogue-states that intend to use force at will.

Apart from Israel, two other nuclear-armed states refuse to join the NPT: Pakistan and India. All three have been assisted by the US. Israel, obviously. India was granted a special exemption by the US in the 2007 nuclear cooperation agreement, which provided India with the benefits of the NPT "without assuming any of the NPT's obligations," as reported in the June 2015 issue of *Arms Control Today*, the authoritative publication of the Arms Control Association. It concludes that India has "reneged on its commitment," made by Prime Minister Manmohan Singh, "to assume the same responsibilities and practices and acquire the same benefits and advantages as other leading countries with advanced nuclear technology, such as the United States." The benefits and advantages have come, but not the responsibilities and practices, as the review details. Pakistan's nuclear weapons programmes, developed with tacit US support in the Reagan years, are particularly dangerous because of the concerns expressed by leading Pakistani nuclear scientists that *jihadis* might have access to Pakistani nuclear weapons, a horrible prospect to add to many others.

The term "benefits" should not mislead. In the September 2014 issue of Britain's journal *International Affairs*, Ramesh Thakur (on India), and Pervez Hoodbhoy and Zia Mian (on Pakistan) argue convincingly that the nuclear programmes have made South Asians less secure and subject to much more severe threats.

Looking back over his long career as a nuclear weapons planner, the former head of the US Strategic Command, General Lee Butler, concludes that we have so far survived the nuclear age "by some combination of skill, luck, and divine intervention, and I suspect the latter in greatest proportion." Anyone who reviews the appalling record can easily understand his words. It is a record of hundreds of near-accidents, some prevented only moments from utter disaster, and shocking decisions of political leaders. That we have escaped destruction is a near-miracle, and right now the drums are beating again.

For the nuclear weapons threat, at least we know the answer: eliminate them, as directed by the Non-Proliferation Treaty of 1970 and the 1996 World Court decision endorsing it as a legal obligation. In dramatic contrast, the US has just announced a trillion-dollar programme of nuclear weapons modernization, and lesser powers are doing likewise.

In the case of environmental catastrophe, it is not at all clear that we know the answer, though there are ways to mitigate and perhaps to overcome the crisis. They are being pursued far too timidly, and at the same time, society is racing ever more rapidly towards the precipice, like the proverbial lemmings. It is a well-established conclusion of contemporary science that most of the fossil fuels in the ground must remain there if our grandchildren are to have some hope of decent survival. Meanwhile the major energy corporations are expending every effort to extract the last possible drop of fossil fuels, governments are opening new zones for extraction, and political leaders and the media are euphoric about the wonders of the technology that accelerates the race to disaster. The IMF has just reported that global energy subsidies are costing governments over $5 trillion annually. Species destruction is already at the level of 65 million years ago, when a huge asteroid hit the earth, ending the age of the dinosaurs and opening the way for mammals to proliferate, finally *Homo sapiens*, which is now the asteroid.

All of this is exactly what we should expect within the logic of market societies, reinforced by a doctrinal system which declares that "it is generally agreed that the use of private property and the pricing system is in the public interest," to quote Nobel Laureate in economics Ronald Coase, articulating the "religion that markets know best," to borrow the words of Nobel Laureate in economics and former World Bank chief economist Joseph Stiglitz, ridiculing the prevailing dogmas of the profession and the neoliberal culture. Among the numerous market failures is ignoring externalities, the impact of a transaction on those not involved in it – in this case, the impact of fossil fuel extraction on our grandchildren, a deficiency of doctrine that is not merely very harmful in this case but lethal.

In our global plutocracies, it is of great importance to understand the thinking of those who the business press call "the masters of mankind." They had their annual meeting in Davos, Switzerland in January – by instructive coincidence, just as the Doomsday Clock was moved two minutes closer to midnight. An annual poll was taken of chief executives of leading corporations, asking them to rank the risks they faced. Climate change did not make it into the list because of their lack of interest in the subject. Worse still, at the top of their perceived risks was over-regulation. It should be transparent that it is the weakness of the regulatory system now in place that is a serious threat to survival.

The risks of nuclear and environment catastrophe are so extreme that they would not be accepted by any sane decision-maker. They are being accepted by leaders who are perfectly sane, trapped by an institutional logic that is deeply pathological and that must be cured, and quickly, if the human experiment is to proceed.

Notes

1 This piece was written in 2015, before the election of President Trump. – *Editor*
2 In 2017, after the election of President Trump, the clock was moved to two-and-a-half minutes to midnight. – *Editor*

Promises to Keep: Science and Scientific Temper in India

T. Jayaraman

Two political projects have characterized India over the last two-and-a-half decades. The first is the advance of *Hindutva*, India's own brand of religious majoritarianism, featuring elements of fundamentalism and obscurantism, and linked to a revanchist view of the origins of the Indian state. The second is the neoliberal turn in the economic policy of the Indian state, often benignly described as economic reform. Both gained ground rather rapidly in the early 1990s, and were strikingly similar in their common characteristic of a radical departure from the ideals that, in the previous nearly half-century, had been taken for granted as underpinning the idea of India. Today, more than twenty-five years since their emergence, both appear to be projects that are still under way – especially from the standpoint of their active proponents, who consider that their gains have not yet been consolidated in a stable form. Despite the apparently irreversible changes that have been made to the economy and economic policy-making in the country by so-called "reform," there is still constant clamour for further advance. As for the proponents of *Hindutva*, in view of their agenda of recasting the entire ideological basis of contemporary India in pursuit of a majoritarian vision of the future, it is evident that they must constantly seek new avenues and arenas of confrontation with the secular, pluralistic and inclusive trends in Indian society.

To those who have viewed the emergence of these two projects with concern and alarm, both appear to have made significant advances, giving rise to the danger of a dual polarization in Indian society. Economic reform, on the one hand, can be argued to have significantly contributed to widening inequalities in society: large-scale deprivation persists alongside the creation of a relatively narrow stratum of beneficiaries of reform; and even within the ranks of the latter, apart from a small section of the super-rich, increase in incomes is accompanied by greater insecurity. On the other hand, the *Hindutva* project holds out the threat of long-term polarization on the basis of religion, while also intensifying caste divisions, setting aside even the modest gains obtained over the years in terms of creating a democratic and inclusive economic, social and political order.

Both these projects strike at other core elements of what one may call a "national" vision that, for a few decades after Independence, was taken for granted. Perhaps their most harmful effect has been on the development of science and a scientific temper in Indian society, an objective that was among the most positive aspects of India's path of development in the first decades after Independence. This is not to suggest that the development of science or a scientific temper in India prior to the 1990s was not beset with difficulties. But that was also a period when there was clear vision on what needed to be done to overcome those difficulties, and a degree of hope that the configuration of social and political forces required for realizing those goals could eventually be mobilized.

It is my contention in this article that science and scientific temper in India are on the threshold of a crisis that is unprecedented in its gravity. I shall elaborate my critical understanding of the origins of this crisis through an impressionistic account – based on personal experience, and on lessons learnt from my involvement with science and science movements. Although this account may not entirely satisfy the more analytically minded reader, I trust she will consider it as a series of working hypotheses that await further detailed study.

Early Strengths

For a measure of the contemporary challenges faced by science in our country, it is worth reminding ourselves how propitious the conditions seemed for its rapid advance at the time of Independence. And how, even if scientific temper was only an ideal, often not matched by the reality of social practices and everyday life, it nevertheless commanded respect as a desired goal and instrument of progressive nation-building.

At the helm of affairs of the newly independent nation was Jawaharlal Nehru, remarkable – among leaders of the national liberation movements of his time and in the decades to follow – for his concern for science and his vision of a secular society: a society that would set aside scriptural injunctions, rituals and blind belief in favour of a rational view of the world fashioned through scientific enquiry. Nehru drew attention, perhaps most eloquently in his *Discovery of India*, both to the instrumental significance of science as a necessity for a modern, industrial nation, and to the importance of a scientific attitude for understanding and transforming society (Nehru 1989). It was not a naive vision, for Nehru was aware of the burden of the past in Indian society; but in his vision, the development of science and scientific temper was the only possible response to casting off this burden and moving forward.

India's first prime minister would have known that building science in a newly independent nation was not a matter of starting with a blank slate. In the record of nations newly liberated from colonial rule in the twentieth century, India was perhaps the only one that possessed a rudimentary scientific infrastructure. British colonial rule had developed, in halting fashion, a range of institutions that, though inadequate in scale, could be extended and given substance in the years to come. Of these, the survey institutions and the development of research in agriculture were perhaps the most developed examples.

India at the time of Independence already had a Nobel laureate in science in C.V. Raman. Raman and the legendary Srinivasan Ramanujan – both testimonies to the capacities of home-grown scientists in a colonial state – were an inspiration to many. The young Homi Bhabha, who would emerge as a visionary leader in the years to come, was waiting in the wings, while his older colleague, Meghnad Saha, was already associated with planning for a modern, industrial state through the National Planning Committee. India's entrepreneurial class, or at least some sections of it, displayed an awareness of the need for science, of which the enthusiasm of the Tatas in founding institutions of scientific research was perhaps the most outstanding example (Lala 2006). The university system displayed early on the symptoms of dysfunctionality in promoting research (this weakness was to become more pronounced as the years went by),[1] but despite this, universities sheltered scientists of substantial calibre, who in turn drew around them small schools of dedicated and well-trained scientific workers.[2]

Nehru developed a close association with science, scientists and scientific institutions in India. He was the first president of the Indian Science Congress, an institution that brought scientists as well as laypersons interested in science from all over the country to regular gatherings. The relationship between Nehru and the Science Congress continued in later years, with him inaugurating their bi-annual meetings as prime minister – a tradition that subsequent prime ministers have continued to this day (Mukerji and Bose 1963).

Nehru's vision of a society imbued with a scientific temper was by no means an isolated one: a wide spectrum of leaders of India's freedom struggle shared his desire to promote a rational, modern view of the social world. But Nehru was perhaps unique in the link he drew between science and a rational view of the social world, and perhaps he did so with greater emphasis than others. Rabindranath Tagore set this vision in verse, and the lines of his celebrated poem, "Where the mind is without fear" – written at the very beginning of the twentieth century and published in

1901 – are remarkable for their articulation of what can well be described as an anthem of the Indian enlightenment.[3] Tagore himself was not uninterested in science, though from a philosophical perspective, as his encounter with Einstein in 1930 demonstrates.[4]

B.R. Ambedkar represented another strain of the scientific temper, taking Nehru's vision of a rational view of the social world even farther by means of an unsparing critique of the caste system and the articulation of a need for thoroughgoing social transformation to annihilate it. Ambedkar's connection with science *per se* appears to have been primarily through economics rather than the natural sciences. But he clearly had much in common with Nehru on the subject, as his unsparing and acerbic critique of Gandhi's romantic views on technology demonstrates (Ambedkar 1946). The most significant of Ambedkar's contributions, namely, his insistence on the eradication of social oppression, especially caste discrimination in the form of untouchability, was not taken up in earnest by the mainstream nationalist movement. That this was to prove disastrous for the progress of science and scientific temper in post-Independence India is one of the main points of this article. We shall return to this in more detail shortly.

India also had a small but significant number of rationalists, including some notable social personalities. Among them was E.V. Ramasamy Naicker, better known as "Periyar," whose message perhaps had the widest political and social reach. Last but not least, there were the communist and Left movements, which were firmly committed to a scientific and rational world-view. This segment of India's political and social thought had an intellectual influence that extended well beyond its political following on the ground. It drew from the Marxist tradition to study science and society on Indian soil, and was rooted in the larger anti-imperialist struggles of that time. In later years it took forward the Bernalian tradition in the Indian context, especially by means of the so-called people's science movements.

At the highest level of leadership of the freedom struggle, Gandhi alone struck a different note. He was highly critical of modern technology – and critical too of science, though not in as explicit a manner (Gandhi 1984). Nevertheless he was neither insular regarding the sources that fashioned his world-view, nor did he promote an overtly anti-rational stance in negotiating contemporary political questions. Gandhi laid a claim, in a limited sense, to the Enlightenment viewpoint in his political thinking. But once Independence came and his views increasingly appeared to be not of overwhelming import to the business of governing the independent nation, there was little need to fear that Gandhian ideals would stand in the way of the advance of science and technology in the country. In retrospect, however, this was perhaps not true: as we shall note below, the Gandhian perspective was to contribute to the resurgence of anti-scientific perspectives in later years.

Science in a Developing Economy

The years between the passage of the Science Policy Resolution of 1958 and the end of the 1980s, or even the early part of the 1990s, were the best and most hopeful period for Indian science. Scientific institutions burgeoned all over the country; a number of advanced research groups began to operate in universities; new scientific departments of government, notably of atomic energy and space, were formed and began to function actively; and an active leadership emerged in many disciplines of science and technology. This network of scientific institutions was to grow substantially over the years, though levels of achievement varied across sectors and across institutions within a sector. The extent to which different scientific departments and institutions managed to integrate high-quality science with the country's developmental needs was, however, a different matter.[5] Agricultural research was certainly by far the most successful in this regard and space followed suit a few years later, but other sectors were not as well-connected to developmental needs – industrial and defence research being specific examples.

The Indian state began to encounter periodic economic crises, and the support for science tended to decrease during such phases. Perhaps the most consistently successful period of institutional growth was the 1980s, lasting well into the first half of the 1990s. The second generation of scientists, after the immediate post-Independence generation, came to assume greater influence in the scientific community, assuring the country of a stratum of scientific managers who had some acquaintance with current trends in science and the management of institutions. New fields came into prominence, among them molecular biology and environmental science.

Self-reliance was the slogan that guided India's science and technology policy, especially after the formal inauguration of the era of public sector-led development during the Second Five-Year Plan. The appeal of this slogan to the generation of Indians who had experienced colonial rule and who came of age in the immediate aftermath of Independence should not be underestimated. The slogan also commanded wide consensus across the political spectrum, leading to the scientific, engineering and medical professions being held in high regard as a part of the frontline of India's development efforts. In actual practice, though, self-reliance was limited to sectors where there was active denial of technology by the advanced industrialized nations (or the imposition of onerous conditions in terms of high royalty payments, denial of transfer of know-how, or restrictions on overseas marketing of the products of such investment). In many sectors self-reliance was ignored, especially by the private sector, and an integral part of the public discourse on technology was heated debate on the relative merits of different technologies that were to be imported.[6]

The Nehruvian enthusiasm for a scientific temper did not find much resonance in the public arena in the initial decades after Independence. But in the late 1960s, the renewed enthusiasm for the study of science and society in the wake of a wave of radical thought that swept the globe had an influence on Indian intellectuals as well. As this influence merged with various currents of radical and Left politics in India in the 1970s, there was a rise of both direct involvement of scientists in questions of science and society, and of popular science movements, most notably the Kerala Shastra Sahitya Parishad (KSSP) in Kerala. These currents met with sympathetic interest from a section of science administrators in the country, who had begun to sense that there was need for greater investment in popularizing science as well as greater effort to improve the quality of science education.

The second half of the 1970s and the 1980s thus saw the formation of a loose coalition of research scientists from laboratories and universities, science teachers and students, and popular science movements, that worked fairly systematically at popularizing science and science education. This coalition had a strong interest in issues of science and society, and the call for a scientific temper was one of its key rallying slogans (see Vaidyanathan *et al.* 1979, and Kannan 1990). Another rallying point of this coalition was self-reliance, interpreted not in any parochial or cultural-relativist sense, but very much in a spirit of economic independence, which would inspire Indian scientists and technologists to develop their capacities without slipping into a neo-colonial, copycat dependence.

One must, of course, be careful not to overstate the reach and influence of this coalition. The media rarely paid attention to its work, apart from the exceptional case of Kerala where it was truly a mass movement (Zachariah and Sooryamoorthy 1994). In the intervening years, the original example that Nehru had set with his own life was to be diluted in the time of his daughter Indira Gandhi and grandson Rajiv Gandhi, who were known to visit heads of Hindu religious cults and sects, and assorted mystics known in India as "god-men." During the brief tenure of the coalition government headed by the Janata Party after the Emergency ended in 1977, an exhibition on science and scientific temper set up by the molecular biologist

P.M. Bhargava was dismantled by the government, an act widely believed to have been instigated by the *Hindutva* lobby – a term that was still to acquire currency then among the English media – which was a part of the Janata Party at that time (see *Business Line* 2003, and Bhargava and Chakrabarti 2007). The first attack on the writings of Left historians also began in this period, with objections being raised to the new textbooks being prepared for the syllabi of schools that came under the Central Board of Secondary Education (Mukherjee and Mukherjee 2001).

That these were portents of more intensified attacks in the future was hardly anticipated at the time. This was not entirely unjustified. In 1976, the 42nd Amendment to the Constitution of India was passed, which included in Article 51A the injunction: It shall be the duty of every citizen of India "to develop the scientific temper, humanism and the spirit of enquiry and reform."[7] This was no doubt a positive development even if it was implemented in the period of the Emergency.

Overall, by the late 1980s, it appeared that India had, notwithstanding many gaps, the attributes of a scientific power in the making. What was needed was greater investment and expansion, a greater link to industry and productive activity, greater attention to quality especially in human resources, and greater attention to the expansion of both the quantity and quality of scientific research in universities. But each one of these, which seemed to be operational problems on the surface, were actually major structural problems for Indian science, problems that could not easily be overcome.

Structural Issues of Indian Science

One of the most significant barriers faced by Indian science has been the slow advance of literacy and universal school education, and the failure to achieve even majority opinion, let alone a consensus, in favour of compulsory education. In the early decades after Independence even universal literacy was not given due attention. Although that situation changed in the 1980s, the reality has still to fully match the rhetoric. In striking contrast to Southeast Asia and East Asia, South Asia is a laggard in the field of education. As a consequence, Indian science was able to draw its talent from only a narrow stratum of Indian society. Investment in higher education has also been below global norms, with the gross enrolment ratio in higher education in India remaining below the average for developing countries.[8]

There are other aspects to education that have not been considered in the context of the development of science. The quality of science education, for example, has remained persistently below the levels needed to keep pace with scientific advance. This is no doubt a problem that affects many education systems, even in the developed countries, but the gap in India is striking. Another problem, more insidious, is the general influence of a slow pace of modernization on the penetration of scientific knowledge among the population at large.

Those trained in science have often been found wanting in terms of a scientific or rational attitude. Total solar eclipses, for instance, have been occasions when collective irrationality seemed to grip Indian society at large. Similarly, a couple of decades ago, the entire country was swayed by accounts of idols of Ganesha "drinking" milk, echoed by similar reports from the Indian diaspora in the United States and uncritical accounts of the phenomenon in the television media. On such occasions, it has proven difficult to find a counter-statement from educated sections of society that counsels against the breathless, bordering-on-hysterical acceptance of all manner of superstitious and obscurantist interpretations. Astrology continues to retain a remarkable hold on Indian society, with its penetration in the ranks of those who are scientifically educated being significant. A recent survey found that a majority of students of the Indian Institute of Technology (IIT) in Mumbai still retain faith in astrological advice and practices, though some did resort to the excuse that it is their family that insists on such practices (Pathak 2013). Notably, the adherence to astrology in these cases is not restricted to its entertainment value, as is often the case in the developed countries, but is an integral part of decision-making in significant, life-changing situations.[9] Scientists of some standing, or notable figures in science-based professions such as medicine or engineering, are sometimes found to be ardent devotees of particular god-men or believers in active religious cults. The sociological significance of such adherence notwithstanding, it is nevertheless a telling comment on the continuing hold of the unscientific and the irrational on India's intellectual class.

Alongside obscurantism rooted in tradition is a general attitude of reverence towards received wisdom at the expense of critical assimilation. The scientific community has often noted this sharply (Balaram 2010). It is well known among teachers of science, for instance, that students tend to be passive recipients of lectures in classrooms. A good deal of the current pedagogical research in India focuses on teacher–student transactions in the classroom. But this is one-sided, clearly, and ignores the fact that teachers labour under very difficult social and economic conditions, which affects both the educational system in particular and society in general. Students too bear the brunt of the pressure of family aspirations for upward social and economic mobility in a milieu marked by insufficient employment generation that would guarantee minimum income security. Reform of science education, especially its less tangible aspects, is an uphill task in this milieu.

Serving as a backdrop, as it were, is the enormous deprivation in access to knowledge, especially in rural India, which is home to 69 per cent of India's population of approximately 1.2 billion. The virtually sole universal medium of knowledge is television, which covers approximately 76 million rural households, or 45 per cent of rural households. The urban–rural divide is clear as almost 98 per cent of urban households own a television set. Television, however, has been a sore disappointment in its educational function, more so with respect to science, while its entertainment function, typically pandering to existing social and cultural mores without a transformational agenda, has dominated. What little knowledge delivery exists is restricted to instrumental purposes such as agricultural extension. The result has been that more than two-thirds of India has no more than a cursory engagement with the enterprise of science in any form whatsoever. Small wonder, then, that this social milieu constantly reproduces and sustains, both in ideology and practice, the most backward forms of social oppression and retrogressive practices associated with caste, class and gender.

Another aspect of science in India, of education and research, is the lag between experiment and theory. Theoretical work appears to attract a disproportionate number of successful students, and striking examples of high-quality experimental work seem to be less frequent in Indian science than outstanding theoretical work. While, no doubt, C.V. Raman's Nobel-winning work was experimental, it illustrates precisely this point – the bulk of subsequent achievements have been theoretical. Two later Nobel awards to scientists of Indian origin, though based on experimental work, related to work that had been done entirely outside the country. Part of this is due, no doubt, to the expenditure entailed in setting up laboratories and the consequent paucity of experimental science institutions, especially in a developing country like India. But even after several decades of investment in chains of scientific institutions focused on various branches of experimental science, from pure or applied science to technology, the returns on investment in terms of forging ahead in experimental work are quite meagre.

The gap between experiment and theory is the tip of the iceberg. The development of science and technology in India also suffers from a huge gap between research and teaching, and industrial production. Agricultural science and technology has achieved some success in narrowing this gap. Some sectors like space have managed to maintain success in converting knowledge into successful delivery in tangible benefits within the scope of their mandate. Overall, from the poor footprint that India has in the realm of patents, copyright and royalties, it is clear that innovation in India lags far behind that of scientifically advanced countries. This is also clear from the data on India's share in high-technology product exports.[10] In the earlier, public sector-dominated era, sectors such as agriculture undoubtedly achieved some success in innovation, even if much of it was not patented – partly because agricultural research, by its very nature, cannot be transferred to production without considerable innovation to adapt to local conditions. However, the links between science and productive activity as a whole have always been weak.

Apart from the science–production linkage, it is worth considering the role of the social-cultural milieu in a society that still fundamentally has not overcome the downgrading of productive labour vis-à-vis purely mental or intellectual labour. Even with respect to the latter, speculative thought in a variety of forms, including traditional religious teachings, mysticism and magical speculation, receives as much recognition as scientific enquiry.

Modern science and technology owe a great deal to the linkage between science and production that was developed during the scientific and industrial revolutions in Western Europe, and later in the erstwhile Soviet Union and Japan.[11] There is a gap in this regard in India's trajectory of development. Both scientific and industrial activity began in this country through the transplanting and eventual assimilation of knowledge and methods of knowledge generation that were already developed elsewhere, that were readymade as it were. Unfortunately, as a consequence, it has become much more difficult to grasp the linkage between the two streams that emerged in different spheres of activity. In practice, industrial knowhow or technology was acquired by an emergent industrial class with little development of such knowledge on their own. In science, to some extent, independent generation of new knowledge, of a quality that was competitive with the best work globally, was the ideal. Nevertheless, this ideal was rarely realized in practice, except in a few centres and among a small number of scientific groups.

The gap between science and productive activity is nowhere more strikingly illustrated than in the Science Policy Resolution of 1958.[12] The text, at first reading, is a remarkably inspirational call for the development of science – striking especially when viewed against the state of the Indian economy at that time. On the positive side, it locates science as a necessity for India's development, acknowledging not only its instrumental necessity but also its larger role in fashioning a modern world-view. In the tradition of the national movement for Independence, it sees science and scientific development as essential to the building of a self-reliant, modern nation.

In retrospect, there were three problems with the text of the Resolution. First, it has a simplistic, linear view of the relationship between science and technology, seeing technology as somehow a direct product of scientific activity – which misses the relative autonomy of technological knowledge, especially in its development. This is evident in the opening paragraph itself, which proclaims, "But technology can only grow out of science and its applications." Secondly, it does not see any serious obstacle to the rapid dissemination of scientific knowledge in the country, whether in the realm of education *per se*, including both the eradication of illiteracy and the spread of formal education, or in the larger socio-cultural milieu. While acknowledging the need for education to enhance the supply of scientific manpower, it does not concretely connect the development of science to a programme of universal, compulsory education (which, in any case, was to lag behind tremendously in the years to follow). The third is an implicitly uncritical view of the issues relating to traditional knowledge in India's history, as stated in the following words: "It is an inherent obligation of India, with its traditions of scholarship and original thinking and great cultural heritage, to participate fully in the march of science, which is probably mankind's greatest enterprise today." Though at first sight thoroughly inspirational in the best traditions of Nehruvian rhetoric, it also betrays, as one may remark in hindsight, an uncritical view that misses what is problematic with this tradition. Nowhere in the Resolution is there a call for the more critical view of the past that marked Nehru's engagement with science and a scientific temper in the pre-Independence era.

Science without Radical Transformation

Even in the 1980s it was evident to many commentators that the fundamental problem for science in India was that it did not develop in the context of a sweeping economic, social and political transformation of society. In contrast to the scientific and industrial revolution in Europe following on the rise of capitalism in the bourgeois revolutions, the development of science in Japan following the Meiji revolution, or the development of science and technology in China following the installation of the People's Republic in 1948, the driving inspiration for science in India was the freedom struggle. While acknowledging this influence, freedom from colonial rule did not necessarily mark social and economic transformation, directed above all at a transformation of rural society and at opening the doors to a thoroughgoing modernization of Indian society. We will not go into the nature and dimensions of this failure here, as this has been extensively written about. From the viewpoint of science, the fundamental conditions for its development, namely, the creation of conditions for rapid development of industrialization and modern techniques of production, were never adequately realized. The most striking contrast, perhaps, is with China. The gap between India and China in the first four decades after Independence did not seem large, especially after the setbacks that science in China suffered during the Cultural Revolution. Subsequently, the substantially different foundations for the development of science and technology in India and China have been brought home sharply.

As a consequence of the absence of radical social transformation, the Nehruvian view of scientific temper, despite its many merits, avoided direct confrontation with the fundamental irrationality of India's social and economic life, namely, the caste system. It is a striking fact that the many votaries of scientific temper, in Nehru's own lifetime as well as later, did not explicitly link their ideals with annihilation of the caste system. Critically, Nehru's own view of caste missed its inherently exploitative aspect, especially in its very construction. The following lines from *Discovery of India* illustrate the nature of Nehru's apologia for caste:

> Caste was a group system based on services and functions. It was meant to be an all-inclusive order without any common dogma and allowing the fullest latitude to each group . . . [it was] infinitely better than slavery even for those lowest in the scale. Within each caste there was equality and a measure of freedom; each caste was occupational and applied itself to its own particular work. This led to a high degree of specialization and skill in handicrafts and craftsmanship . . . [caste] kept up the democratic habit in each group.[13]

Elsewhere, caste "was an attempt at the social organization of different races, a rationalization of the facts as they existed at the time." Nehru went on to add: "It brought degradation in its train afterwards, and it is still a burden and a curse, but we can hardly judge it from subsequent standards or later developments."[14]

Clearly, with such a problematic understanding even in Nehru's mind, it is not surprising that the scientific temper debate never truly took into account the phenomenon of caste. Scientific temper was counterposed to religious obscurantism, but it was rarely recognized that the caste system, grounded ideologically in Hinduism, was a more deep-rooted manifestation of such obscurantism, and the scriptural, dogmatic aspect of an epiphenomenon. Even on the left of the political spectrum, whose leading figures articulated opposition to both religious obscurantism and the caste system, the intimate connection between these two forms of irrationality in Indian society did not always form the core of the fight against obscurantism.

A rare exception is to be seen in the writings of the Indian communist leader, E.M.S. Nambooridipad, who pointed out that:

> one has to abandon all ideas of paying tributes to the "age-old" civilization and culture of India. One has to realize that the rebuilding of India on modern democratic and secular lines requires an uncompromising struggle against the caste-based Hindu society and its culture. There is no question of secular democracy, not to speak of socialism, unless the very citadel of India's "age-old" civilization and culture – the division of society into a hierarchy of castes – is broken. In other words, the struggle for radical democracy and socialism cannot be separated from the struggle against caste society.

Ambedkar had a far superior understanding of the need to eradicate the caste system than Nehru, noting as he did, on the eve of the inauguration of the republic, the fundamental contradiction between the ideal of political democracy, and the oppressive social and economic reality of Indian society. Ambedkar was forthright too in his criticism of Gandhi's opposition to technology and machine-based industry in particular (Ambedkar 1946), a rarity at a time when Gandhi's views were increasingly beyond criticism in the mainstream of the national movement.[15] With Nehru's unwavering allegiance to Gandhi and his own role in the leadership of the national movement, it was not on the cards that Ambedkar's thoroughgoing commitment to rationality in the nation's social life would link up with the Nehruvian agenda of scientific temper.[16] The link between Ambedkar and the struggle to uphold secularism and a scientific temper has been discussed in some detail by Meera Nanda (Nanda 2006). She has also noted the failure of the mainstream of the national movement to be consistently secular, and the several compromises they made with obscurantism – conflating it with religion, especially Hinduism.

Latter-day critics of the Nehruvian view of scientific temper, led by social scientists such as Ashis Nandy and Shiv Viswanathan, frame their criticism in the language of cultural relativism, counterposing science as a form of "western rationality" to an "indigenous" world-view intrinsic to Indian society (Nandy 1988). However much it is dressed in modern philosophical and sociological jargon, it is clear that such criticism recycles the backward-looking response to British colonialism that has a long history in India's intellectual life. Equally, despite their rhetorical celebration of the "subaltern," such cultural relativists have little to say on the fundamentally oppressive structures of India's social fabric inherited from pre-colonial days.

In sum, the long-term challenge to science in India, both in its instrumental sense as part of the development of its productive forces and in its role as part of the intellectual underpinnings of a new vision of Indian society, is to be sought in the failure of agrarian transformation, the key to the eradication of the fundamental contradictions of Indian society that both the Left and Ambedkarite viewpoints have long alluded to. Failure to address this in adequate fashion in practice, it must be recognized, set the stage for the crisis of science in contemporary India.

Contemporary Challenges to Science

In the background of the structural problems that science in India continued to face even when the overall development of science seemed to be set on a positive track, the radical shift in the economic development strategy of the Indian state has been nothing short of disastrous for the long-term future of science in India. Much has been written about the consequences of this shift and the manner in which it marked a break from the past (see Chandrasekhar and Ghosh 2002). Some specific aspects of this in relation to science are worth noting. First, the general downgrading of public sector investment and the call for a general withdrawal of the state from many sectors of development implied that science would no longer receive the kind of support it used to. Secondly, the few attempts at promoting the development of technological self-reliance were to be set aside. Economic reform was to usher in access to advanced technologies from elsewhere in the world (in contrast to the "license raj" of the preceding era), and "competition" with such advanced technology, so it was claimed, would assist in strengthening technological development in India. Thirdly, science in India was to be a part of India's thrust to join the global "knowledge economy," implicitly giving up the earlier emphasis in policy of a balance between scientific development and the agenda of poverty eradication.

The twenty-five years that have passed since the initiation of "reform" have seen the gradual impact of this new agenda.[17] It would be simplistic to think that the impact of this new policy turn was immediate. Public sector investment in science has declined gradually, even as the state's investment in specific sectors such as atomic energy and space continued to be maintained or even grow in real terms in certain years. However, the engagement of the state in scientific activity was increasingly limited to a few "strategic sectors." The launch of an open and active nuclear weapons programme after the nuclear weapons tests of 1998 was the signal for a decisive shift in the meaning of the term "self-reliance" to a narrow interpretation purely in strategic terms.[18] Even this has in practice been subverted by the concurrent abandoning of the ideal of non-alignment in favour of an increasing strategic alliance with the United States.

The poster-boy of "reform" in technological terms is undoubtedly the information technology (IT) sector, which has registered impressive growth over the last two decades.[19] However, even here it is worth noting the overwhelming dominance of routine work, obtained through "outsourcing" contracts from corporations of the advanced industrial nations; the absence of a genuinely indigenous IT hardware industry; and the poor footprint this sector has in the actual innovation of new software or new technology products. Overall, in the "reform" era, innovation has been slow to pick up. India remains an also-ran in global exports of advanced technology.[20] Public sector investments of an earlier era in select scientific and technological institutions, such as the Indian Institutes of Technology, have made India a global source of high-quality human resources for scientific research, but with little of the benefits from these resources accruing to the domestic economy apart from the creation of a narrow high-wage sector in terms of employment in select metropolitan centres. As the research base in the university system (never substantial to begin with) continues to shrink, state investment in advanced scientific and technological research and training is being limited to a few high-profile institutions.[21]

While the scientific agenda of the Indian state has shrunk in scope in the last two decades, *Hindutva* has mounted a parallel attack on scientific temper and rationality in Indian society. We use the term *Hindutva* here to denote a broad political coalition (also referred to as the *Sangh Parivar*) that includes the Rashtriya Swayamsevak Sangh (RSS), the Bharatiya Janata Party (BJP), and an assortment of other organizations that have grown in number over the last three decades. While they maintain formally separate organizational structures, ideological affinities and a close coordination in their activities can easily be identified.

The first spell of BJP rule in India, from 1998 to 2004, was when the *Hindutva* agenda began to directly intrude into the science and technology policy agenda of the country. Its most dramatic manifestation was the nuclear weapons tests at Pokhran in 1998, which we have already noted. While the shift in India's nuclear weapons stance represents an overall shift in the policies of the Indian state, the role of the *Hindutva* world-view in the immediate process of decision-making that led up to the shift in policy should not be underestimated.

The second spell of the BJP's rule from New Delhi under the leadership of Narendra Modi, which has run its course now for almost four years, has begun to see a dramatic slashing of India's scientific and technological research and higher education budgets. Some of these cuts are as yet only proposals but are likely to be implemented soon. While these may as yet be reversed, they are only a sharp accentuation of a trend that has been in effect for a much longer period.

Increasingly, in the last few years, *Hindutva*'s attacks on rationality and a scientific temper have assumed a direct and physical dimension, exemplified by the assassinations of three prominent advocates of rationality and of a scientific study of India's history, society and polity, and campaigners against superstition in public life (*Economic and Political Weekly* 2015). These attacks have focused in particular on three issues. The first is the systematic, evidence-based and scientific study of India's history. Secondly, uncritical glorification of the "achievements" of science in ancient India, where mythology in several Sanskrit texts is taken for fact and following which wild conclusions are drawn (see *The Hindu* 2015). Thirdly, an insistence on the "values" of Indian "culture," where culture is conflated with all manner of rituals and practices, whether religious or social, especially on issues of caste, religion and gender.

While these are the areas of concentration of *Hindutva*'s ideological efforts, this is not to suggest an entirely coherent campaign of a homogenous character. Many of *Hindutva*'s efforts are opportunistic in character: it may be an attack on the adoption of modern attire or a modern lifestyle by women in Bengaluru; or it may be incendiary protests at an event to celebrate the legacy of Tipu Sultan, the legendary ruler of Mysore who was perhaps the last determined opposition to the onward march of colonial British rule. It could be the claim that "aircraft" that could "fly backward" existed in ancient India; or the celebration by a section of the "legacy" of Nathuram Godse, the assassin of Gandhi. The *Manusmriti*, an arch-reactionary exposition of the rules of the caste system composed of a melange of the most absurd rules of hierarchical social behaviour,[22] is another *Hindutva* favourite, while astrology and its introduction into university curricula as a course of study is a *Hindutva* success story, achieved under the first spell of the BJP's rule.

These instances of outright obscurantism have met with protests from a wide cross-section of Indian intellectuals, strident media criticism, and even expressions of concern and condemnation from sections of India's managerial class and corporate leaders. Nevertheless, for reasons that I believe we still do not understand entirely, *Hindutva*'s campaign also strikes a chord among significant sections of Indian society.[23] Even among sections that do protest, such as intellectuals, there are many who are sympathetic to *Hindutva*'s blandishments. And there is a significant section of India's elite that does not see the prevalence of obscurantism on a wide scale as something reprehensible or as a state of affairs that calls for urgent redressal.

One might argue that this is in effect the other side of the same coin that has led to the Indian elite's historic disregard of the imperative of mass education. As we have indicated earlier, it would be to underestimate the intensity of the problem if we try to understand this disregard purely in terms of the "policy" of the Indian state or the "policies" of successive governments in power, though better policies at the local, regional or national scale can provide forward movement to some extent. But what such policy expresses or manifests in the ultimate analysis is, arguably, the deep-rooted backwardness of the Indian elite, or ruling classes to put it more accurately, whose world-view does not encompass the need for unleashing the potential of India's people. It is perhaps even fearful of doing so, wary that such a social and political upsurge would sweep its own dominance away, and hence only promotes modernization in such moderate doses as do not endanger its own existence. At the same time, this elite seeks a seat at the high table in the global political order, and actively pursues the accoutrements of global power status. What else can explain the strange spectacle of some of the leading figures of Indian industry being prepared to gift hundreds of millions of dollars to some of the world's wealthiest educational institutions in the world's wealthiest nations, even while maintaining an uncritical silence in the face of mass educational deprivation and rampant obscurantism at home, promoted by governments that they could well influence in the right direction?

A Divided Opposition

Why is it that this crisis of science and scientific temper in India has not been tackled with greater political energy and intellectual vigour? Why has it not received the opposition that it merits? Apart from the larger political questions involved, there are a number of current intellectual trends that have partially blocked an adequate response to this crisis.

One is the rise of a general scepticism regarding science and technology among a section of the intellectual class, in which mainstream social scientists find prominent representation. Two influences have fed this trend in India. The first is a general scepticism of science that has been current and perhaps even dominant among mainstream social scientists globally for more than thirty years now. Among these sceptical tendencies may be included an assortment of viewpoints such as postmodernism (of which, of course, there are many variants), cultural relativism, political ecology and social constructivism. The starting point of these critiques vary, but they share a broad understanding that all science and technology has "social genes," that the claims of science to producing objective knowledge of the natural world are suspect, that objectivity itself is an incoherent notion while all truth-claims are merely expressions of class or other forms of oppressive ideological domination, and that there is no basis for the notion that science produces any knowledge that is universally valid. These viewpoints have had a significant influence on the Indian academic community.

The second influence is a more up-to-date and refurbished version of the debate over the so-called Nehruvian versus Gandhian "model" of development. In this debate, in its original form, the former is presented as a "model" that relies on development through industrialization (to the neglect of agriculture and rural livelihoods, and hence the well-being of the mass of the population), while the latter is presented as one that eschews large-scale industrialization, focuses on the development of the rural "community," promotes local industry especially in craft and artisanal forms, and hence is more attuned to ensuring general well-being. In its current version this debate is over the "development model," and it has a more abstract form without the specificity of the earlier version. Both sides to the debate continue to conflate industrialization, and the role of science and technology in development, with the socio-economic transformations that are a necessary aspect of development in general, and in particular, the need for an agrarian transformation.

Thus, it is science that is the source of the problem rather than science in a society that has not undergone any radical transformation. In the more benign critiques, modern science is at best irrelevant, while in the harsher versions, science is seen as indeed the villain in a romantic fable where the stable equilibrium of a pre-capitalist order, portrayed romantically as free of exploitation and oppression, has been destabilized as a consequence of a modernity imposed by the west and subsequently continued by the Indian elite. It is evident that such views undermine the scientific temper, and, in romanticizing the past (and glorifying "indigenous" knowledge), allows *Hindutva*'s obscurantism to acquire intellectual pretensions.[24]

Another trend that threatens scientific advance and opens the door to new forms of obscurantism comes from the rise of environmental concerns and environmental movements. While environmental movements have by and large originated with unexceptionably significant issues such as conserving and protecting the environment, preventing pollution, banning hazardous substances, and gaining access to forest resources by those who have traditionally used them and depend on them for livelihoods, they have also been accompanied by romantic anti-scientific views that have increasingly become more dominant. The crux of the problem with environmentalism as a whole, except for a minority viewpoint, is to see environmental concerns as trumping all other socio-economic and political considerations. Thus, all questions of social transformation are set aside or made secondary to immediate environmental action. As a result, environmental movements are complicit in glorifying rural "communities," especially those with low levels of mechanization or modernization of agriculture, without regard to the deep inequalities and oppression that are characteristic of such communities in general. Caste, in particular, is explained away, as it were, or simply ignored. Shockingly, the socio-biological interpretation of caste – justifying it on grounds of ecological sustainability (with no mention of its oppressive character) – by Madhav Gadgil, a noted environmental scientist and activist, has met with little criticism.[25] It is unsurprising that the committee headed by him that was appointed to enquire into the preservation of biodiversity in the Western Ghat hill ranges in western India paid no heed, in its sweeping recommendations for environmental conservation, to the question of the livelihoods of millions who inhabit the region.[26] Environmentalists and environmental activists of note routinely include obscurantist factors in their appeals,[27] and even those who are otherwise critical of obscurantism tend to concede ground if it is linked to environmental concerns.

Environmentalism has also given rise to a new "secular" obscurantism that makes claims against particular technologies (often, it would seem, whimsically) or particular projects without any evidence, based often on gross misrepresentation of scientific facts. A case in point is the opposition to the project to detect and measure the properties of elementary particles known as neutrinos, coming from cosmic rays, which was proposed to be set up in the state of Tamil Nadu. A wild campaign in opposition was initiated by environmentalists from the state, who succeeded in stalling the project with the assistance of ill-informed judicial pronouncements and uninformed political support. The allegations included charges that the neutrinos were capable of causing radiation damage to persons in surrounding areas. This, of course, is a piece of laughable nonsense. The neutrinos would have caused no radiation damage, for the following reasons: first, because they only very "weakly" interact with any other matter; secondly, because they are not artificially produced but occur naturally in cosmic rays; and thirdly, because the experiment is proposed to be housed under a few hundred metres of solid rock.[28] Ironically, soon after the project was definitively stalled by a judicial verdict came the announcement of the award of that year's Nobel

Prize in physics, precisely for the study of the kind of phenomena the proposed experiment was to investigate.

These are by no means isolated instances. As in the rest of the world, there is rising opposition in India to the introduction of genetically modified crops, which has stalled further research of potential value to Indian agriculture. While it is true that such "secular" obscurantism is a global phenomenon,[29] in India it links up with the general prevalence of obscurantism of the traditional kind, and the widespread lack of scientific awareness in society, to form a formidable reactionary force.

Regrettably, such views have also gained a few adherents among the Left in India. While the traditional critique of the Left has focused on the need for equitable access to modern science and technology, and social control over technology to mitigate its unexpected consequences, such issues have tended to encompass questions of the risk associated with many modern technologies. However, while in its initial stages such questions of risk and safety have been linked to the ownership of technology, in later stages the questions of risk and safety acquire a life of their own (intrinsic to the nature of technology itself), while the predominantly socio-economic questions are relegated to the background.

In many instances it even appears that such anti-technology movements are visible manifestations of a deep-rooted frustration arising from the inability to organize effectively for radical social transformation. The sustained agitation against the completion and start up of a nuclear power plant on the eastern coast, south of the city of Chennai, dominated by protests of the local fisherfolk, expresses this contradiction clearly. The way in which the issue of long-term nuclear risk (which is of very low probability, but of potentially catastrophic consequence if indeed it occurs) overshadows and pushes aside every other issue, socio-economic or political, that is of significance in the short or medium term, suggests that the nuclear power plant is not the real focus of the local population's ire. It appears to be more the lightning rod that draws to itself the accumulated frustrations with respect to many other problems of greater import in their daily lives, problems that they believe to be intractable.[30]

THE WAY AHEAD

Our assessment of the current state of science and scientific temper in Indian society is not a positive one. This bleak view does, however, require some qualification. Obviously, all of science will not come to a grinding halt. A modern state and elite in the twenty-first century cannot exist without any science at all. And, as sectors like agriculture and space research have shown, this level of activity need not be insubstantial. Nor is it impossible for high levels of individual scientific achievement to be registered in scientific institutions, departments and research groups across the country – or for the current state of affairs to permit a few sectors of high competence, if not innovation, as in the information technology sector.

But there is little guarantee that in the years to come, India's science will achieve the levels that the country needs and deserves. Nor is it likely, judging by current trends, that the widening gap between India and other emerging scientific powers – such as Brazil, South Korea and China – will be closed. For the last four to five decades, the fortunes of science have altered between potential and hope, on the one hand, and crisis and despair, on the other. If a few individuals or institutions did well or better, the state of the rest has been a matter of concern. Among institutions that have done well, some have managed to retain something of their original purpose and élan, or, in the best cases, to improve their standing, even if there is an inescapable sense of fragility about their well-being.

More subtly, though, the agenda of these scientific institutions and broad sectors of research will continue to change, driven by the imperative of raising funds and resources from large private or public institutional donors from outside India, of collaborating with institutions from advanced scientific countries, and of meeting the demands of large private and institutional players within India. This may, of course, promote substantial scientific activity, but activity that is in a fundamental sense misaligned to the needs of the country.[31]

Much can be done in the short and medium term to improve science and technology in the country if successive governments increase public expenditure on science and technology, provide a more optimistic atmosphere in the way they manage scientific institutions and their needs, and ensure that the private sector meets its commitment to the promotion of knowledge generation. A return to the dominance of the public sector in the management of the economy seems a difficult prospect given the far-reaching changes of the last two decades and a half, unless a radical change takes place in economic policy. Even in such a situation, it is not self-evident that science will receive its due, as the advance of unscientific attitudes on the left of the political spectrum indicates.

For science to regain its rightful place in a vision of India's future, it is most important to revisit and re-emphasize its liberatory role. In doing so, two issues regarding the received notion of scientific temper need to be confronted head on. The first is the need to revisit the classical notion of secularism as separation of religion from the public sphere. In India, the practice of caste has deep roots, particularly in the various dogmas and practices that make up what is referred to as the Hindu religion. In this context, the right to personal practice of the Hindu religion cannot be allowed to encompass the practice of caste even in the private sphere. The extent to which this is to be dealt with by legal means may be a subject of discussion. No movement for the secularization of Indian society, or for ensuring the secular ideal in the economic, social and political life of the country, can ignore confronting the practice of caste discrimination, even in the so-called personal sphere.[32]

The second issue is that the agenda of promoting secularization and the scientific temper cannot be restricted to science in the restricted sense of the natural or engineering sciences, but must encompass the role of science in social transformation. To be sure, such an emphasis has not been entirely absent, but it has often been presented in the abstract as a broad appeal to rational thinking and application of scientific analysis. Today, the limitations of this approach are evident, and the agenda of scientific temper cannot move forward without focusing on all the oppressive, exploitative forms of the irrational in the sphere of the social.

Science must be linked not merely to poverty eradication, as in the Nehruvian agenda, but to an agenda of liberation from exploitation and oppression, especially of the pre-modern social oppression that is India's special burden, and the promotion of universal well-being, based on advance of the material basis of such well-being. Whether this vision will be realized in practice is a matter for the future. But of its necessity, as seen from the experience of the last seventy years and as this article has tried to argue, there can be little doubt.

Notes

1. Meghnad Saha's woes as a professor at the University of Allahabad in the 1930s, before his move to Kolkata, have quite a contemporary feel to them. They are briefly recounted in Anderson (2010).

2. This is not to deny the increase in the number of departments in several universities, or even in some colleges, that produce research work of good or excellent quality, but their relatively small numbers in the university system, it can be argued, continues to be a feature of contemporary higher education in India.

3. The poem was first published in English in 1913 as part of Tagore's famous collection, *Gitanjali*, and has been reproduced since on innumerable occasions in print and more recently on the internet. For the poem in full in English and the Bengali original, see http://en.wikipedia.org/wiki/Chitto_Jetha_Bhayshunyo.

4 An account of the original conversation is described in *The New York Times*, Marianoff (1930). A more detailed description and context of the meeting is provided in a special issue of *The Kenyon Review*: Einstein and Tagore (2001).

5 For more, see Government of India (1958), Mukhopadhyay (1983).

6 For an authoritative account of self-reliance as part of India's economic policy in the first few decades after Independence, see Nayar (1983).

7 The Constitution (Forty-Second Ammendment) Act 1976; available at http://www.constitution.org/cons/india/tamnd42.html

8 See data from the following reports: Government of India (2012; 2014).

9 I am indebted to Shailaja Pathak for stressing this point in numerous discussions.

10 World Bank data on high-technology exports with high R&D intensity, such as aerospace, computers, pharmaceuticals, scientific instruments and electrical machinery, are available at http://data.worldbank.org/indicator/TX.VAL.TECH.CD

11 There is sometimes the mistaken perception that the industrial revolution did not owe very much to the scientific revolution which preceded it. While it is undoubtedly true that the development of technology may proceed in relative autonomy from specifically scientific advance, the close connection historically between the scientific and industrial revolutions has been amply demonstrated by Margaret Jacob in her work. See for instance, Jacob (1997).

12 For the text of this seminal document in the evolution of India's science policy, see http://unesdoc.unesco.org/images/0015/001543/154344eb.pdf

13 I am indebted to R. Ramakumar for bringing this to my attention.

14 Nehru's views on the historical origins of caste elsewhere in the volume are remarkable for their sweeping generalizations and historical naivete. They recall D.D. Kosambi's excoriation of national leaders who, ill-equipped, spent their time in prison producing "pop" versions of history.

15 Gandhi was also capable of justifying his social agenda with a deeply obscurantist argument. An outstanding example of this was his attribution of the Bihar earthquake of 1934 to divine retribution for the widespread practice of the sin of untouchability. This drew a sharp response from Rabindranath Tagore, who was shocked by Gandhi's reasoning. See Bhattacharya (1997).

16 For a critique of Nehru's *Discovery of India* from the viewpoint of its limitation in dealing with caste, see Guru (2016).

17 For a more detailed assessment of the "reform" agenda in science, see Jayaraman (2009).

18 For an early critique of the nuclear weapons programme and its significance, see Ram (1999).

19 For an up-to-date review of the IT sector, see, for instance, Mani (2013). See also Chandrasekhar (2006).

20 See, for instance, data on global trade in advanced technology from successive reports of the US National Science Board (2014; 2016). See also the review of innovation in India in Mani (2009).

21 There appears to be little evidence of a concerted effort at advanced scientific research in the new generation of privately funded institutions of higher education.

22 The full text of the *Manusmriti* merits reading. For a critical edition of the *Manusmriti* see Olivelle (2004). An easy English translation is available at http://www.ahandfulofleaves.org/documents/Dharmasutras_Olivelle_1999.pdf

23 There are very few studies that explore this question adequately. See, for instance, Raza and Singh (2004). For some other efforts with which the author himself was associated, see Pathak (2013) and Raj (2016).

24 For a recent example of this, see Aravindhan (2016).

25 For a sampling of Gadgil's views, see Gadgil and Malhotra (1982; 1983; 1994). A rare critique is to be found in Guha (2002).

26 For a critique of the Western Ghats report of the Madhav Gadgil committee, see Aravindhan *et al.* (2015).

27 For instance, I have heard Sunderlal Bahuguna, almost thirty years ago, refer to Mount Kailash in his lectures as the "abode of Siva and Parvati." While a similar statement by anyone from the Sangh Parivar, referring to Ayodhya as the birthplace of the mythological god Rama of the *Ramayana*, would rightfully draw fire as obscurantist, such statements by environmentalists do not draw similar criticism.

28 See Jayaraman (2015), and for an up-to-date review of the state of the project, Ramachandran (2015).

29 For a recent account of such views in the west, see the book *Science Left Behind*: Berezow and Campbell (2012).

30 For a discussion of this issue, see Aravindhan and Jayaraman (2013). The paper was based on fieldwork and interviews by Aravindhan for his M.A. dissertation.

31 A dramatic example is provided by the health sector, where high-technology hospitals offering world-class treatment enable India to emerge as a medical tourism destination for many developing and developed nations, whereas the majority of the population still lacks adequate basic health care.

32 Indeed, the natural tendency of Hinduism to conflate so-called religious belief with the practices of everyday social life is evident in the ban on the production, sale and consumption of beef by non-Hindus in different parts of the country sought to be imposed by the forces of Hindutva.

References

Ambedkar, B.R. (1946), *What Congress and Gandhi Have Done to the Untouchables*, Bombay: Thacker & Co.

Anderson, R.S. (2010), *Nucleus and Nation: Scientists, International Networks, and Power in India*, Chicago: University of Chicago Press.

Aravindhan, N. (2016), "A rebuttal to Rajiv Malhotra, by an 'elite leftist goon activist'," *scroll.in*, available at http://scroll.in/article/802962/a-rebuttal-to-rajiv-malhotra-by-an-elite-leftist-goon-activist, viewed on February 4.

Aravindhan, N. and T. Jayaraman (2013), "Risk and the Role of Science in Conflict Resolution: A case study of the Kudankulam Nuclear Power Plant in Southern India," paper presented at the national conference on "Science in Society and Development: Nehru and Beyond," Centre for Jawaharlal Nehru Studies, Jamia Millia Islamia, New Delhi.

Aravindhan, N., K.K. Murari, T. Jayaraman and G. Radhakrishnan (2015), "Appraising the Debate on Biodiversity Conservation in the Western Ghats," *Economic and Political Weekly*, Vol. 50, No. 30, p. 49.

Balaram, P. (2010), "Irreverence and Advancement," *Current Science*, Vol. 98, No. 9; available at http://www.currentscience.ac.in/Downloads/article_id_098_09_1155_1156_0.pdf, viewed on 10 May 2010.

Berezow, A.B. and H. Campbell (2012), "Science left behind: Feel-good fallacies and the rise of the anti-scientific left," *Public Affairs*.

Bhargava, P.M. and C. Chakrabarti (2007), *Angels, Devil, and Science: A Collection of Articles on Scientific Temper*, New Delhi: National Book Trust.

Bhattacharya, S. (1997), *Mahatma and the Poet: Letters and Debates Between Gandhi and Tagore 1915–1941*, New Delhi: National Book Trust.

Business Line (2003), "Homeopaths vandalize critic's house," available at http://www.thehindubusinessline.com/bline/2003/07/08/stories/2003070802201700.html, viewed on April 27, 2016.

Chandrasekhar, C.P. (2006), "Who Needs a "Knowledge Economy"?: Information Knowledge and Flexible Labour," *Social Scientist*, Vol. 34, Nos.1–2, pp. 70–87, available at http://www.jstor.org/stable/3518172

Chandrasekhar, C.P. and J. Ghosh (2002), *The Market that Failed: A decade of neoliberal economic reforms in India*, New Delhi: Leftword Books.

Economic and Political Weekly (2015), Editorial: "A Chill Wind," Vol. 50, No. 37; available at http://dev.epw.in/system/files/pdf/2015_50/37/A_Chill_Wind.pdf

Einstein and Tagore (2001), "'Endless Dawns' of Imagination," *The Kenyon Review*, Vol. 23, No. 2, pp. 7–33; available at http://www.jstor.org/stable/4338196

Gadgil, M. and K.C. Malhotra (1982), "Ecology of a Pastoral Caste: Gavli Dhangars of Peninsular India," *Human Ecology*, Vol. 10, No. 1, pp. 107–43.

Gadgil, M. and K.C. Malhotra (1983), "Adaptive Significance of the Indian Caste System: An Ecological Perspective," *Annals of Human Biology*, Vol. 10, No. 5, pp. 465–77.

Gadgil, M. and K.C. Malhotra (1994), "The ecological significance of caste," *Social Ecology*.

Gandhi, M.K. ([1909] 1984), *Hind Swaraj*, Ahmedabad: Navjivan.

Government of India (1958), "Scientific Policy Resolution," New Delhi: Ministry of Science and Technology, Government of India, 4 March; available at http://www.nrdms.gov.in/sci_policy.asp

Government of India (2012), *All India Survey on Higher Education*, New Delhi: Department of Higher Education, Ministry of Human Resource Development,

Government of India; available at http://mhrd.gov.in/sites/upload_files/mhrd/files/statistics/AISHE2011-12P_1.pdf

Government of India (2014), *Educational Statistics at a Glance*, New Delhi: Bureau of Planning, Monitoring and Statistics, Ministry of Human Resource Development, Government of India; available at http://mhrd.gov.in/sites/upload_files/mhrd/files/statistics/EAG2014.pdf

Guha, S. (2002), "Claims on the Commons: Political Power and Natural Resources in Pre-Colonial India," *Indian Economic and Social History Review*, Vol. 39, Nos. 2–3, pp. 181–96.

Guru, G. (2016), "The Indian Nation in Its Egalitarian Conception," in R.S. Rawat and K. Satyanarayana, eds, *Dalit Studies*, Durham: Duke University Press.

Jacob, M.C. (1997), *Scientific Culture and the Making of the Industrial West*, Oxford University Press.

Jayaraman, T. (2009), "Science, Technology and Innovation Policy in India under Economic Reform: A Survey," paper presented at the international conference on "The Crisis of Neo-liberalism in India: Challenges and Alternatives," Mumbai; available at http://www.networkideas.org/ideasact/jan09/pdf/jayaraman.pdf.

Jayaraman, T. (2015), "Tunnel vision blocks neutrino lab progress," *The Times of India*, 24 February; available at http://timesofindia.indiatimes.com/india/Tunnel-vision-blocks-neutrino-lab progress/articleshow/46358125.cms

Kannan, K.P. (1990), "Secularism and People's Science Movement in India," *Economic and Political Weekly*, Vol. 25, No. 6, pp. 311–13; available at http://www.jstor.org/stable/4395925

Kumar, D. (1995), *Science and the Raj, 1857–1905*, New Delhi: Oxford University Press.

Lala, R.M. (2006), *The Creation of Wealth: The Tatas from the 19th to the 21st Century*, New Delhi: Penguin Books.

Mani, Sunil (2009), "Is India Becoming More Innovative since 1991? Some Disquieting Features," *Economic and Political Weekly*, Vol. 44, No. 46, pp. 41–51; available at http://www.jstor.org/stable/25663789

Mani, Sunil (2013), "Changing Leadership in Computer and Information Services, Emergence of India as the Current World Leader in Computer and Information Services," Working Paper Series no. 453, Thiruvananthapuram: Centre for Development Studies, September; available at http://cds.edu/wp-content/uploads/2013/10/WP453.pdf

Marianoff, D. (1930), "Einstein and Tagore Plumb the Truth," *The New York Times*, 10 August.

Mukerji, B. and P.K. Bose (1963), *A Short History of the Indian Science Congress Association (with life-sketches of general presidents) 1914–1963*, Calcutta: Indian Science Congress Association.

Mukherjee, M. and A. Mukherjee (2001), *Communalization of Education: The History Textbook Controversy*, New Delhi: Delhi Historians' Group.

Mukhopadhyay, D. (2014), "Post-Independence Science Policy and Science Funding in India," *Current Science*, Vol. 7, No. 12, 25 December; available at http://www.currentscience.ac.in/volumes/107/12/1983.pdf

Nanda, M. (2006), *Prophets Facing Backward*, New Delhi: Orient Blackswan.

Nandy, A. (1988), *Science, Hegemony and Violence: A Requiem for Modernity*, United Nations University.

National Science Board (2014), *Science and Engineering Indicators 2014 Arlington VA*, National Science Foundation (NSB 14-01), available at http://www.nsf.gov/statistics/seind14/content/etc/nsb1401.pdf

National Science Board (2016), *Science and Engineering Indicators 2016 Arlington VA*, National Science Foundation (NSB 16-01), available at https://www.nsf.gov/statistics/2016/nsb20161/uploads/1/nsb20161.pdf

Nayar, B.R. (1983), *India's Quest for Technological Independence*, Vols. 1 and 2, New Delhi: Lancers.

Nehru, J. ([1946] 1989), *The Discovery of India*, New Delhi: Oxford University Press.

Olivelle, P. (2004), *Manu's Code of Law: A Critical Edition and Translation of the Manava-Dharmasastra*, Oxford University Press.

Pathak, S. (2013), "Astrological Belief in Contemporary Indian Society," unpublished M.Phil. dissertation, Tata Institute of Social Sciences, Mumbai; available at http://192.168.194.112/handle/1/7060

Raj, A. (2016), "Study of Scientific Temper amongst Youth in Kerala: A Study in Thrissur District Kerala," unpublished MA dissertation, Tata Institute of Social Sciences, Mumbai.

Ram, N. (1999), *Riding the Nuclear Tiger*, New Delhi: LeftWord Books.

Ramachandran, R. (2015), "Neutrino scare', *Frontline*, 5 March; available at http://www.frontline.in/science-and-technology/neutrino-scare/article6901605.ece

Raza, G. and S. Singh (2004), "Cultural Distance Between Peoples' Worldview and Scientific Knowledge in the Area of Public Health," *Journal of Science Communication*, Vol. 3, No. 4.

Sridhar, V. and S. Singh (2010), "Rural India's Communication Divide," *The Hindu*, available at http://www.thehindu.com/opinion/op-ed/rural-indias-communication-divide/article598333.ece

The Constitution (Forty-Second Amendment) Act (1976), http://www.constitution.org/cons/india/tamnd42.htm

"Mythology and Science" (2016), *The Hindu*, 6 January; available at http://www.thehindu.com/opinion/editorial/editorial-mythology-and-science/article6757521.ece

Vaidyanathan, A., N. Krishnaji and K.P. Kannan (1979), "People's Science Movements," *Economic and Political Weekly*, Vol. 14, No. 2, pp. 57–58; available at http://www.jstor.org/stable/4367242

Zachariah, M. and R. Sooryamoorthy (1994), *Achievements and Dilemmas of a Development Movement: The Kerala Shastra Sahitya Parishad*, New Delhi: Vistaar Publications.

The Story of Kamala Ratnaveli: Caste in Sri Lanka and Left Intervention

Kumari Jayawardena

"Welcome home, Kamala!"

"Goodbye, Kamala!"

The women's voices called out both the greeting and the farewell as the earthenware vessel containing the ashes was gently dropped into the water. They watched the length of muslin in which it had been wrapped swirl as it floated slowly to where the Kelani river meets the Indian Ocean. Among the small group on the bridge were Kamala's daughter Melanie and granddaughter Imogen (who had brought the ashes from England), and her childhood companions Suriya and Kumari. The year was 2012.

The story of Kamala Ratnaveli started some 85 years earlier in a very different Sri Lanka – or Ceylon, as it was then called. Born of a poor village family of the Rodi caste, Kamala was brought as a child to Colombo by Left activists to be educated in the English medium. The Rodi were not merely considered the lowest caste among the Sinhalese, they were treated as untouchables to be shunned by society. This intervention did not simply aim to show that those at the bottom of the social hierarchy, who were marginalized and poor, could overcome these obstacles through access to education. It was a frontal attack on the mindset that the Rodi were afflicted by some sort of inborn characteristic that made them forever outcasts, something that was unchangeable and immutable. The Leftists, while believing with Marx that only industrial growth would in the long run eliminate caste as a system, adopted humanitarian policies such as organizing relief during an epidemic in which "low-caste" groups were particularly badly affected. Educating Kamala Ratnaveli was a part of this approach.

The "Hidden Agenda" of Caste

One of the "hidden agendas" of Sri Lanka's much-proclaimed democracy is the continued existence of the undemocratic caste system, which has survived feudalism and colonial rule. J. Uyangoda refers to this as "the inner courtyard," arguing that: "In Sinhalese and Tamil societies, extreme forms of social inequalities are practised in caste relations that seem to reproduce themselves under conditions of the post-colonial state, post-colonial capitalism, and liberal regimes following the rule of law" (Uyangoda 2000: 14). Mobility from one caste to another is not possible. Persons of low income can leave their class, but not their caste, of origin, and through income and education change their class status.

While the exclusion of Sri Lankans from political power produced an agitation for constitutional reform in the early twentieth century, opposition to the issue of social exclusion based on caste was not a concern of local political leaders, who did not want to tamper with the status quo on traditional social structures and values. Caste thus remained unchallenged until the 1930s, but continues even today to be what Uyangoda calls "a subterranean force" (*ibid.*: 17).

In India, there existed a strong and somewhat independent bourgeoisie, based mainly on industrial ventures. Many of its members had enlightened views on reformist issues and social evils, also opposing social exclusion based on caste. This was not the case, however, in Sri Lanka, where the bourgeoisie's economic involvements were different. They only ventured into investment under the protective shadow of the state. The first capital accumulation of any significance was in the liquor trade, which was state-regulated. The large profits were reinvested in plantations, graphite mining and the education of sons abroad (Jayawardena 2007a). As a result, members of the wealthy bourgeoisie that emerged were not only collaborative with British rule, but also disinclined to take up contentious social issues that would be controversial and disturb the status quo, issues such as caste.

In Sri Lanka, caste, which in pre-colonial times was linked to occupational stratification, had eroded by the nineteenth century with the growth of commercialization and the availability of caste-free employment in the government and private sectors. Occupational caste names persisted, however, as did certain discriminatory practices. The newly emergent local bourgeoisie, while campaigning for more political reform and speaking out on Liberty and the Rights of Man, were indifferent to issues such as caste oppression. The absence of national leaders in the vanguard of social change was a void that was filled by members of the nascent radical movements in the north and the south in the early 1930s. They drew attention to the feudal nature of the caste system and denounced its undemocratic aspects. Such protests against caste did not originate from the oppressed themselves but from "outsiders."

The "outsiders" who called attention to the severe exploitation and slave-like conditions on the tea plantations of Sri Lanka included urban lawyers and professionals, Indian nationalists, women political activists, British liberals and local Left leaders (Jayawardena and Kurian 2015: 69–126, Part 2). But on the caste issue, many of the local elite showed no concern – either because they themselves accepted the system of caste or because they felt the subject was too sensitive for public discourse. Colonial officials also treaded warily. While enacting laws against discrimination, they did not interfere in established social systems, adopting a policy of non-interference in local structures and customs. But by the nineteenth century, Euro–Asian radicals had denounced caste; and in the twentieth century, the country's first Left party – the Lanka Sama Samaja Party – exposed social exclusion and campaigned openly against the caste system, calling for its abolition in the Party's first manifesto in 1935. In the north of Sri Lanka, in the early 1930s, a parallel movement was led by young radicals of the Jaffna Youth Congress.

Even by the twentieth century, pockets of social exclusion based on caste prevailed in religious institutions and schools. As Tudor Kalinga Silva notes, in many so-called "depressed" caste groups, "poverty, landlessness, low dignity, unemployment and poor living conditions exist ... with continued discrimination on the part of surrounding communities ... government institutions [and] schools" (Silva 2009: xvi). Two national leaders of the 1930s who spoke on labour and political questions were George E. de Silva, a radical nationalist politician from Kandy, and A.E. Goonesinha, a militant leader of the Colombo working class. But even they never became champions of the underprivileged castes, although they themselves belonged to such communities. Goonesinha claimed in 1927 that his Ceylon Labour Union insisted on adult franchise "without any discrimination because of sex, race, religion or caste" (Jayawardena 1972: 255). Yet he never specifically highlighted the caste system, the most primordial of these divisions.

While Sinhalese and Tamil political leaders were indifferent, some young rebels and radicals of both communities brought the caste issue into prominence. In the north, the radicals of the Jaffna Youth Congress campaigned vigorously against caste, making it the central issue of its 1930 sessions.[1] After the Department of Education had enforced equal seating in school classrooms, this issue could not be ignored in the north. Children used to be segregated by caste in classrooms, with those of "low" caste being made to sit on the floor or on separate benches. Attempts to change this were met by acts of arson, and within a period of two months a dozen schools with equal seating were attacked, while minority Tamils burned down schools that did not enforce equal seating (Kadirgamar 2012: 73). The Congress resolution of 1930 reaffirmed its emphatic views "against the social disabilities based on birth, occupation or wealth," and resolved to "secure equal opportunities to all and to cooperate with other agencies engaged in the same work." It recorded its appreciation of "the equitable rule introduced by the Department of Education requiring equal seating in all schools," and appealed "to all our countrymen to do away with all such distinctions" (*ibid.*). On the other hand, there were Tamil conservative leaders, notably Sir P. Ramanathan, who opposed the move and led a delegation to the Colonial Secretary in protest.

Another minority, the Euro–Asians (Burghers and Eurasians), who were of mixed European and local origin, took a progressive stand and deplored the caste system. This was especially true of radical Burghers, who, from the mid-nineteenth century onwards, campaigned for an enlightened and forward-looking society. The earliest proto-nationalists in Sri Lanka, belonging to a group known as "Young Ceylon," were led by a Burgher, the charismatic Charles Lorenz (Jayawardena 2007b). One of Lorenz's colleagues, Frederic Nell (1828–1867), who edited *Young Ceylon* from 1850 to 1852, wrote on "The Social Improvement of the Ceylonese." He did not mince words and criticized the local caste system, blaming the British for not eradicating "the leprosy of CASTE" (capitalized in the original) (Roberts *et al.* 1989: 83; Jayawardena 2007b: 152–53).

While in pre-capitalist Sri Lanka the system of social stratification based on occupation was caste, changes took place in the nineteenth century, when access to education, employment, the legal system and political participation became available irrespective of caste. As Uyangoda states, what resulted was a "colonial caste system . . . new wine in old bottles, where the archaic system has been accentuated by the incursion of new forces, economic, political and cultural" (cited in Jayawardena 2007a: 160). But in spite of the "new forces," the caste system itself certainly did not vanish, but remained surprisingly resilient to economic and political changes.

Uyangoda, writing in 2012 on "social exclusion based on caste marginalization" in the Kurunegala district, argues that "this is not only the denial of the individual's rights, but also the rights of social groups . . . to fully participate in the political, social, cultural, associational and economic life in society." Their "extreme social marginalization" compelled the people to "live in a regime of incomplete citizenship and incomplete democracy," combined with other "social, cultural and political violations" as well as "poverty and social disabilities" (Uyangoda 2012: 34, 37–38).

A significant social change affecting caste was the rise of a local bourgeoisie composed of persons of different castes. The emphasis now seemed to shift from caste to class. As Newton Gunasinghe observed: "There is the disintegration of the caste system as a mode of division of labour . . . without leading to the disappearance of caste as a social group or [of] caste consciousness" (Gunasinghe 2007: 145–46). Persons of different castes benefited from the expansion of the colonial economy, and the local bourgeoisie itself, which emerged in the nineteenth and early twentieth centuries, was a multi-caste phenomenon. However, the "new wine" in the form of the bourgeoisie, which resulted in the development of a "consciousness of class," did not obliterate caste consciousness. Caste rivalry continued in several ways, often expressed through contradictions between the old rich and the new rich (Jayawardena 2007a).

Among the Sinhalese and the Tamils, caste distinctions and caste discrimination continued at the village level. Some of the radical leaders of the emerging Left of the 1930s who had roots in the village were conversant with the caste system and the indignities it imposed. Dr S.A. Wickremasinghe, born in Atureliya in Akuressa district of the Southern Province, was the son of rural "high caste" gentry, his father Thedias Ferdinandis Abeywardena Wickremasinghe being known in village parlance as Nasnaranketiye Ralahamy, referring to his status as well as the land on which he lived. Similarly, Philip and Robert Gunawardena, sons of Boralugoda Ralahamy in Avissawella district, were privileged and equally aware of caste discrimination in their areas. Another Left leader, Colvin R. de Silva of Randombe in Galle district, where there were large numbers of the "lower" castes, was also conscious of the working of the caste system. Members of the Left were used to taking a stand on questions related to caste. They would address "low"-caste party members as "comrades" in the presence of "higher"-caste persons. This was all the more telling as the Sinhala word for comrade, *sahodaraya*, connotes a sibling relationship. Left leaders would also intervene in violent clashes between castes (A. Abeywickrema, personal communication, 15 May 2015). The caste issue, which had come up forcefully in both southern and northern Sri Lanka during this period, was linked to the Donoughmore Commission's report advocating universal franchise. This was implemented in 1931, when most of the "depressed" castes were to vote for the first time. In some areas where they were concentrated, their vote was crucial to the outcome of the election.

This consciousness of the Left leaders was reinforced by the influence of Marxism while they were students in the west. Marx, writing in 1853, had made his celebrated reference to caste and social backwardness in India. He noted that communities in India "were contaminated by distinctions of caste and by slavery that subjected men to external circumstances in a never-ending natural destiny, and thus brought about a brutalizing worship of nature. Man, the sovereign of nature, fell down on his knees in adoration of Hanuman, the monkey, and Sabbala, the cow" (Marx 1972: 41). He also predicted that modern industry would "dissolve the hereditary divisions of labour, upon which rest the Indian castes, those decisive impediments to Indian progress" (*ibid.*: 85).

The young socialists who returned to Sri Lanka in the early 1930s and joined the Youth Leagues were shocked to witness first-hand the inequalities of the caste system. This occurred especially when they joined the Suriya Mal movement, which, in 1933–34, distributed food and medication to malaria-stricken persons of the Kegalle and Kurunegala districts, where much caste oppression prevailed. By 1935, an estimated 100,000 or more are said to have died in the malaria epidemic. Particularly affected were the poorest people of the "lowest" castes, already debilitated by the economic depression. Thus, in the oppression of the people, against which the Leftists firmly stood, caste and class were intertwined.

The Suriya Mal Movement

An important political episode of the early 1930s was the formation of the Youth League movement composed of young radicals. Many of them were avowed socialists. The most prominent Youth Leagues were in Jaffna and Colombo. In 1931 the Youth Leagues of Colombo formed the Youth Congress, which campaigned for political and economic freedom. Socialist students returning from abroad found in the Youth Congress a readymade organization through which to express their views. Prominent among the students were Dr S.A. Wickremasinghe, Philip Gunawardena, N.M. Perera, Colvin R. de Silva, Leslie Goonewardena and Robin Rutnam. Others in the Colombo Youth Leagues who were to become notable in Left politics were Terence de Zylva, George Caldera, Susan de Silva, Vernon Gunasekera and Jack Kotalawala.

An annual event in colonial Sri Lanka was the sale of poppy flowers on 11 November (Armistice Day), with the proceeds being used to benefit British soldiers wounded in the First World War. This aroused nationalist feelings among radical Sri Lankans and they formed a rival movement in 1931, originally led by local ex-servicemen. The movement was taken over by Leftists of the Youth Leagues, who boycotted the poppy and instead promoted the sale of a yellow flower – the *suriya mala*. The new radical leadership included the principal of a Buddhist girls' school, Doreen Young (later Doreen Wickremasinghe), who became the Suriya Mal president, with S.W.R.D. Bandaranaike as the trustee of the movement's fund. Other Suriya Mal supporters who provided relief to the poor during the malaria epidemic were Dr S.A. Wickremasinghe, N.M. Perera, Selina Perera, Colvin R. de Silva, Philip, Robert and Harry Gunawardena, Terence de Zylva, Robin Rutnam, his mother Dr Mary Rutnam, and many Ananda Balika teachers.

The Suriya Mal movement was led by an incipient anti-imperialist group that was also the nucleus of the country's first Left party, formed in 1935: the Lanka Sama Samaja Party (LSSP). Writing about the movement, Terence de Zylva, the founder of Kolonnawa Vidyalaya, claimed that it was "definitely anti-war," and was intended to "prevent money going out of the country to help the British Empire wage wars for the purpose of partitioning the world" (Jayawardena 1973). Doreen Young wrote in the *Ceylon Daily News* (11 November 1932) on "Suriya Mal or Poppy?' Posing the question, "whose need is more dire, the ex-servicemen in England or the poor of this country?," she said it was useless "to sigh as you think of the glorious dead and ignore the duty you owe to the living whose inglorious conditions are in part the responsibility of every citizen."

Two teachers, Eileen Wirasekera and Helen D'Alwis, wrote a pamphlet urging people to wear the *suriya* flower on 11 November "for freedom and peace," and thereby "register your refusal to encourage participation in Imperialist War. Every Suriya Mala is a blow against Imperialism, Fascism and War" (Jayawardena 1991). Students also were attracted to the movement. The trade union leader Bala Tampoe recalled that as a schoolboy at Royal College, he was influenced by a classmate, Dannister Gunatilake (brother of Vivienne Goonewardena), to join the Suriya Mal movement. Tampoe had joined students selling *suriya mal* near Royal College in 1935, confronting British women who were selling the rival poppy. This experience, he says, was the earliest demonstration "of the rebel in him" (Pasqualge 2012a). Action was taken against the Suriya Mal movement by some schools. Miss Gwen Opie, principal of the Ceylon Missionary Society School, Ladies' College, addressed the students at assembly, denouncing the Suriya Mal movement and its president Doreen Young.

There was outrage among the Suriya Mal workers when D.B. Jayatilake, the leader of the State Council, said that the malaria epidemic was due to the people's *karma*. The Suriya Mal Relief Committee charged Jayatilake with avoiding the political implications of the epidemic and using funds to celebrate the Jubilee of the King of England in 1935, "while the country was being reduced to a graveyard." The report of the Relief Committee emphasized that the actual relief given was less important than the political interaction between the stricken peasants and Suriya Mal activists. This interaction also stirred the consciousness of the peasantry to an extent previously unknown. As the report stated:

> Not until now did we really begin to understand and appreciate the full implications of a *crude feudalism, and the nature and extent of the oppression, misery, want and moral degradation that could prevail within such a system* ... our sympathetic treatment of the villager as our equal was a revelation to him, accustomed as he was to be bossed, abused, and treated like a dog by his so-called social superiors. (Emphasis added; cited in Jayawardena 1980)

The Lanka Sama Samaja Party

Many of the radicals of the Youth Leagues and Suriya Mal movement, and those who led the strike at the Wellawatte Spinning and Weaving Mills in 1933, came together to form a new party in 1935 – the Lanka Sama Samaja Party (LSSP). The issue of caste oppression was very much in the forefront at that time. Apart from the influence of the northern anti-caste agitation, the radicals were aware of similar movements in south India. These included the movement of E.V. Ramasamy Naicker, known as "Periyar," who assailed Hindu gods and the domination and tyranny of brahmins. He visited Sri Lanka in 1932 and spoke at several meetings. There was also the leader of oppressed castes in Kerala, Narayana Guru, who visited Colombo to meet Malayali workers at the Wellawatte Spinning and Weaving Mills and elsewhere.

In the LSSP manifesto, the fundamental objective of the party was declared to be "the establishment of a Socialist Society," which entailed "the Socialization of the means of Production, Distribution and Exchange of Commodities"; it also involved "the attainment of National Independence and the Abolition of Economic and Political Inequality and Oppression arising from Differences of Class, Race, Caste, Creed and Sex" (*Young Socialist*, March 1980). This was the first time that caste was mentioned publicly in a political document as a system that should be "abolished," as it perpetuated "inequality and oppression."

During these years when caste was being openly denounced, a decision was made to use Suriya Mal funds for the education of a child of the most oppressed caste (Rodi), to prove that with equality of opportunity and access to quality education such children could perform as well as those from privileged groups. The intention was to seek a very young child, but when a six-year-old girl jumped into the car and would not leave it, she was brought to Colombo with her parents' consent to begin a new life. The girl's father (Hulavali Sonpalliyawattege Redi Ratnaveli) was a leader (*hulavaliya*) in the area, and he and her mother would have valued the prospects that opened up for their daughter. Doreen and Dr S.A. Wickremasinghe, who had decided on the education of a child from a Rodi village in Eheliyagoda, were keen proponents of this idea.

The Wickremasinghes

Dr S.A. Wickremasinghe (1901–1981) qualified as a doctor in Sri Lanka and went to Britain for further medical studies in 1926. He was from a prosperous rural family of Atureliya in the Southern Province and had studied at Mahinda College, Galle. The college principal, F.L. Woodward, was a Buddhist theosophist with liberal political views who influenced Wickremasinghe, as did another theosophist, vice-principal F.G. Pearce. Wickremasinghe, while in Britain, interacted with Indian and British socialists and communists, and worked with like-minded Sri Lankan students. On returning to Sri Lanka, he won a seat in the State Council (1931–36), where he highlighted the economic and social problems facing the country and campaigned against British colonialism.

Doreen Wickremasinghe née Young (1908–2000) was from Cheshire, Britain; her mother was the daughter of Robert Weare, a well-known socialist of Bristol. Doreen attended the "progressive" theosophist school St. Christopher's in Letchworth and graduated from the London School of Economics with a B.Sc. (Econ.) degree. She worked with Krishna Menon in the India Freedom League in London. In 1930, hoping to proceed to find employment in India, she came to Sri Lanka with a friend, and unexpectedly, found herself made the principal of Sujatha Vidyalaya, a Buddhist girls' school in Matara in the south. There she was politically active, among other issues championing the public protest of the "scavenging" workers of Matara, a "low-caste" Indian community. It made her understand their degraded condition and that of others who were considered "untouchables," shunned by the rest of society. In 1933, Doreen married Dr Wickremasinghe. She moved to Colombo and became the principal of Ananda Balika, a Buddhist girls' secondary school; she also engaged actively in the Suriya Mal movement and Left politics.

The Rodi Community

The Suriya Mal group chose to educate a child from the Rodi community because of the exceptional degradation suffered by that community. In the 1930s it was still ostracized socially, economically and politically. Its members gained a livelihood mainly by begging, besides weaving mats and coir rope (Denham 1912: 212).[2] Robert Knox wrote of the Rodi caste in the sixteenth century: "They do beg for their living . . . and that with so much importunity as if they had a patent for it from the King" (*ibid.*: 215). They also made brooms and drums, and cleaned streets after religious events. Such work, having "an aura of disgrace and ritual impurity," led them to be ostracized and feared (Silva 2011: 108).

The social degradation of the Rodi imposed on them certain conditions of behaviour that affirmed their low position in society. When begging, they had to stand away from houses, and money was placed in their bowls made of leaves. Rodi children did not attend school in the past, and they were excluded from the social life of the village. Their housing, known as *kuppayamas*, consisted of separate hamlets on the fringes of the village. The Rodi legend of origin, however, states that their ancestors were royal persons who had been banished from society as punishment for wrongdoing. They also claim to be the descendants of a banished princess, Ratnavalli. As Uyangoda writes, caste myths and ideas of a "historic fall" are direct responses to "conditions of inequality, injustice, and marginality," and "a belief in a glorious, golden past is usually a strategy among oppressed communities to come to terms with inescapable deprivation" (Uyangoda 2000: 18).

Weeratunga writes that the Rodi form less than 1 per cent of the population, and that they have a language and "a mythical tradition of their own" (Weeratunga 1988: 18–19).[3] "The community have kept their identity and language," and "a sense of group consciousness is very much evident" (*ibid.*: 19). The Rodi language is not a dialect of Sinhala but has its own history. Raghavan claims that it belongs neither to the Indo-Aryan nor to the Dravidian group, but is linked to "the dialects of the Munda group of language spoken by the hill tribes . . . around Orissa and Bihar . . . and hill tracts of Chittagong" (Raghavan 1957: 106). He quotes Wilhelm Schmidt who says that the Munda languages are a part of the languages referred to as Austro-Asiatic.

Weeratunga also identifies the dominance of patriarchy among the Rodi community. She states: "Rodi women live in a patriarchal, patrilocal community defined by a gender ideology hostile to them." The strength of the women was in "the persistence of their struggle to retain control over their day-to-day lives" (Weeratunga 1988: 75–76). A Rodi man, expressing his views to Weeratunga, said: "Only sons are our own. The daughters have been raised to give away to other families" (*ibid.*: 71).

Between the Rodi community and the "gypsies" in Europe (known as the Roma), there are some striking parallels. Both were considered "outsiders", as belonging to the lowest rank, feared and yet romanticized in literature. Numerous novels, dramas, operas, songs, films and folklore in Europe portrayed the Roma as both physically attractive and seductive. Prosper Merimée's "Carmen", the tale of a "gypsy", was made into a popular opera by Bizet. Another famous poem, Mathew Arnold's "The Scholar Gypsy" (1853), recounts the story of a poor Oxford University student who abandoned his studies to join a band of "gypsies" and learn their traditional knowledge. The hostility to both Rodi and Roma was similar, based on unproven assertions. Both were suspected not only of kidnapping children, but also of enticing the high-born with their spells; a popular folk song in Britain was about a woman who abandoned "her newly wedded lord" to run "off with the raggle-taggle gypsies."

Apart from preserving their own languages, the Rodi community and the Roma had other features in common. They claimed to be able to read fortunes, predict the future, practise charms and cast spells. In both cases the resort to magic was a "weapon of the weak," a phrase used by James Scott to explain the resort to non-traditional forms of protest by people otherwise ostracized or marginalized.

Both Roma and Rodi women were thought by some to be clairvoyants, as seen in the ubiquitous Roma fortune-tellers in Europe. The Rodi community was, according to Bryce Ryan, "the most publicized caste in Ceylon," their very "depressed condition" attracting the attention of writers (Ryan 1953: 225). M.D. Raghavan commented, "no other group has stirred the imagination of the people as the Rodiya" (Raghavan 1957: 1). The reputed physical charms of Rodi women made them a subject for writers. Stories about them included Dr Lucien de Zilva's novel, *A Chandala Woman* (1923), and J. Vijayatunga's short story, "The Rodiya Girl" (1960). Ryan also remarked, "The beauty of Rodi women is proverbial in Ceylon and mentioned in every account of the caste" (Ryan 1953: 235, note 20). Postcards of bare-breasted Rodi women were sold from the early twentieth century onwards. The anthropologist M.D. Raghavan's book on the Rodi is called *Handsome Beggars* (1957). In the folklore of Sri Lanka, a famous episode is the romance between Asokamala of the Rodi caste and King Dutugemunu's son Saliya, who thereby lost his claim to the throne. This legend, which has captured the Sinhalese imagination, was made into a popular film entitled *Asokamala*.[4]

The Rodi community attracted the attention of ethnographers and writers. Much valuable ethnological material and many suggestions for amelioration of their lives came from civil servants. Outstanding among these was the contribution of Hugh Nevill, who in 1887 wrote in detail in *The Taprobanian* on "The Gadi or Rodi Race in Ceylon." This is regarded as the first important piece of ethnographical writing on the Rodi.[5] Another civil servant, Ponnambalam Arunachalam, headed a commission in 1904 to "inquire and report on the measures that should be taken for the education of the Rodiyas of Ceylon." He urged that their education was a "noble and urgent task," adding that "no change in the popular feeling towards the Rodiya, no real improvement of his condition, can be expected until by special efforts a fair number of them is sufficiently educated to realize their degradation and to desire to better themselves" (cited in Raghavan 1957: 70). Arunachalam also stressed that the Rodi should have land for cultivation in order to be self-supporting (*ibid.*: 95).

Alongside the romanticization of their lives, and the interest shown by writers, ethnographers and anthropologists, the social exclusion of and discrimination against the Rodi community aroused the concern of those who were politically conscious and egalitarian in outlook, especially young radicals of all communities. In this concern, religious motivation also played a part. Some Buddhists and Christians were among those who reacted against the plight of the Rodi and the attitudes towards them. Christians who carried out education and proselytization had opened a school for Rodi children in the Kotmale Valley, Pussellawa, but with meagre success due to non-attendance (*ibid.*: 70). Another group of Christians tried to resettle Rodi families outside their traditional *kuppayamas*. Canon Ivan Corea and his wife Ouida pioneered assistance to the Rodi community when he was the vicar of St. Luke's Church, Borella, in the 1960s. The Dunwatta Settlement (church property) was started by them in Sarasvati Lane off Castle Street, Borella, where several Rodi families were settled.[6] Raghavan, however, was sceptical of these "well intentioned" efforts (Raghavan 1957: 36). A large number of persons from the Rodi community participated in Canon Corea's funeral and one of their leaders conducted the last rites according to Rodi tradition. Concerned Buddhists too have recriminated against the treatment of the Rodi community and against instances where *bhikkhus* would not accept food (*danê*) from Rodi persons. One positive Buddhist intervention was the temple founded by Ven. Narada Thero in a Rodi settlement at Vallandera in Sabaragamuwa (*ibid.*: 97).

Nireka Weeratunga, who studied the Rodi community in 1988, recorded older members' memories of five types of discrimination. They were "restricted to wear their caste attire, being refused entry to temples, served tea in (disposable) coconut shells at tea shops, being insulted and beaten up if they attended school and being confronted by violence if they had dared to hire a vehicle" (Weeratunga 1988: 77). It was such discrimination that inspired the Suriya Mal leaders to choose to educate a girl from the most deprived caste. They sought to demonstrate through education the practicality of eradicating social marginalization of the Rodi and patriarchal attitudes towards Rodi girls.

Some Marxists may have thought that the aim of educating one Rodi child was a limited one, for they believed that the caste system itself would only disappear with industrial growth. R. Palme Dutt, one of the theoreticians of the British Communist Party, had written: "The crippling institutions of caste will only be overcome, not by preaching and denunciation, but by the advance of modern industry and political democracy as new social ties and common interest replace the old bonds" (Dutt 1940: 263).

Kamala
The Rodi girl chosen to be educated was Kamala Ratnaveli, born on 4 August 1928 and brought to Colombo at the age of six. She settled into the totally new environment with help from many persons. Doreen said it was amazing that she never shed a tear or said she wanted to go home. Doreen's mother Lily Young, who had come to Ceylon to help look after the newborn Suriya, also took Kamala under her wing (Suriya Wickremasinghe, personal communication). In placing Kamala in school, Doreen Wickremasinghe had to proceed carefully – for even urban society had not accepted caste equality, and a Rodi child in school with their own children was unthinkable for prejudiced parents. Doreen chose schools for Kamala that had foreign principals: Alethea School, Wellawatte, run by Elizabeth Preston, a British theosophist and a member of the Ceylon Labour Party; Ananda Balika, where Doreen herself was principal; and Visakha Vidyalaya, whose principal was an American, Clara Motwani. Catherine Hapugalle, who with Elizabeth Preston conducted the Alethea School, was sympathetic, as were the young teachers at Ananda Balika who had been active in the Suriya Mal movement. Kamala had the goodwill of many others, including Lionel Wendt, the foremost aesthete in Sri Lanka at that time, who gave her piano lessons.[7]

Under British rule, education in the English language was the key to social and economic advancement. It ensured white collar employment in the government and private sectors, and carried social prestige. Education limited to a rural Sinhala or Tamil school in the 1930s would not have produced these results. Kamala Ratnaveli was educated in urban, English-medium boarding schools, and during the holidays she lived with the Wickremasinghes. Kamala thus underwent several crucial changes in her life. One was the move to an English-speaking environment, both in Doreen Wickremasinghe's home and in the school where Doreen was principal. Kamala adapted well to the challenge, being bright and socially outgoing, and making friends while undergoing new experiences. Her family visited her occasionally, while Doreen Wickremasinghe, her daughter Suriya and Kamala visited Kamala's family in their village. Suriya's last visit was in the 1950s; she remembers that they had to go on foot for the last part of the journey, and that the village and its people, including the language they spoke, did not strike her as any different from the several small, poor villages she had visited in the Southern Province. Doreen had told her that she could expect Kamala's mother to cook the tastiest rice-and-curry meal she would ever eat in her life, and this proved to be no exaggeration (Suriya Wickremasinghe, personal communication, 21 April and 4 December 2015).

Crisis
Kamala studied at Ananda Balika up to 1936. That was a crisis year for the Wickremasinghes, at whose home she was living. Dr S.A. Wickremasinghe, who had earlier been retrenched from government medical service, lost his seat in the State Council, which had provided him with a monthly allowance of Rs 500. Doreen Wickremasinghe's continued job possibilities were negated by conservative Buddhist school managers, on the ground that she had married a leading Leftist and so was unsuited to head a school for Buddhist girls. The rapidity of these events led to Dr Wickremasinghe and Doreen moving to Britain, where he obtained a medical practice in Camberwell, London. Kamala was sent to stay with the family of Harold Peiris, and later with Vivienne and Leslie Goonewardena (of the Lanka Sama Samaja Party), and she attended Visakha Vidyalaya during these years. It was a difficult period for the LSSP, which was suspected of sedition by the colonial government and subjected to surveillance during the late 1930s. The top leaders were detained after the beginning of the Second World War, in 1939. After the LSSP leaders broke jail and fled to India, Kamala was moved to the home of the mother of Selina Perera, Dr N.M. Perera's wife. This did not work out well, however, and ultimately Kamala was sent back to her village.

Education Resumed
Doreen Wickremasinghe learned of this some time after her return to Sri Lanka, and she contacted Kamala and her family. These were tense

moments for the country as Singapore had fallen to Japan and a Japanese occupation of Sri Lanka was feared to be imminent. Dr Wickremasinghe was in jail and Doreen was expecting her second child. Colombo being unsafe, she arranged for her confinement in Kandy General Hospital, and also rented a small house near Bandarawela in the hill country. It was to this house that in 1942 Kamala was brought to stay once again with the Wickremasinghes. Her education was resumed at the Bandarawela branch of Visakha Vidyalaya.

My mother told me later that she learned of Kamala's situation through Susantha de Fonseka; he had been walking along a village road when he met this young girl carrying a bundle of firewood on her head. She recognized him from before, smiled at him and said, "Do you remember me? I'm Kamala!"

> I recall clearly the day Kamala was brought by her father to rejoin us. I was a precocious seven-year-old. Kamala's father seemed to me like any of the villagers who used to frequent our home in Matara. Our cottage had no electricity or water, and though we had the use of the communal village well, my mother found a wonderful bathing spot in the forest – also used communally – with a waterfall and pool, and flat stones on which we washed our clothes. That first day, after her father had left, a group of us were walking there and I happened to look up at Kamala. I saw tears rolling down her cheeks, while she remained totally silent. I was puzzled and embarrassed; crying was something only babies and little children did. I had long stopped crying myself, and seeing a big girl of fourteen weep was a shock to me. I pretended not to notice and did not tell a soul. But decades later the memory returned to haunt me. (Suriya Wickremasinghe, written communication, January 2016)

In 1942, after Dr Wickremasinghe's release, he and Doreen, with Suriya and the new baby (Surendra), lived for a while in the Bandarawela cottage; then they went back to live in the south in Wellamadama village near Matara, in an isolated Dutch bungalow on a hill by the sea. They were given it rent-free because it was reputed to be haunted, the villagers refusing to go near even in daytime. Suriya, Kamala and Kumari spent every school holiday together, either in that marvellous house at Wellamadama (now the site of the Ruhuna University Vice-Chancellor's Lodge) or at Kumari's equally exciting house by the sea in Kollupitiya. The sturdy disbelief of superstition and the paranormal on the part of both Suriya's and Kumari's parents stood all three children in good stead, and they had happy carefree times in both homes, where they were allowed to roam the neighbourhood at will.

Nurses' Training School

Kamala passed the Junior School Certificate (JSC), a creditable achievement considering the break in her education for a crucial few years. This qualified her to enter the Nurses' Training School in Colombo, which she decided she wanted to do. Doreen made all the arrangements for her joining: she had her clothes and uniforms made, provided her with other necessities, and took her for admission to the school (Suriya Wickremasinghe, personal communication). It was another milestone in Kamala's life. Barbara Seneviratne poignantly recalled her own early days at the Nurses' Training School (NTS) and her friendship with Kamala:

> I remember Kamala as a nurse who was very helpful to me. In September 1949 when I joined the NTS, I missed my father very much and here walks in an angel to my room. She was more like a sister I never had. First thing she did was to make two cups of tea. . . . I told her about myself but she was very quiet; then she smiled, took me downstairs, and introduced me to her friends. That was the beginning of a wonderful friendship. (Barbara Seneviratne, personal communication, 12 February 2014)

She further described aspects of their social life together: "She was my dearest friend. We went for walks round de Saram Road. There were days we were taken out by my father on his motorbike which had a sidecar. Our first stop was the Maliban Hotel in Borella, where we finished about 30 string-hoppers" (*ibid.*).

As a nurse, Kamala worked in the operating theatre of the Ragama TB Hospital. The next great change in her life was when she was awarded a Colombo Plan scholarship for nursing studies in Britain. The policy of the Colombo Plan organization, which included training programmes, was to strengthen economic and social development in the Asia-Pacific region. Kamala's move to Britain for further training with nine other Sri Lankan nurses laid the foundation for what later proved to be a permanent life in Britain. She came back to government service in Sri Lanka, visited England again, returned and worked for a time in Dr Wickremasinghe's Matara medical practice and maternity home. This was a period of restlessness for Kamala. Returning to Britain once more, she served in several hospitals, including the Women's Hospital, a branch of the London Chest Hospital, and the Sorrento Hospital and East Birmingham Hospital (later Heartlands), in the operating theatre and eye department. She continued in her nursing career and achieved the rank of nursing sister (Melanie Harris, personal communication, 24 April 2015).

Alienation from Sri Lanka

In London, Kamala – known as Kim to her family and friends – socialized with people of many nationalities who had migrated to Britain; and she met her future husband, Malfonso Morris, who had come to Britain in 1962. He was one of a wave of West Indian migrants who arrived in Britain at a time when there was a shortage of "blue collar" labour in a range of skilled and unskilled jobs. These included transport services – bus, train and the London underground, as well as postal and hospital services, and other skilled and unskilled work. Malfonso (Mal) was a postal sorter, and was later employed as a mental health worker and a television engineer; between 1985 and 1995 he worked at Citibank in New York (*ibid.*).

Kamala's marriage in 1966 was a multicultural event, but there were no Sri Lankans present as she was by then almost entirely alienated from Sri Lanka. Even for her wedding she did not wear a sari, but a long, white lace dress and veil. Kamala and Mal had two children, Gary in 1967 and Melanie in 1969. Mal was a Christian, the son of a pastor, but Kamala, born a Buddhist, did not convert; her children, however, went to Sunday School for a short period.

In those years, Kamala lived in a neighbourhood where there were hardly any Sri Lankans. Her only Sri Lankan friend was Olga Perera (known as Peggy), whom she befriended while shopping and who helped babysit Kamala's children while she was at work. Kamala soon became a close friend of Olga, who was ethnically of the Burgher (mixed European and Asian) community, and indifferent about Sri Lankans' social practices and origins.

With the passage of time Doreen and S.A. Wickremasinghe, who had contributed significantly to moulding Kamala's early life, lost touch with her. But Kamala wrote to tell their daughter Suriya of her marriage in 1966. When Dr Wickremasinghe died in 1981, Suriya wrote to Kamala at the same address she had given in her 1966 letter, and she received a reply. Thereafter Suriya, who visited London frequently in the 1980s due to her position on the International Executive Committee of Amnesty International, contacted Kamala and visited the family in their home in the Midlands.

Kamala's history was not known to her family and friends in England, as she never spoke of her social origins in Sri Lanka. Her husband, on meeting Suriya Wickremasinghe, asked her what the mystery was about Kamala – but it remained a closed book.

> When I visited Kamala in the Midlands around 1982, I stayed overnight at her home and met her husband Mal – to whom I took a great liking – and

her two delightful teenaged children. They were friendly and affectionate. However, during this visit it became clear to me that Kamala had told them very little of her Sri Lanka background, and they were not sure of her relationship to me. "Is Mum your sister?" the 13-year-old asked me as she took me to the bus-stop the day I left. "As good as a sister, as we grew up together," I explained as best I could. That Kamala had distanced herself from her past even in relation to her own family puzzled and troubled me for many years. Although she had greeted me warmly, I wondered whether my visit had in fact been an embarrassment to her. (Suriya Wickremasinghe, personal communication, January 2016)

Kamala's Children
While engrossed in her work as a nurse, Kamala attended to her children's education. She no doubt had learned the value of education from her own experience. Her daughter Melanie studied at Solihull Sixth Form College, then obtained a degree in Dance from the University of Leeds. She taught dance at Solihull College for several years and later worked for Walsall Council in the Virtual School for Looked after Children.[9] The aim was to ensure that children taken into care by the Social Services Department were educationally in line with their peers. Melanie currently works for Wolverhampton University managing a mentoring programme to support Looked after Children to aspire to university education.[10] She has herself just obtained a Master's degree in education.

Kamala's son Gary, having also done "A" Levels at Solihull Sixth Form College, left for America to join his father who had obtained employment there. Gary initially worked at Macy's department store, New York; he later joined the US Marines and was posted to Hawaii; and subsequently was employed as a driver for United Parcel Service in New York. Gary presently lives in North Carolina with his wife Nadia and their son Chris (Melanie Harris, personal communication, 1 May 2015).

Forty-seven Years Later
Many years later, in 1997, Kamala made a trip to Sri Lanka with her daughter Melanie and friend Olga Perera. She was visiting her homeland after a gap of forty-seven years. There was a warm reunion with Doreen, in whose home they stayed, and a joyful exchange of reminiscences with Suriya and Kumari about their joint childhood adventures. Kamala recounted how, being "the eldest," she used to be assigned the fearsome responsibility of seeing that the other two behaved sensibly. Fascinated, they also learned, or re-learned, many details about their escapades that only Kamala remembered.

Melanie, a young woman in her twenties with a lovable and outgoing personality, promptly became enthralled by her mother's homeland. Later, when she was to marry, she was adamant that the wedding had to be in Sri Lanka. In 2001, therefore, Kamala, Melanie, Melanie's English fiancé Nigel and Nigel's mother Margaret, all came to Sri Lanka. Doreen had died in 2000. They stayed at Suriya's home in Colombo, where the marriage registration and informal reception were held. Suriya, who had no experience in organizing such an event, invited a close friend, Barbara Seneviratne, to be there and help out. Barbara and Kamala, who had not met since their Nurses' Training School days, did not realize they had known each other before till Barbara suddenly exclaimed, "You are Kamala Ratnaveli!" Her subsequent account of what Kamala had meant to her is described above.

At forty-two years of age Kamala had her first heart attack, and she later underwent a triple bypass. She died in Birmingham in 2002, aged 74 (Melanie Harris, personal communication, 10 May 2015). Melanie was determined that her mother's ashes should return to Sri Lanka, but this became possible only ten years later, when they were brought by Melanie and her daughter Imogen. At a small memorial gathering of family and friends, several speakers, including the trade union veteran Bala Tampoe, emphasized the historic importance of Kamala's story. Tampoe also described his participation in the Suriya Mal movement (Pasqualge 2012a). The urn containing Kamala's ashes was immersed in the waters of the Kelani Ganga in Colombo North, where the river meets the sea. After Kamala's death Melanie continued her links with Sri Lanka and visited again with Imogen.

CASTE TODAY

Intervention by the government after independence (1948) did take the caste issue some steps forward with the Social Disabilities Act. Rather than help unite the Sinhalese and Tamil radical intelligentsia, as occurred in the 1930s, the 1957 Act was regarded by some politicians as aimed at Tamil society and as an unwanted interference in Tamil practices in Jaffna. It is reported that certain caste issues which had been in abeyance during the armed conflict now emerged afresh in the north, in the context of reconstruction and rehabilitation. On the issue of caste, the struggle certainly continues.

The extent to which caste continues to be a significant factor throughout our society is beyond the scope of this article. One aspect is worth looking at, however, in so far as it reflects the position of the Rodi people. Caste features in prolific newspaper advertisements for marriage partners inserted by both Sinhala and Tamil parents (though one does occasionally find a welcome "caste immaterial"). But one would not expect to find the Rodi caste mentioned in such advertisements.

There has however been an intriguing and ironic development. Some Rodi women, cashing in on the Sri Lankan weakness for superstitious practices, have begun to publicize their livelihoods in this area through advertisements in the Sinhala national press. One such instance is that of Kusumvalli Maniyo, who promises to "bring relief to your suffering as a mother would" (*mavakmen numbalage dukata pihita*, *Divaina*, 12 January 2014, supplement, 51). She advertised *niche kula gurukam* (low-caste spells) that could mesmerize women and men (*sthree purusha vashi*). Also advertising were Iswaranestilaka Gurumeniyo, Ratnavali Gurumeniya and Sunethravalli Gurumeniya – all women boasting of their Rodi origins and occult skills (*Irida Lankadipa*, 26 April 2015, Nimthera 4).

In Retrospect
This was a historic initiative of the Suriya Mal movement, which needs to be recorded and placed in the public domain. But assessing it is not simple. It has two aspects: the public and the personal.

The public aspect
The question of social exclusion had been discussed by radicals in both the north and the south in the 1930s, and this issue had brought them together. The Left succeeded in making the point that education is a crucial factor in emancipating oppressed groups in society. In bringing the caste issue into the public domain, however, some might suggest, with hindsight, that the venture was misconceived. It soon became apparent that Kamala's social origin could not be broadcast wide and loud. It was common in Sri Lanka society, where there is an extended family system, for a family to bring up a child from a disadvantaged background, and nobody would have thought to question the presence of Kamala in the Wickremasinghe household.

To announce that this was a Rodi child, however, would have been an entirely different matter in the atmosphere of the time. As noted earlier, Doreen had to choose schools for Kamala that had foreign principals; society had not accepted caste equality, and a Rodi child in school with their own children would have been unthinkable for many parents. That said, one cannot estimate the extent to which, over the years, the story of Kamala spread and affected later generations. Certainly, close associates of the Leftists in the know, and in particular the teachers of Sujatha and Ananda Balika, would have passed on egalitarian values in their own circles including families and pupils. Moreover, published histories of the Left movement have for long referred, albeit briefly and without detail, to the successful education and career of a Rodi child.

One can surmise that by leaving their villages for towns and changing family names, members of the Rodi caste may have merged into the wider society. After so many years of free education from primary school to university, there should certainly be at least a few Rodi government servants, teachers, doctors and other professionals, but one never seems to hear of them. Perhaps this very article will encourage Rodi people, in occupations other than those claiming occult skills, to come forward and boldly claim their heritage. Only by such actions might a reality be made of egalitarianism in a society which still, in many respects, pays it only lip service.

The personal side
This aspect has already surfaced from time to time during the recounting of the story above, and is not repeated here. Suriya Wickremasinghe adds:

> In later life, and especially after my visit to Kamala's home in England, when I found that she was distancing herself from her past, I began to agonize about whether the whole idea had not been misconceived and caused unnecessary grief. Kamala being sent back to the village half-way through her schooling was particularly unfortunate, and I recalled her silent tears after being brought back to us in Bandarawela. Although my parents robustly rallied round and supported her, including in adulthood, whenever the need arose, I could not help recalling certain unhappy experiences when Kamala was still living and working as a nurse in Sri Lanka. Was it just her equable nature that prevented her from turning round and echoing Eliza Doolittle, "didn't anyone think of *me*?" These thoughts, which troubled me for decades, were partly assuaged when Kamala wrote saying she was thinking of visiting us, and referred to Sri Lanka as "home." They were finally put to rest when, on her last visit, Kamala, speaking with palpable sincerity of my mother Doreen, conjectured, "what would have happened to me if not for her, *what would have happened to me?*"

The last word, however, should go to Kamala's daughter Melanie. Her comments were sought on the draft of this article, and I quote from her response:

> I am absolutely thrilled with what I have read, I am speechless. It is clear and the contextual aspects of it are second to none. Reading it evoked so many emotions, happiness, sadness but the ultimate feeling it left in me was

pride. I am so proud of my mum and my heritage, and am so thankful to the Wickremasinghes, who are my "grandparents", and others like them, for giving my mum a chance.

Author's acknowledgements: Many thanks to J. Uyangoda, S.B.D. de Silva, Wes Ervin, B. Skanthakumar, Vijay Nagaraj and Premakumara de Silva for their valuable contributions and comments on this article. I am grateful to Barbara Seneviratne for her contributions, Judy Waters Pasqualge and May Yee for their excellent editing. I thank Rasika Chandrasekera and Quintus Fernando for their help with the manuscript, and Chandrika Widanapathirane, Dilan Godapitiya and others of the SSA for their support.

Of those who had been close to Kamala Ratnaveli, I thank her husband Malfonso and daughter Melanie for answering Suriya Wickremasinghe's and my queries, and sending us photographs. A special thanks to Suriya Wickremasinghe who urged me to write this article, and whose contributions, advice and guidance were indispensable.

NOTES

1 There had been many caste controversies in Jaffna, as the "low" castes were not allowed temple entry and access to wells used by the "high" castes. Pfaffenberger (1990).

2 In later years, the community advanced through education and other forms of employment. See Raghavan (1957); Ryan (1953); Silva (2011).

3 M.D. Raghavan estimated their number in 1956 at 3,122, but they are counted in the census as Sinhalese (Weeratunga 1988: 1).

4 I thank Miss Manisha Alwis for this information.

5 Hugh Nevill, 1848–1897, was a civil servant for thirty-two years in various posts in the island. He was the founder of and a main contributor to the *Taprobanian*. Nevill was referred to by Dr P.E.P. Deraniyagala as "one of the most outstanding English intellects ever to serve in Ceylon."

6 Canon Corea belonged to the famous Corea family in Chilaw, known for their activist nationalism in politics in the colonial period.

7 Kamala was a frequent visitor to my parents' home. I met her in 1936 when my parents, A.P. and Eleanor de Zoysa, and the Wickremasinghes shared a house. In later years, when Suriya Wickremasinghe stayed with us or when I went to stay with them at Wellamadama, Kamala was often there too. I also met her when she visited Sri Lanka in 1997, and at her daughter's wedding in 2001, where I was able to talk to her about the past.

8 A national figure and former State Councillor who moved among politicians including in Leftist circles.

9 The Virtual School gives educational support to all children who have been removed from their home and are now in the care of the local authority. It works

with Looked after Children, their foster carers, social workers and designated teachers, wherever a child may live or go to school.

10 Social services are services provided by the local authority to help people who have serious family or financial problems. They have the power to remove children from their parents if they are being neglected or abused within the home. These children are referred to as Looked after Children.

REFERENCES

Denham, E.B. (1912), *Ceylon at the Census of 1911*, Colombo: Government Printer.

Dutt, Rajani Palme (1940), *India Today*, London: Victor Gollancz Ltd.

Jayawardena, Kumari (1973), "The Origins of the Left Movement in Sri Lanka," *Modern Ceylon Studies*, Vol. 63, No. 2.

Jayawardena, Kumari (1980), "Background to the Formation of the Lanka Sama Samaja Party," *Young Socialist*, March.

Jayawardena, Kumari (1991), *Doreen Wickremasinghe: Western Radical in Sri Lanka*, Colombo: Women's Education and Research Centre.

Jayawardena, Kumari (2007a), *Nobodies to Somebodies: The Rise of the Colonial Bourgeoisie in Sri Lanka*, Colombo: Social Scientists' Association, Colombo.

Jayawardena, Kumari (2007b), *The Erasure of the Euro-Asian: Recovering Early Radicalism and Feminism in South Asia*, Colombo: Social Scientists' Association.

Jayawardena, Kumari and Rachel Kurian (2015), *Class Patriarchy and Ethnicity on Sri Lankan Plantations*, Orient BlackSwan.

Kadirgamar, Santasilan, ed. (2012), *Handy Perinbanayagam: A Memorial Volume*, Colombo: Kumaran Book House.

Lanka Sama Samaja Party (1980), "The Manifesto of the Lanka Sama Samaja Party 1935," *Young Socialist*, March.

Marx, Karl (1972), "British Rule in Asia" [1853], in *Colonialism: Articles from the New York Times and Other Writings*, New York: International Publishers.

Marx, Karl (1972), "Future Results of British Rule in India" [1853], in *Colonialism: Articles from the New York Times and Other Writings*, New York: International Publishers.

Nevill, Hugh (1887), "The Gadi or Rodi Race in Ceylon," *The Taprobanian*, Vols. 1 and 2, Colombo.

Pasqualge, Judy Waters (2012a), "Suriya Mal and Kamala," notes on gathering held on 15 October 2012, Hendala, Sri Lanka.

Pasqualge, Judy Waters (2012b), "Interview with Bala Tampoe on the Suriya Mal Movement," Colombo, October.

Pfaffenberger, Bryan (1990), "The Political Constructions of Defensive Nationalism:

The 1968 Temple Entry Crisis," *The Journal of Asian Studies*, Vol. 49, No. 1, pp. 78–96.

Raghavan, M.D. (1952), *Handsome Beggars*, Colombo: Colombo Book Centre.

Ryan, Bryce (1953), *Caste in Modern Ceylon: The Sinhala System in Transition*, New Jersey: Rutgers University Press.

Scott, James (1985), *Weapons of the Weak: Everyday Forms of Peasant Resistance*, New Haven: Yale University Press.

Silva, Kalinga Tudor, P. Kotikabadde and D.M. Chandima Abeywickrema (2009), "Caste Discrimination in Sinhala Society,' in Kalinga Tudor Silva, P.P. Sivapragasam and Paramsothy Thanges, eds., *Casteless or Caste-blind? Dynamics of Concealed Caste Discrimination, Social Exclusion and Protest in Sri Lanka*, Colombo: Kumaran Book House.

Silva, Kalinga Tudor (2011), "Globalization, Marginality and Cultural Challenges of the Rodiya Communities in Sri Lanka," in *Diminishing Cultures in South Asia*, Vol. 2, Colombo: SAARC Cultural Centre.

Uyangoda, J. (1998), *Caste, Social Justice and Political Change in Sri Lanka*, Colombo: Social Scientists' Association.

Uyangoda, J. (2000), "The Inner Courtyard: Political Discourse of Caste, Justice and Equality', *Pravada*, 6, Nos. 9–10, pp. 14–19.

Vijayatunge, J. (1960), *The Rodiya Girl and Other Stories*, Maharagama: Saman Press.

Weeratunga, Nireka (1988), *Aspects of Ethnicity and Gender among the Rodi of Sri Lanka*, Colombo: International Centre for Ethnic Studies.

The Rise of the Bharatiya Janata Party: Two Essays and an Introduction

Prakash Karat

This contribution is in three parts: an introductory essay written in 2016, an article written in 1992, and an article written in May 2014. – Editor

INTRODUCTION

N. Ram has been a friend and comrade for the last forty-five years. We first met in 1969, at a time when we were both attracted to Marxism and the communist movement. Throughout his career as a student activist, journalist and editor, Ram has distinguished himself by intellectual work of the highest calibre. The two essays about the Bharatiya Janata Party (BJP) that I am dedicating to N. Ram were written in 1992 and 2015. Both address the rise of the BJP, its evolution and bid for power. The first piece was written at a time when the *Hindutva* offensive was under way and the BJP had emerged as the biggest opposition party in the Lok Sabha. It was written just a few months before the demolition of the Babri Masjid in December 1992. The second essay was written on the eve of the sixteenth Lok Sabha election, which saw the second coming of *Hindutva*. The article deals with the rise of Narendra Modi as the pre-eminent leader of the BJP and its prime ministerial candidate.

The rise of the BJP as a major force in the early 1990s and its becoming the largest political party (in terms of vote share) in the 2014 Lok Sabha elections have occasioned a vast amount of commentary and analysis. The BJP has variously been described as a Hindu nationalist party, a right-wing populist party, a conservative communal party and a communal-fascist party.

In class terms, the BJP represents the big bourgeois-led capitalist class. The days when the Jana Sangh, the predecessor of the BJP, represented the trader and commercial sections of the bourgeoisie are long over. In the political spectrum, the BJP is right-wing in its economic and social philosophy. But the complexity involved in defining the BJP as a party stems from its organic links with the Rashtriya Swayamsevak Sangh (RSS). The RSS is an authoritarian organization with a semi-fascist ideology. The

BJP is a creation of the RSS, and it draws its ideological and organizational sustenance from the parent body. This is what sets it apart from any other right-wing or conservative party.

The nationalism of the RSS is based on a Hindu-chauvinist outlook that makes it devoid of any anti-imperialism. This was evident during the national struggle for freedom. As such, the BJP lineage was from those social forces who represented the old landlord and mercantile commercial interests in pre-Independence society. However, with capitalist development under a bourgeois–landlord state, the BJP, when it emerged in 1980, became the quintessential party of the big capitalists. At the same time, its RSS link led it to adopt right-wing populist and Hindu-nationalist postures which were at times in conflict with the overall interests of the big bourgeoisie. Till the end of the 1980s, the Congress Party remained the premier party of the big bourgeoisie.

The end of the 1980s heralded major changes both internationally and nationally. The liquidation of the Soviet Union and the socialist bloc brought about a change in the outlook of the Indian bourgeoisie. Within the country, the ruling classes opted for liberalization and ushered in a new phase of capitalism aligned with the dominant finance-driven globalization. The neoliberal regime and its main sponsors, big business and monopoly capital, found new virtues in the BJP, which had always been a staunch votary of privatization and free enterprise. Another factor for its gaining ground among the ruling classes is that the "cultural nationalism" of the BJP is not anti-imperialist. Rather, the RSS–*Hindutva* ideology is conducive to India integrating with global finance capital. The BJP utilized the *Hindutva* agenda to garner popular support and divert the people's discontent away from the pernicious effects of neoliberalism. This endeared it further to the ruling classes. Thus, the first break in big bourgeois support to the Congress took place precisely at a time when both liberalization and communalism gained ground, in 1990–91.

For the first time, a significant section of big business swung their support to the BJP in the 1991 Lok Sabha elections – an event that is analysed in my first essay. What this period saw was the emergence of two all-India parties, the Congress and the BJP, which vied and competed for the support of the most powerful strata of the ruling classes. Since then they have been parties of alternate choice for the ruling classes. The *Hindutva* moorings of the BJP and the communal platform have their uses whenever the ruling classes require this disruptive ideology and politics to buttress their class rule, and to counter any perceived threat or challenge in terms of popular discontent or organized resistance.

After a decade of Congress-led UPA (United Progressive Alliance) rule, such a juncture arrived. The economic slowdown which was directly connected to the global financial crisis of 2007–08, the perceived failure of the Manmohan Singh government to protect the interests of big capital in the wake of massive corruption scandals that singed the big corporates also, and what was considered the slow pace of neoliberal reforms because of concerted resistance – all contributed to the big switch. There was an unprecedented surge of support from the big bourgeoisie and the entire corporate sector for Narendra Modi.

In opting for Narendra Modi and the BJP, an important consideration was Modi's record as Chief Minister of Gujarat. Gujarat was the first state in which the *Hindutva* experiment was launched. This occurred in the 1980s. It paved the way for the ultra-capitalism of Narendra Modi during his fifteen-year tenure as Chief Minister. This was the "Gujarat model" which attracted the support of the corporate sector as a whole. To sum up, the BJP has been able, since the 1990s, to become an alternate pole to the Congress in the eyes of the leading constituent of the ruling classes. This has given the BJP a tremendous advantage.

The other vital feature of the BJP is its link with the RSS. Notwithstanding its self-description as an apolitical cultural organization, the RSS is an intensely political organization. The Bharatiya Jana Sangh was set up by the RSS in order to have a political party that could work towards the goal of a "Hindu *rashtra.*" The RSS negotiated with the All India Hindu Mahasabha to ensure that there was a unified political platform of Hindu nationalism. The Jana Sangh merged with the Janata Party in 1977. After the break with the Janata Party, erstwhile Jana Sangh leaders consulted with the RSS in order to set up the Bharatiya Janata Party. The RSS is the guide and eventual controller of the BJP. In the initial days, the BJP experimented with becoming a centre-right party. But after the electoral debacle in 1984, when it got only two seats in the Lok Sabha, it fell back on its hardcore *Hindutva* agenda. This was the period of the presidentship of L.K. Advani, between 1986 and 1990. The RSS link with the BJP was made open by Advani during this time.

From the outset, the RSS played a key role in shaping the organization and policies of the party. It placed its cadres in the key post of organizational secretary at different levels of the party organization. It may be argued that without the steel frame of the RSS, the BJP would not have been able to withstand the setbacks suffered in two successive Lok Sabha elections. In the 2009 election, the BJP's vote share sank to a low of 18.8 per cent. This is to be compared with the high of 25.6 per cent in 1998. The RSS had to intervene in the leadership crisis after the 2004 election. It ensured that Advani stepped down from presidentship towards the end of 2005. Subsequently, it played a key role in getting Narendra Modi projected as the prime ministerial candidate for the 2014 Lok Sabha election. It was the RSS that sustained the machinery of the party throughout the difficult period. The election success of the BJP in 2014 has to be attributed as much to the groundwork of the RSS as to the effective projection of Modi by the corporate media.

Much of political science literature and even those who have studied the BJP closely tend to underplay the integral relationship between the RSS and the BJP. Some attribute a degree of autonomy to the BJP vis-à-vis the RSS that is not unwarranted. The BJP, as the political front of the RSS, has sought to shape its politics and programmes keeping in mind the necessity to become a mainstream party with broad electoral support. But the direction, ideological and organizational, has always emanated from the RSS. It was the RSS that anchored the *Hindutva* vision, articulated as "cultural nationalism" by Advani. It was the RSS that initiated the "social engineering" required to broadbase the social support of the party. The impetus to attract Other Backward Classes (OBCs) and Dalits to the BJP was motivated by the pan-Hindu concept of Hindu *samaj* and "*sama rasta*" of the RSS.

There is no change whatsoever in the communal outlook of the RSS, which still considers Islam and Christianity to be alien to Hindu civilization and culture. The nationalism that the BJP espouses is moored in the Hindu-chauvinist nationalism of the RSS. This finds reflection in the foreign policy postulates of the BJP. For the BJP, Israel is a valuable friend and ally, given the RSS's predilection for Jewish racist nationalism which is anti-Muslim and anti-Arab.

With the installation of the Narendra Modi government, and the BJP for the first time getting an absolute majority in the Lok Sabha, the relationship between the RSS and the BJP government has assumed more explicit forms, something that was not so open at the time of the National Democratic Alliance (NDA) government. The problem of characterizing the BJP is precisely because of its organic link with the RSS. *It would be appropriate to characterize the BJP as a right-wing party of majoritarian communalism.* However, the fact that it is an instrument of the RSS gives it the potential to become an authoritarian party if circumstances warrant it.

II

The BJP–RSS combine achieved its biggest success in the sixteenth Lok Sabha elections held in April–May 2014. The BJP became the largest political party in terms of vote share, overtaking the Congress for the first time. Even though it got only 31 per cent of the votes, it was able to achieve an absolute majority in the Lok Sabha. The fact that the *Hindutva* mascot Narendra Modi won the popular mandate provided an aura of legitimacy for the right-wing communal platform.

It will be instructive to see what happened during the earlier stint of the BJP in the central government, when Atal Behari Vajpayee was the prime minister. There is a striking consistency in the basic policies and thrust of the two governments. The six-year period of the earlier BJP-led government rule was marked by a privatization spree of public sector units, opening up of the financial sector to foreign capital, and big cutbacks in public investment in agriculture. The high-level corruption that accompanies a neoliberal regime became a regular feature during the NDA rule. The government facilitated RSS penetration of educational and cultural institutions to vitiate the content of education and culture. Prominent intellectuals and artists were targeted by *Hindutva* outfits. The Pokhran nuclear tests and an overt effort to become a natural ally of the United States of America ensued.

The Modi government has pursued the same path, but more vigorously. It has aggressively pushed neoliberal policies; it is taking privatization into new areas, even to the Indian Railways. There have been massive cuts in the budgetary outlays and expenditure on education, health, agriculture, the Mahatma Gandhi National Rural Employment Guarantee Scheme (MGNREGS) and Integrated Child Development Scheme (ICDS). Coordination between the BJP government and the RSS has been given an institutional shape. An ambitious plan to re-shape the educational system and the curriculum has been set in motion. The nexus of crony capitalism and corruption has already manifested itself under the Modi regime.

Narendra Modi has gone further in tying India to the Asia-Pacific strategy of the US. The state is targeting dissent and putting curbs on democratic rights. Parliamentary procedures are being given short shrift. The symptoms of authoritarianism are being manifested in all spheres.

In the case of the Vajpayee government, its eagerness to pursue pro-rich, neoliberal policies led to large-scale agrarian distress, loss of livelihood and growing unemployment. This led to widespread discontent and the puncturing of the "Shining India" campaign of the BJP, and the defeat of the party in the 2004 Lok Sabha election. After two years of the Modi government, there is already widespread distress among farmers. The steps to tame labour and undermine the land rights of farmers are meeting with growing united resistance. The *Hindutva* project of the BJP–RSS combine is headed for stormy times.

THE BJP: A REACTIONARY RESPONSE TO THE PRESENT CRISIS
(1992)

Any discussion on the Bharatiya Janata Party (BJP) must begin with the question: how is the BJP to be characterized? From 1986, what stands out about this party is its strident advocacy of Hindu-majoritarian communalism. But in Marxist terms, while it is necessary to underline its communal features, that alone is not sufficient to define the party's character. It would not be correct to see the BJP, as many analysts do, as a nationalist party which is right of the centre.

The BJP is definitely a right-wing party, but it is distinguished by its reactionary communal platform. In that sense, it is different from ordinary conservative parties of the right. Classically, such right-wing parties are characterized by open advocacy of the interests of the ruling classes and defence of the status quo. This stance differentiates them from other ruling class parties who disguise their class interests when putting out their party programmes, and strive in varying degrees to build a coalition of support based on welfare state or social democratic prescriptions.

In contrast to conservative right-wing parties, there is very often a phenomenon of neo-right parties which are marked by radicalism; that is, they take to mass politics and launch mass movements with a critique of extant society that breaks the boundaries of the traditional right. The mass politics generated by such parties are primarily motivated by a reactionary-sectarian platform that targets an "enemy": the other ethnic/religious community, which is held responsible for all the problems of society. Le Pen's National Front in France registered growth mainly through its virulent campaigns against immigrants and by projecting a French ultra-nationalism tinged with racism; the new parties in Germany are making a dent in the Christian Democratic base with their chauvinist anti-foreigner appeal; in the Middle East, the parties of Islamic fundamentalism have a mass radical character, whether it be the Khomeinism of Iran or the Islamic party in Algeria. Most of these parties flourish when societies are in acute crisis and the traditional ruling class prescriptions to run society have reached a dead-end. The BJP has to be placed at this end of the spectrum in the Indian context.

The Enemy Identified
In the political terrain of India, a conservative party of the right has no immediate foreseeable future. Given the mass poverty, the sharp economic and social inequalities, and the compulsions of electoral politics, all

bourgeois–landlord parties have to pay obeisance to the slogans of social equality and removal of economic disparities.

The BJP, in its quest to function as a viable party of the right in the Indian political milieu, has finally arrived at what it considers to be the key to its success. Hindu nationalism articulated with an internal enemy – the Muslim minority – gives the BJP its communal character. Alongside this cutting edge to its platform is the right-wing character of its economic policy: support to the liberalization and privatization drive. It is the combination of these two features that makes the BJP a unique political force at the national level: a right-wing communal party which represents the reactionary sections of the big bourgeoisie and landlords.

In arriving at this point in the evolution of the BJP, the party has been influenced and facilitated by external factors, and also by its own internal compulsions. The external factors can be defined as: the new stage reached in the crisis of the bourgeois–landlord system in the 1980s, which necessitated a turn away from the Nehruvian path by substantial sections of the ruling classes; the changes internationally exemplified by the worldwide right-wing offensive and its ascendancy, as seen in the Reagan era in the US, and the Thatcherite and Kohl regimes in Europe; the dramatic shift in the international correlation of forces with the events in Eastern Europe and the dismantling of the Soviet Union, and the rise of religious fundamentalism in the third world as a whole in the 1980s.

Internally, the BJP found itself at a dead-end after the 1984 general elections, when it got just two seats in the Lok Sabha. Its very identity and existence seemed threatened. The party had to reassess its basic programmatic and ideological outlook to chalk out a new strategy.

Search for a Potent Platform
The BJP came into being in 1980 after the collapse of the Janata experiment. The resurrection of the Bharatiya Janata Sangh in the form of the BJP seemed to be a qualitative transformation wherein the party marked a break from the old Jana Sangh–Rashtriya Swayamsevak Sangh (RSS) ideology. This brief interregnum when the party adopted the plank of Gandhian socialism sat ill upon its RSS-dominated cadres. The presidentship of A.B. Vajpayee (1980–86) saw an underplaying of the Hindu communal rhetoric, and an attempt to broadbase the party's platform by taking up issues affecting the tribals, the Scheduled Castes, the rural and urban poor. The trauma of the experience within the Janata Party and the controversy regarding dual membership (of the BJP and RSS), which ended the marriage, resulted in a lingering effort to imitate the centrist bourgeois parties. The 1984 debacle

put paid to these efforts. The phase of Indira Gandhi's appeal to Hindu votes and the strong reaction to her assassination were seen by the BJP as the success of the Congress (I) in stealing its original platform and prospering from it. It must be recalled that the RSS worked to ensure the success of the Congress (I) in many areas during the 1980 elections.

Metamorphosis into Hindutva

The journey from an amorphous, right-of-centre bourgeois platform to *Hindutva* was systematically accomplished in three years, from 1986 to 1989. L.K. Advani's presidentship coincided with this period. The transition was effected on directions of the RSS with Advani as the pilot. It was under Advani's stewardship that the links with the RSS were declared, *Hindutva* defended and finally the Ram temple adopted as the BJP's main plank.

What were the ingredients of the Hindu communal platform? Some of the issues were no doubt rooted in the traditional stance of the Jana Sangh and the RSS: the effort to project the party as the only nationalist force; the typical petty-bourgeois ploy of advocating a third path that is neither capitalism or communism – part of Deendayal Upadhyay's "integral humanism"; the alacrity in picking up any issue that showed a potential for rousing anti-Muslim feelings. All this was part of the ideological–political baggage bequeathed by the RSS and the Jana Sangh to the BJP.

But the post-1986 phase showed a more aggressive approach to old issues, and the addition of new ones to the repertoire. The Meenakshipuram conversions saw the BJP lining up with the RSS and the VHP (Vishwa Hindu Parishad) to raise the bogey of Islamic subversion of Hindu *samaj* from within. The groundswell of support built up by the VHP for the Ram temple at Ayodhya was ultimately cashed in by the BJP after a three-year period when, in 1989, at its Palampur national executive session, it formally adopted the temple demand. The resurgence of separatist terrorism in Kashmir saw vocal reiteration of the demand to scrap Article 370 from the Constitution. The infiltration of Muslim migrants from Bangladesh became the basis for whipping up anti-Muslim feelings, while Hindu migrants were welcomed back. The Minorities Commission was condemned as appeasement of minorities.

All the above issues are woven around the central theme of targeting the Muslim minority as the enemy. The BJP thesis is put out as follows. The BJP is against pseudo-secularism – which, it says, amounts to "minorityism". Pseudo-secularism is the practice of all parties, which denies the essentially Hindu character of the country and therefore pampers the minorities and appeases minority communalism for garnering votes. Genuine secularism requires recognition that Hinduism is the cultural essence of Indian society and its binding force. Advani set out this thesis in his first presidential address to the National Council session in May 1986: "Unfortunately, for many politicians and political parties, secularism has become only a euphemism for appeasement of minority sections which tend to vote en bloc." In the next presidential address, he called for rejection of pseudo-secularism and declared: "Truth is that for many politicians and intellectuals, secularism is only a euphemism to cloak their allergy to Hinduism."

The two pet terms, pseudo-secularism and minorityism, were utilized as part of the offensive against secularism, and to cover up the BJP's advocacy of *Hindutva* and majority communalism. By the BJP's specious reasoning, only acceptance of *Hindutva* could make one a genuine secularist – what it calls positive secularism. Any defence of legitimate minority rights becomes minorityism. As for manifestations of minority communalism, they become useful grounds for championing majority communalism.

The success that the BJP attained in putting out these distorted concepts has surprised many people. Why was the response to these old slogans in a new garb so receptive? What gave these slogans a resonance among wide sections of the people? To answer these questions, we must go back to the conjuncture of events that catapulted the communal agenda on to the mainstream political agenda.

Bourgeois–Landlord Crisis: A Response
The turning away of the ruling classes from the path of development framed in the days of Nehru elicited different responses from the political forces representing these classes. In the case of the Congress (I), the Rajiv Gandhi regime symbolized the new outlook and values that were sought to be embraced. Liberalization and market values were glorified. This phase of liberalization floundered by 1988–89, with the economy in a deep state of financial crisis. Politically, the retrenchment of the Nehruvian model led to increasing compromises on secularism and with the divisive forces who severely threatened national unity.

Faced with this systemic crisis, an alternative was put out by the BJP, advocating *Hindutva* as the basis for protecting national unity and to counter divisiveness; for abandoning the Nehruvian framework and advocating liberalization Indian-style, which is supposed to lead to the building of a strong capitalist India under the aegis of Hindu majoritarian interests.

It is a matter of conjecture how much of the bankrupcty and venality of the Rajiv Gandhi regime helped the BJP gather significant support from sections of the middle classes and the rural elites. But quick disillusionment with the Congress of the Rajiv era sparked off the process of the BJP's resurgence. At first it was masked by the V.P. Singh/Janata Dal phenomenon, which appeared to provide a secular-bourgeois alternative, but the clear ideological alternative of the BJP thrived by initially utilizing broad anti-Congressism in alliance with the National Front and the Janata Dal.

At the outward level, the Bofors scandal brought out the venality of the new dispensation, while the Shah Bano case served to expose the worst aspect of appeasement of minority communalism. The BJP cultivated the image of a clean variant of the Congress (I) within the system. Its claim of putting "the nation first" was supposed to be a guarantee against corruption and degeneration. As for the Congress (I)'s opportunist bouts of surrender to communalism, it went hammer and tongs at the unprincipled compromise with Muslim fundamentalism on the Shah Bano case, but welcomed the Rajiv concession to Hindu communalism of opening the locks at the disputed site in Ayodhya.

For a substantial section of the middle classes, the spurning of the Rajiv Gandhi dream was adequate to turn them to the BJP's false rhetoric, now that the the Nehruvian framework no longer provided them a stable perspective. The promise of quick benefits through liberalization were belied. The vicious attacks on national unity and the Hindu minority in Punjab and Kashmir reinforced the BJP propaganda that the minorities are being pampered. The frustration on the economic front after arousing glittering hopes, coupled with the onslaught on national unity, provided fertile soil for the BJP's distorted appeal on nationalism and secularism.

Whatever defence of secular values was in place for this vocal strata got breached dangerously with the implementation of the Mandal Commission's recommendations by the V.P. Singh government in August 1990. In the perception of these predominantly upper-caste, educated sections, the Janata Dal regime represented a direct threat to their main avenue of advancement: education and employment. This drove them to the anti-democratic position of denying the protection to be accorded to historically and socially oppressed sections. The anti-reservation movement provided the thrust for the BJP to win over large sections to its shrill temple campaign through Advani's *rath yatra*.

The year 1990 marked the culmination of the maturing of the *Hindutva* platform with its attendant responses from significant sections of the middle classes and elite sections. The procession of retired and serving bureaucrats, military officers and intellectuals to the BJP underlined this shift.

Big Bourgeois Reaction
Sections of the big bourgeoisie who were dismayed by the inept government of the National Front, as seen from its class point, were prone to pro-BJP sentiments. The anti-Mandal feelings influenced these sections also. In fact, traditional sections of the big bourgeoisie, such as Marwari big business houses, were deeply religious and supportive of Hindu interests, but they demarcated when it came to secular class interests and had always predominantly supported the Congress. The 1990–91 period saw the first major break. Advani, on his first visit to Kolkata after the *rath yatra*, was feted at a lunch hosted by the Birlas with top industrialists attending. A public entertainment programme followed in the evening with children from Birla-run schools performing. This public display of support and recognition was extended to the 1991 Lok Sabha elections, when, for the first time, a section of the big bourgeoise saw the BJP as a credible alternative to the Congress (I). The supply of funds that followed found the BJP outstripping the Congress (I) in resources in many places, especially since the latter was handicapped by being out of power.

This situation has not lasted long. There is a discernible shift back to the Congress (I) after the new economic policies were initiated by the Narasimha Rao government. This has restored the confidence of big business circles in the Congress (I) regime, and, consequently, dampened the enthusiasm of support to the BJP. The big bourgeoisie now hankers for stability to facilitate the new economic policies. It sees the Achilles' heel of the BJP: the mish-mash of its economic philosophy which oscillates between naked support to big business and landlord interests, a petty-bourgeois critique of economic policy, and opportunist slogans to retain popular support.

Economic Policy
The BJP is for liberalization and privatization. This is clear from its policy pronouncements and actions in Parliament. Though its recent economic policy statement (adopted at Gandhinagar in May 1992) has tried to muffle this naked stand in a lot of verbiage, the BJP stands for the following.

Freeing all controls on monopolies. The 1991 election manifesto of the BJP called for drastic dilution of the MRTP (Monopolies and Restrictive Trade Practices) Act, i.e. raising the ceiling defining monopoly houses from Rs 100 crores to Rs 1,000 crores. In line with this, the BJP voted for a virtual scrapping of restrictions on monopolies in the MRTP amendment bills moved by the Narasimha Rao government in 1991, ensuring its passage.

Dismantling the public sector. The BJP is for dismantling the public sector, except in some limited areas like defence and certain infrastructural industries. It wants disinvestment of public sector units' shares. In fact, after the recent scandal about the first round of disinvestment when the shares were sold at incredibly low prices, the BJP came forward to bail out the government, with the suggestion that a disinvestment corporation be set up so that the sale of shares can be conducted properly.

Privatization of banks and the finance sector. The BJP wants nationalized banks to be restricted and private banks to be encouraged. In line with its bogus *swadeshi* slogan, it now also demands restrictions on foreign banks and encouragement to private Indian banks.

Hostility to land reforms. Though the BJP talks of land reforms in a very perfunctory fashion, it has been notably hostile to the implementation of land reforms; the record of BJP-run governments in this respect is dismal.

The retreat of the Congress (I) from the Nehruvian path of economic development is seen by the BJP as a vindication of its backward economic philosophy. The Jana Sangh–RSS stream has been consistently opposed to the concomitants of the Nehruvian model of planning, public sector and rapid industrialization from their right-wing point of view. BJP spokesmen in Parliament, like Advani and Jaswant Singh, have gone on record welcoming the new economic policy by stating that the Congress (I) is only implementing what the BJP had been long advocating.

It is evident to all perceptive observers that the BJP does not differ from the Congress (I) in its basic economic policy positions. It has, however, in the past few months, tried to sell the slogan of *swadeshi*, taking the cue from the RSS campaign to oppose the entry of multinationals. The absurdity of propagating *swadeshi* by calling upon people to patronize Indian big business and not multinationals, when Indian big bourgeoisie is eagerly welcoming collaboration with these very multinational corporations, has confused even the BJP cadres. It is a pedestrian and hollow attempt to talk of "liberalization with self-reliance," as the BJP has done at its Bhopal national executive meeting in August 1992, when the very process of liberalization will undermine self-reliance in the Indian situation.

The hallmark of the BJP's economic policy is ambiguity and obfuscation of the real economic issues before the people. The economic policy document adopted in May 1992 is grandiloquently titled "A Humanistic Approach to Economic Development (A Swadeshi Approach)." It does not talk of concentration of wealth in the hands of the monopolies, or of concentration of land in the hands of the landlords; it does not advocate taxing the rich, nor does it want any regulation of the corporate sector. It spends pages talking of farmers, but does not devote even one sentence to the roots of agrarian exploitation. It seeks to mask its class stance by such opaque and meaningless passages as:

> This then is the credo of the BJP. Rapid economic development with full employment and reasonable stability in price level – through "Swadeshi" and "Swalambhan" judiciously combined with self confidence. . . . We believe that the development of the nation depends on the mobilization, galvanization and optimization of national will, national potential, national energy, national resources, national self-confidence, national pride, national effort with people's involvement.

No amount of "national" common sense can decipher what this means.

BJP president M.M. Joshi carries on in the same vein: "We must liberalize, industrialize and modernize – but it has to be done in the Indian way." The dismal record of the BJP-run state governments on the economic front stems from the pro-big business–landlord–trader bias of the BJP. A detailed examination of these governments' economic performance is however outside the purview of this article.

The BJP represents a reactionary counter-force to the opposition mounting against the new economic policies. The BJP's opposition to the 29 November 1991 industrial strike and 16 June 1992 general strikes, and the significant refusal of the RSS-directed Bharatiya Mazdoor Sangh (BMS) to join the united protests, are graphic illustrations of its right-wing approach.

Pseudo-Nationalism: Distorted Defence of National Unity
The BJP's concept of nationalism has not outgrown the old Jana Sangh formula of Hindi–Hindu–Hindustan. The RSS's concept of a Hindu *rashtra* is now set out as the cultural concept of *Hindutva*.

The BJP was aided in projecting its idea of a Hindu-majoritarian nation in the decade of the 1980s, when serious threats to national unity developed. The growth of secessionist forces and fundamentalist ideas among the minorities in Punjab and Kashmir, and earlier in the North East, have been the most serious challenge to national unity since independence. The BJP and Hindu communal forces have responded to this threat by launching the offensive of *Hindutva*. In contrast to the working class and democratic response, which defends national unity while recognizing the cultural and national diversity of India, the BJP stands for defending national unity by imposing a Hindu-majoritarian state. Instead of seeing the root cause of the strains on national unity within the undemocratic state structure, which denies federalism and fosters uneven development due to capitalist growth, the BJP is actually for a more centralized, authoritarian structure.

Against the Federal Set-up
The BJP has been hostile to any restructuring of centre–state relations that might lead to more autonomy for the states and the creation of a genuinely federal set-up. That is why it talks about the formation of small states by breaking up existing states on the basis of administrative convenience. It would like to see at least 60 such states in India. The weakening and division of existing linguistic states would destroy the basis for states' autonomy, and strengthen the centre's hold and powers over the states. The BJP wants a strong centre and weak states without any cohesive linguistic–nationality principle. It must be recalled that the Jana Sangh had bitterly opposed the formation of linguistic states in the 1950s. The BJP's allergy to strong linguistic states with more powers stems from its authoritarian concept of Indian nationhood, which denies the linguistic/cultural/religious diversity of the country. Similarly, it advocates a presidential form of government, which, in a diverse and complex country like India, is an invitation to authoritarianism.

The success that the BJP has registered in recent years is partly due to the growth of separatist trends among the minorities. This plays upon the apprehensions of the majority community who are targeted in states like Punjab and Kashmir, where they are in a minority. Playing upon the fears of the majority community conceals the fact that the BJP's response to threats to national unity is a profoundly disruptive and distorted one. Harping on Hindu interests strengthens separatist and fundamentalist threats among the minority communities. Making the building of a Ram temple at Ayodhya an issue of "national unity" and "national honour" is pernicious, as it excludes non-Hindus from the national integrative process.

The BJP has, in fact, a vested interest in the perpetuation and fostering of fundamentalism and separatism amongst the minorities, as these provide it with the target of an enemy against whom communal mobilization is possible. What needs to be realized is that any step or advance made by the BJP in mobilizing the people or influencing public opinion in favour of *Hindutva* is a sure step towards the disunity and disintegration of India. The more the BJP harps on the Hindu communal platform, the more sectarian elements among the minorities get active – and both these forces feed and nurture each other. The result is damage to Indian unity and fertile ground for all varieties of divisive forces.

The BJP's stance on the vital question of national unity therefore has to be concretely exposed. Its nationalism is pseudo-nationalism, as it leads to striking at the roots of Indian unity. The Khalistanis, the Hizb-e-Islami or the North Eastern separatist forces find in Hindu majority communalism a validity for their disruptive activities.

Feeding on Communal Violence
There is a considerable body of liberal opinion in the country that sees the BJP as basically a right-of-centre party which can be persuaded to adopt a more moderate tone on the communal question. It sees the stridency of the BJP on the Ayodhya issue as an aberration; it expects to see the BJP evolve as a party which takes up other economic and social issues, and emerge as a responsible centre–right party. This is a naive expectation. The BJP has tasted blood with its Muslim-baiting, anti-minority platform. The mix of distorted nationalism and catering to Hindu apprehensions in a period of deep societal and economic crisis has helped it garner new support away from the secular constituency.

At the core of the BJP's electoral expansion is the groundwork put in by the RSS and its allied organizations: a sustained period of propaganda and activities which target the Muslim community as the enemy, and the organization of communal riots. A study of the incidence of communal violence and communal polarization in different parts would show a close correlation between the BJP's electoral gains and the outbreak of communal violence. Gujarat is a classic example. For the past two decades, Hindu–Muslim riots have become a regular occurrence in the cities and towns of Gujarat. Ahmedabad, Baroda, Surat – all are periodically convulsed by riots and bloodshed which have systematically led to communal polarization, steady accretion of the strength of the BJP, and communalization of the police and other state institutions. The BJP polled 51 per cent votes in Gujarat in the 1991 Lok Sabha elections.

Further south, the BJP has been struggling to establish its political presence for long without much success. It has now made major gains in Karnataka. Here also, the recent period has seen riots in Belgaum, Davangere and many other areas. The RSS has spread out from its traditional area of influence in South Kanara. The BJP polled 28 per cent votes in the last Lok Sabha elections. An electoral shift was evident in Uttar Pradesh towns in the ninth general elections, consequent to the worst rioting since independence in the November–December 1990 period.

The BJP has literally reaped a harvest of votes on the sufferings and hatred fomented by spreading communal poison. It is this menacing quality of the party that makes it an implacable enemy of Indian democracy and secularism – both of which are vital to sustain India as we know it since Independence.

There can be no illusions about the BJP being a right-wing communal party. It is, further, a reactionary force, being a party of majority communalism. Despite its rhetoric and active work to woo the Scheduled Castes, tribals and other socially oppressed sections, it is a party grounded in the defence of the moribund Hindu social order. In this sense, it is profoundly hostile to the social emancipation of sections, including women, who were ordained a low social status in the caste-oppressive Hindu order.

Organic Link with the RSS
No discussion on the BJP can be complete or accurate without underlining its unique feature – its link with the RSS. The BJP in its present incarnation is tied to the RSS by an umbilical cord. The advent of Advani as president of the party in 1986 made this link explicit. He justified the relations with the RSS and looking up to it for guidance by likening this to Congress leaders consulting Gandhiji for guidance during the freedom struggle even when he was not a formally elected leader of the Congress. The BJP makes no bones about belonging to the *Sangh Parivar*. That the RSS is the fount of authority and sustenance is made clear by the open summoning of BJP leaders to RSS conclaves to report and discuss matters with the RSS leadership.

The RSS dictates the BJP's stance on the Ram temple issue, and coordinates the overall campaign conducted by other front organizations such as the VHP. Increasingly, the RSS is directing various aspects of the BJP's organizational functioning including government activities. Whether it is the Kalyan Singh or Patwa ministries, the RSS has a say in all major government policies.

The RSS, while posing to be above the mundane level of politics, keeps the strategic interests of a Hindu *rashtra* in view. It sees the BJP in its present avatar as a convenient instrument. But it should not be forgotten that the RSS has often come out in appreciation of the Congress (I) when it feels that the tactical interests of Hindu communalism demands it. It would ideally want the major national party to become Hindu-oriented. In 1987, RSS *sarsanghchalak* Balasaheb Deoras, in his *Vijayadashami* address, said: "We are not anti-Congress. Our founder leader was a Congressman. Our organization is opposed only to the Congress policy of appeasing the minorities." More recently, the late Bhaurao Deoras, Balasaheb's influential brother, went on record to state that Narasimha Rao was the best prime minister the country had ever had. The RSS was clearly hoping that Rao, heading a minority government, would work out an entente with the BJP to remain in power.

The autonomous growth of the VHP, another front of the RSS, also has enabled it to tighten its grip on the BJP. The RSS, with the enhanced clout of a mass movement for the Ram temple, is now in a better position to influence the electorally oriented BJP and direct the drive towards *Hindutva*.

Anti-Communism
The BJP's anti-communist virulence derives from the clear-sighted view of the RSS that the communists are sworn opponents of Hindu *rashtra* and obstacles to the establishment of *Hindutva*.

The RSS has been concentrating on developing its base in Kerala and West Bengal, bastions of the Left movement. The annual report of the RSS general secretary, H.V. Seshadiri, presented at the RSS *Prathinidhi Sabha* in Lucknow in March 1992, targets the two states. The report states that RSS programmes in Kerala and West Bengal have signalled that "Communists, whose ideological-cum-power base had already collapsed at the global level, have started losing out fast to the nationalist forces here."

Much before the current offensive, the BJP–RSS had perfected the art of combining with the Congress (I) and the United Democratic Front (UDF) to defeat the Left Democratic Front (LDF) and the Communist Party of India (Marxist) (CPI[M]) in Kerala. In local elections in 1988, the Lok Sabha elections in 1989 and Assembly elections in 1991, the RSS–BJP shifted votes in favour of selected UDF candidates.

Second only to their *bête noire*, the Muslim minorities, the BJP–RSS targets the communists for attack. In Kerala, they have been waging a systematic campaign of violence against CPI(M) cadres and supporters, to win for themselves a militant anti-communist constituency. The recent killing of a sixteen-year-old SFI (Students Federation of India) student in Kottayam illustrates this visceral hate campaign.

The BJP thinks the current international climate of anti-communism with reverses in the socialist countries can be utilized to step up its domestic anti-communist campaign. In fact, among all the bourgeois–landlord parties, only the BJP has been sustaining a systematic anti-communist campaign in the wake of the collapse of the Soviet Union. The BJP, backed by the RSS, sees this as a golden opportunity to defame socialism and Marxism, and woo sections who were attracted to the socialist ideal. The CPI(M) comes in for special attack and abuse as it is perceived to be the main barrier to the BJP's growth in West Bengal and Kerala.

Foreign Policy
The BJP, like its predecessor, the Jana Sangh, adopts basic foreign policy positions that are marked by the absence of any anti-imperialist content, even though the party claims to be a champion of national interest and sovereignty. The integral humanism of Deen Dayal Upadhyay, which has been embraced by the BJP, does not recognize the reality of imperialist exploitation. For the BJP, in the words of its president, M.M. Joshi, "much of the economic inequalities in the present world arise from the belief that it is possible to have unlimited growth on a planet with limited resources and environment. Our experience tells us that a balanced growth model is far less exploitative." In analysing the present economic inequalities in the world, the BJP cannot see imperialist exploitation as the root cause. Instead, its consistent anti-communism makes it naturally tilt towards pro-imperialist positions. In a presidential address to the party in 1986, Advani noted that the Janata government (1977–79) had tried to improve relations with the western bloc, which gave India's non-alignment credibility. He bemoaned the fact that relations with the western bloc were again marked by distrust. The BJP would have welcomed India having a close and strategic partnership with the United States, but for one inhibiting factor – Pakistan. The support given consistently by the Soviet Union to India on the Kashmir issue was the major reason that prevented the BJP from advocating an open alliance with the US, and which reined in its anti-Sovietism to some extent.

Unlike other right-wing forces, the BJP sees the world through the prism of its anti-Muslim outlook. The party's strident advocacy of relations with Israel and its happiness with the Narasimha Rao government establishing full diplomatic relations with Israel are motivated by its intense desire to cultivate Zionism, which it sees as an effective counter-weight to Islam in the Middle East. During the US and allied forces' war on Iraq, the BJP refused to condemn the wanton destruction of that country – and its cadres spontaneously countered anti-US feelings among the people with slogans praising George Bush.

In the current world situation, the BJP sees the reverses for socialism in Eastern Europe and the former Soviet Union as ideological vindication of its anti-communism. Unable to conceal its glee at the happenings in the Soviet Union, the BJP leadership continues to strike its usual, hypocritical posture of steering a path clear of communism or capitalism, which in essence is nothing but deep-rooted adherence to capitalism.

In the absence of the Soviet Union, the BJP would be only too glad to have India as a junior partner in the American scheme of things – if only the latter could jettison Pakistan. L.K. Advani's visit to the US in January 1992 and the speeches he delivered at US right-wing forums like the Heritage Foundation were clear signals to the ruling circles there: that the BJP backs liberalization and privatization; that the BJP welcomes close cooperation with the US; and that the BJP wants the US to back India rather than Pakistan in South Asia.

The BJP was the only opposition party that welcomed the Indo–US joint naval exercises. Advani defended these exercises in a press conference and said it will be in India's interests to conduct such joint exercises.

The BJP has been virulently anti-China in its postures till recently. Now it has reluctantly come around to the view that improving relations with China is important given the changed world situation, though in the same breath it demands a separation of Tibet from China.

The BJP's foreign policy posture has been in stark contrast to the positions adopted by all the other national bourgeois parties. It has never supported non-alignment, anti-imperialism or the fight against neo-colonialism. Its world outlook is flawed by its chronic anti-communist outlook, which makes it see the world in a distorted fashion.

Past Lessons to be Learnt

Any tolerance of or concession to this mix of communal pseudo-nationalism will be disastrous for India's unity and secular democracy. In the past, the exigencies of electoral politics saw unprincipled compromises by secular parties, which enabled the BJP to acquire legitimacy and access to popular discontent against the Congress. The Janata Dal–National Front committed the opportunist mistake of entering into an electoral understanding with the BJP in the eighth general elections. The BJP prospered by this at the expense of the secular parties. In the future also such opportunism will arise in the secular camp as bourgeois parties pay primacy to vote-gathering over basic principles.

The other aspect whereby the BJP gets strengthened is the willingness of secular bourgeois parties to appease minority communalism. The Shah Bano case and Rajiv Gandhi's unscrupulous compromise were a boon for the Hindu communalists. The Janata Dal has also shown itself to be partial to fundamentalist and communal demands of the minorities in order to muster the support of sectarian leaders. V.P. Singh's visit to the Imam of Jama Masjid to solicit support in the ninth general elections was one such damaging instance.

The defence of minority rights must be so conducted that it does not nurture minority communalism and fundamentalism. The BJP bogey of minorityism must be systematically exposed for its reactionary and anti-democratic content. The Muslim minority in India is discriminated against and socially disadvantaged. This truth needs to be substantiated and concretely elaborated with facts and figures. The attitude of the state towards minorities is the acid test of a democracy.

A society that cannot protect its citizens belonging to religious minorities can only be an imperfect and flawed democracy. The secularism practised by the Congress and other bourgeois parties sees it as the right of all religions to be treated equally. It does not conceive of the separation of religion from the state and politics. The BJP uses the definition of "*sarva dharma samabhava*" to argue for the recognition of *Hindutva* as the basis for secularism. Unless the secular forces can be firmed up to defend secularism as the separation of religion from the state and politics, the erosion of secular values cannot be checked or national unity be defended. The Left campaign that no *swamis, mullahs* or *granthis* should be allowed to use religion or religious places for political activity must become a principle for all secular and democratic forces.

Left forces have not registered sufficient growth all over the country in the 1980s through the development of class and mass struggles. This inability to expand their basic classes and to new areas has enabled the BJP to capitalize on the mass discontent arising out of the deepening problems of the bourgeois–landlord system and the decline of the Congress mass base.

The BJP has to be fought at the level of its communal ideology and politics. But this struggle will become effective only when it is simultaneously taken on for its reactionary class platform as a whole. Exposing its economic policies and building up militant mass struggles against the policies of its state governments are of crucial importance. The defence of national unity and the struggle against separatism must not be allowed to be exploited by the BJP and Hindu communal forces. With the consistent role of the Left, secular-democratic forces must be rallied to the cause.

The BJP's authoritarian outlook can be countered by a vigorous struggle to federalize the Indian state structure and to decentralize powers to the states. The BJP talks of more fiscal powers for the states and complains of discrimination by the centre, now that it is running four state governments, but it is against any genuine federal structure through which the forces of separatism can be contained and neutralized.

At the level of ideology, there has to be a sustained campaign to expose the anti-democratic, anti-minority, pro-imperialist and pro-bourgeois–landlord character of the BJP. The vast reservoir of patriotic and democratic consciousness of the people must be harnessed to checkmate the BJP's distorted nationalism which endangers national unity. The advance of the Left and democratic forces will very much depend on how this task is fulfilled while waging a determined struggle against the class policies of the Congress (I) government.

THE RISE OF NARENDRA MODI:
A JOINT ENTERPRISE OF HINDUTVA AND BIG BUSINESS
(May 2014)

Ten years after the National Democratic Alliance (NDA) lost the general election in 2004, the Bharatiya Janata Party (BJP) is now scenting the prospects of a comeback. The combine of the BJP and Rashtriya Swayamsevak Sangh (RSS) is making a determined bid to come to power at the centre in the sixteenth Lok Sabha election. The RSS is salivating at the prospect of Narendra Modi, an RSS *pracharak*, becoming prime minister of the country.

Whatever the outcome of the election, there is no doubt that *Hindutva* is witnessing a second coming, and that there is a shift among the big bourgeoisie in favour of the right-wing communal party, the BJP. It is necessary to understand what has brought about this change in the political situation, and to grasp what the change portends for the future trajectory of the political economy of the country.

In an article published in *The Marxist* in 1992, I had stated:

> The BJP, in its quest to function as a viable party of the right in the Indian political milieu, has finally arrived at what it considers to be the key to its success. Hindu nationalism articulated with an internal enemy – the Muslim minority – gives the BJP its communal character. Alongside this cutting edge to its platform is the right-wing character of its economic policy: support to the liberalization and privatization drive. It is the combination of these two features that makes the BJP a unique political force at the national level: a right-wing communal party which represents the reactionary sections of the big bourgeoisie and landlords. (Karat 1992: 19)

Emergence of a Hindutva Party
In the period 1986–89, the BJP took on an aggressive *Hindutva* platform. The party fashioned its discourse against secularism and traditional bourgeois-democratic nationalism under the presidentship of L.K. Advani. The terms "pseudo-secularism" and "minorityism" were coined and used to condemn bourgeois secular parties and politics. The Ram temple movement and the advocacy of "cultural nationalism" to signify *Hindutva* marked the

apogee of this Hindu-majoritarian platform. This aggressive communal policy led to a wave of communal violence in the period that began with L.K. Advani's *rath yatra* and culminated in the demolition of the Babri Masjid in December 1992.

The rise of right-wing *Hindutva* forces coincided with the economic crisis of 1988–89, which was a product of the new economic policies of the Rajiv Gandhi government and the financial crisis that resulted from the liberalization of that phase. The rise of *Hindutva* and the right-wing economic policy platform of the BJP also marked a turn away from the "Nehruvian" model by the ruling classes, and from an economic policy in which the state played a relatively significant role in directing investment.

The 1990s were years during which this phase of the BJP's rise occurred. It emerged as the largest opposition party for the first time in the tenth Lok Sabha election of 1991. The Ram Janmabhoomi movement had already led to widespread communal violence and polarization in the wake of Advani's *rath yatra*. The Babri Masjid was demolished in December 1992. In the eleventh Lok Sabha election in 1996, the BJP emerged as the largest single party in the Lok Sabha with 161 seats. In the twelfth Lok Sabha election in 1998, it was able to form the first NDA government under A.B. Vajpayee (after a short-lived attempt in 1996).

The six-year rule of the BJP-led NDA government ended with the 2004 Lok Sabha election. The BJP failed again in the 2009 election to wrest power: it won only 116 seats and its share of votes dropped to 18.8 per cent.

The situation has undergone a significant change in the recent period. The BJP has become the major contender for power in the sixteenth Lok Sabha election. What accounts for this resurrection of the BJP's influence and its electoral strength?

Neoliberal Crisis Affects Congress
The neoliberal policies of the United Progressive Alliance (UPA) government have resulted in an economic crisis. After a period of high growth fuelled by debt-financing and speculative bubbles, and consequent to the global financial crisis of 2008, the phase of growth ended and there was a slowdown in the economy, with the annual rate of growth of GDP falling below 5 per cent. Further, growth in the neoliberal regime has been accompanied by joblessness and a lack of employment growth; the country has also witnessed unprecedented levels of inflation for a period of seven years. Agrarian distress has blighted the lives of millions of peasants. Two decades of liberalization have resulted in widening inequalities and a tremendous concentration of wealth in the hands of a few.

A notable outcome of the neoliberal regime has been the spread of high-level corruption. The corporate loot of natural resources, and the venality of the ruling political class and the bureaucracy, became endemic features of Indian society. The middle classes, which had earlier benefited from liberalization, have increasingly been affected by high inflation and corruption. In the 1990s, a large section of the urban middle classes rallied around the BJP. In the elections of 2004, and more so in the elections of 2009, they turned to the Congress. But middle-class discontent grew during the UPA-II rule, and by 2011, this section began to express its disgust and to protest against corruption and high prices. Discontent against the ruling establishment soon became widespread and began to spread to the rural areas.

An important source of support for the Congress and the UPA government came from the big bourgeoisie. During the tenure of the UPA-I government, big business had by and large rallied behind the ruling party – that is, the Congress. Despite reservations the big bourgeoisie had about Left support to the UPA-I government, it was reasonably satisfied with the direction of the economic policies. This period proved to be a bonanza for big private corporations as a result of policies that enabled them to grab natural resources and acquire public assets for a song. Tax concessions for big capitalists and the Mauritius route for the flow of capital in and out of the country kept the corporates and financial circles happy.

Turning Point
But the year 2010 marked a turning point, since a slowdown set in after 2010–11. The rate of growth of GDP halved in the last two years of the UPA-II government. With depreciation of the rupee by over 30 per cent, the cost of external debt-servicing went up sharply for the corporates and profitability came down steadily.

Another feature of 2010 was the exposure of massive corruption scandals that involved the corporate sector. The telecom scandal involving the allocation of 2G spectrum, illegal mining rackets and the coal block allocation case, all affected big private corporations, which included the Anil Ambani group, the Tatas, Birlas, Essars and Jindals. Anil Ambani was questioned by the CBI in the 2G spectrum case, and an FIR was filed against Kumaramangalam Birla and Hindalco in the coal block allocation case. The entire corporate sector reacted with outrage against these anti-corruption cases. The big business houses that had benefited from the largesse provided by the clearances given by the UPA government now turned their ire against Prime Minister Manmohan Singh and his government. The more public anger mounted against the big business–ruling politicians–bureaucrats nexus, the more big business houses turned against their patrons in the government.

Gujarat Model: Big Business Support
As the economic crisis deepened, industrial production fell steeply and the avenues to super-profits dwindled; and the big bourgeoisie turned to looking for another political saviour. The quest did not take long. The corporate bosses homed in on Narendra Modi, chief minister of Gujarat. Ever since the communal pogrom of 2002, Modi had assiduously set about wooing big business houses to invest in Gujarat. The bi-annual "Vibrant Gujarat" summit meetings became the platform from which to showcase the "Gujarat model" sponsored by Modi.

By the 1980s, Gujarat had become one of the most capitalistically developed states in India. Under the neoliberal regime, states were encouraged to compete against each other to attract private investment for infrastructure and industry. What Gujarat did under Narendra Modi was to provide the biggest concessions to private corporations to invest their capital, by means of cheap land allotment, provision of subsidized electricity and tax concessions.

By the time of the fourth Vibrant Gujarat summit in January 2009, the corporate sector had rallied around this new "Saviour" and "Redeemer". It was at this summit that Anil Ambani stated: "Narendrabhai has done good for Gujarat and imagine what will happen if he leads the nation. A person like him should be the next leader of the country." Sunil Mittal, head of the Bharti group, declared: "Chief Minister Modi is known as CEO, but he is actually not a CEO because he is not running a company or a sector. He is running a State and can also run the nation" (Varadarajan 2014).

From then on, at the Vibrant Gujarat summits of 2011 and 2013, the chorus only grew louder and was sung by larger numbers. Mukesh Ambani, Ratan Tata, Adi Godrej, Gautam Adani and the CEOs of other top industrial and banking companies declared their adulation for Narendra Modi and the Gujarat model. In the 2013 summit, Anil Ambani, in a nauseating panegyric, drew the lineage of Modi from Mahatma Gandhi and Sardar Patel, and called him the "King of Kings".

The big bourgeoisie is the most powerful stratum of the ruling classes, which comprise the bourgeoisie and landlords of the country. It has grown enormously after liberalization and has consolidated its leadership of the ruling class. The first time a substantial section of the big bourgeoisie shifted its support away from the Congress was in 1991, when important factions supported the BJP. On his first visit to Kolkata after the *rath yatra* in 1990, the Birlas feted L.K. Advani at lunch. An array of top industrialists attended the event. This public display of support and recognition was extended to the 1991 Lok Sabha elections, when, for the first time, sections of the big bourgeoisie saw the BJP as a credible alternative to the Congress. In the 1991 elections, the BJP outstripped the Congress side in raising resources and spending money.

Big Bourgeoisie for Modi
This is the second time – the first being in the 1990s – that the big bourgeoisie has swung its support to the BJP. The difference, however, is that in the current phase, there is near-unanimous support from big business and the corporate sector for Narendra Modi.

It is not only Indian big business that has endorsed Modi. The 2011 and 2013 Vibrant Gujarat summits were attended by the president of the US–India Business Council, Ron Sommers, who termed the development of Gujarat under Modi "stunning." Narendra Modi enlisted the services of a US lobbying and public relations firm, APCO Worldwide, to drum up support for the Gujarat model, and to lobby with the US government and international finance capital. APCO, which has close links with Israel, has done a commendable job in marketing Modi and his Gujarat model.

The announcement of Modi as the BJP's prime ministerial candidate caused stockmarkets to shoot up. The benchmark BSE Sensex and National Stock Exchange Nifty gained 18 per cent from September 2013 to mid-April 2014. The share of Adani Enterprises (owned by Modi's close ally, Gautam Adani) surged by a whopping 114 per cent since the rally began in February 2014. The markets have categorically signalled who their leader is.

The announcement of Modi as the leader of the BJP's election campaign saw a massive and sustained campaign in the corporate media, both television and print, to project him on a development and good governance platform. This unprecedented campaign is a result of the total backing of the corporate sector, which owns the bulk of the mass media in the country. At the same time, the corporate media have blacked out the communal aspects of the BJP campaign and the big role the RSS is playing in the campaign. At no time has an individual leader received such widespread saturation coverage as has Modi since he embarked on his first rally in June 2013. This campaign explains the genesis of the "Modi wave", which is then re-propagated by the very corporate media that created it. The impact and the appeal that Modi has among educated youth and sections of the middle classes in various parts of the country is a result of this media campaign.

Influx of Personnel

In class terms, both the Congress and the BJP represent the interests of the big bourgeoisie and landlords. The shift towards Narendra Modi and the BJP by the big bourgeoisie has left the Congress enfeebled, enhancing its electoral vulnerability. The shift by the ruling class is reflected in the flow of retired persons from the top echelons of the bureaucracy, security agencies and armed forces to the BJP. For the first time, a retired army chief is contesting as a BJP candidate; also in the ranks of contestants are a former home secretary and a former police commissioner of Mumbai who quit his job to stand. The retired chief of the Research and Analysis Wing (RAW), Sanjeev Tripathi, has joined the BJP.

The 1990–91 period saw a similar influx into the BJP from personnel of the ruling establishment. The BJP's chauvinist nationalism and its call for a strong national security state which rides roughshod over citizen's rights are an attraction for these elements.

Gujarat: Hindutva Laboratory

Narendra Modi's political and ideological life is determined by his being a part of the RSS. From 1986 to 1989, the BJP was moulded by the RSS. L.K. Advani has publicly owned the ideological and organizational links of the party with the RSS. The RSS began a practice of placing its cadres in key organizational posts of the party at various levels. Narendra Modi, who became a *pracharak* (full-time functionary) of the RSS in Gujarat in 1975, rose to become the state organization secretary of the BJP in 1987. This is a post that acts as a bridge between the RSS and its political wing.

This was the period when Gujarat became a laboratory for the *Hindutva* experiment. The Vishwa Hindu Parishad (VHP) became a mass organization, and its tentacles spread across the length and breadth of the state. The 1980s saw a series of major communal riots in Ahmedabad, Vadodara, Surat and other towns. The RSS–VHP combine succeeded in communalizing large sections of the urban middle classes. Narendra Modi was reared and nurtured in this *Hindutva* enterprise.

RSS Pracharak as Chief Minister

Even after Narendra Modi was shifted out of Gujarat to Delhi as the result of a setback due to factional politics within the Gujarat BJP, he never lost the trust of the RSS. In 1998, after Vajpayee became prime minister, Modi was promoted to the position of national organization secretary of the BJP. This was a key position at the national level for maintaining links between the RSS and the party. When Modi assumed chief ministership of Gujarat in October 2011, he was the first RSS *pracharak* to become chief minister of a state. Other RSS men who had filled key governmental positions, including L.K. Advani and Atal Behari Vajpayee, were all *swayamsevaks*, not full-time *pracharaks*.

The first phase of Narendra Modi's chief ministership, from 2002 to 2007, was marked by all the virulent characteristics of a *Hindutva* fanatic. The Godhra train incident in March 2002 provided Modi with a perfect opportunity to sponsor massive "retaliation" against Muslims. The fact that he was able to avoid legal and judicial responsibility for the pogrom has only heightened his image among *Hindutva* followers. From then onwards, the road to his becoming the champion and symbol of *Hindutva* was cleared. That he was unrepentant and unrelenting in his anti-Muslim crusade became evident in the Assembly elections held in December 2002. His campaign speeches were full of anti-Muslim rhetoric: "*Ame Panch, Amara Pachees* (We are five, we have twenty-five). Can Gujarat implement family planning? Which religious sect is coming in the way?" Referring to the closing down of the relief camps, he asked, "What, brothers, should we run relief camps? Should I start children-producing centres there?" (Mukhopadhyay 2013: 298).

After the Gujarat police killed Sohrabuddin and his wife in cold blood and criminal cases were filed in the matter of this false "encounter," Narendra Modi, while addressing election meetings in 2007, would ask, "What did you want me and my men to do with a man like Sohrabuddin?" – and the crowd would roar in answer, "*Kill him*" (*ibid.*: 311).

The dark side of the Gujarat model has always been this *Hindutva* terror and violence against the Muslim minorities. In the wake of the horrific events in Gujarat in 2002, sections of big business reacted adversely. More than the communal violence, what put them off was the insecurity of life and property, which would adversely affect investment.

In February 2003, the Confederation of Indian Industry (CII), the premier organization of industrialists, organized a meeting in Delhi with Narendra Modi, newly elected chief minister of Gujarat. In this meeting, some of the top industrialists, such as Jamshyd Godrej and Rahul Bajaj, expressed concern about insecurity in Gujarat – insecurity that would affect investment. Modi was furious at this criticism. He organized the industrialists of Gujarat to protest. One hundred companies from Gujarat threatened to leave the CII. Faced with this threat, the CII buckled and its director general issued a letter of regret for the misunderstanding (Jose 2012). The class interests of the big bourgeoisie overcame whatever qualms were entertained by its more liberal members. Ratan Tata and Godrej have now come full circle, to a position of wholehearted endorsement of Narendra Modi becoming CEO of the country.

The Marriage of 'Hindutva' and Big Business
The metamorphosis of the RSS *pracharak* into a favourite of private corporations is the most significant phenomenon of the sixteenth Lok Sabha election. The role of the big bourgeoisie in backing fascism as an extreme option is well known. That is what happened in Germany. In India, such a crisis situation has not yet developed for the ruling classes. But the mixture of *Hindutva* communalism and big bourgeois support is a potent and deadly one. It is a recipe for right-wing authoritarianism that spells danger for the secular democratic framework. Neoliberal politics carries within it the seeds of authoritarianism. One of the attractions of Narendra Modi for big capital is the authoritarianism that characterizes his leadership and personality.

The political career of Narendra Modi within the BJP is marked by his ruthless elimination of political rivals and those who do not accept his leadership. Haren Pandya, who was stripped of his ministership and legislative seat, ended up being mysteriously assassinated. Sanjay Joshi, a fellow RSS *pracharak*, was discarded by the BJP–RSS leadership from his post in the party on the insistence of Modi. Keshubhai Patel, Suresh Mehta, Gordhan Zadaphia and, in the latest instance, Haren Pathak were all isolated and driven out.

RSS Plans for Modi
The ascent of Narendra Modi to the position of prime ministerial candidate of the BJP was a result of careful planning. After the RSS decided to dispense with the leadership of L.K. Advani in 2009, its organizational grip over the BJP tightened. Amendments to the BJP constitution were made over the last five to six years to facilitate this enhanced organizational control. The RSS played a direct role in the selection of Nitin Gadkari and Rajnath Singh as successive presidents of the party. The national organization secretary is a direct RSS nominee – so are the two joint general secretaries working under him. The zonal organization secretaries of the BJP are also posts filled by RSS men. An RSS joint general secretary acts as the *Sangh's* liaison with the BJP, a post presently occupied by Suresh Soni.

Nearly a year before the BJP formally declared Narendra Modi as the prime ministerial candidate, Modi went to Nagpur for a meeting with Mohan Bhagwat, the RSS chief. Bhayyaji Joshi and the Sangh's liaison man with the BJP, Suresh Soni, attended the meeting. It was this meeting that set the course for what eventually happened in September 2013, when the BJP parliamentary board decided to declare Narendra Modi the prime ministerial candidate of the party (Joshi 2013).

The RSS played a crucial role in overcoming the resistance of L.K. Advani to their choice. The Goa meeting of the BJP's national executive in June 2014 made Narendra Modi the chairman of the election campaign committee over Advani's opposition, an act that resulted in Advani's short-lived resignation drama. The RSS organ, *The Organiser* (29 September 2013), editorially hailed the decision: "The nation, especially the youth, is looking for decisive, credible and dynamic leadership and popular mood vividly exhibits the undisputable alternative in the form of Modi."

Narendra Modi was to be marketed, in accordance with the ruling-class prescription, as the *vikas purush,* the leader who would deliver development and "good governance." But the RSS planned a back-up for this campaign. The *Hindutva* agenda would be the mainstay of the BJP's election campaign while the corporate media-backed campaign would focus on the aforesaid development and good governance. *Moditva* thus became the signature theme – *Hindutva* modified by the corporate mantra of development and good governance.

The use of the communal weapon to disperse any threat to the ruling classes is a time-tested tactic. The BJP represents a reactionary response to the gathering crisis. The reserve force of the ruling classes, represented by communalism, is now being brought into play. The electoral defeat of the BJP in 2004 did not lead to any basic erosion of the strength of the communal forces. As the Political Resolution of the CPI(M)'s 18th Congress pointed out in April 2005: "The rise of the communal forces in the past one and a half decades and their six-year period in office has enabled the communal ideology and organisations to strike roots in different sections of society. It will be a mistake to underestimate their latent strength" (Communist Party of India [Marxist] 2005, para 2.73).

Communal Game-Plan
The RSS put in place its strategy for the Lok Sabha election well in advance of the election itself. Uttar Pradesh, followed by Bihar, became the focus of an intense communal campaign. Amit Shah, a trusted lieutenant of Modi, was assigned charge of Uttar Pradesh in June 2013, four days after the BJP's national executive meeting in Goa. He had begun unofficially to go to Uttar Pradesh as early as February 2012. Amit Shah was the Minister of State for Home in Gujarat, and in July 2010, he was arrested and charged in the Sohrabuddin fake encounter case, the killing of his wife and the

subsequent murder of a witness. It is this hatchet man of Modi who oversaw the making of the blueprint for the communal campaign in Uttar Pradesh. The BJP, which was not able to get more than 10 seats out of 80 in the 2004 and 2009 elections, had to achieve a breakthrough in Uttar Pradesh, the largest state of India – and the state that had seen the first *Hindutva* wave in the 1990s.

The plan was to create the conditions for a recurrence of communal polarization. The election of the Samajwadi Party government in April 2012 set the stage for what was to occur. A systematic campaign was launched to the effect that the state government was a government for Muslims. Systematic anti-Muslim propaganda was conducted on issues such as cow slaughter, and to the effect that young Muslims were luring Hindu girls away from their homes. From the first communal outbreak in Kosi Kalan to the final major riot in Muzaffarnagar, that is, in a space of two years, twenty-seven major incidents of communal violence took place in the state. The VHP sought to raise the Ram temple issue by undertaking *shobha yatras*. The Vishwa Hindu Sammelan held in Allahabad in December 2012 declared Narendra Modi as the symbol of *Hindutva*. The same pattern of communal campaign and polarization was attempted in Bihar, especially after the Janata Dal (United) (JD[U]) broke its alliance with the BJP.

Halt the BJP
In all spheres of government, the NDA government of 1999–2004 led by A.B. Vajpayee was an undiluted failure. It represented a period of setback to the nation with respect to domestic and foreign policy. Its economic policy was disastrous for the people of India; indeed, with regard to rural India, the years of the NDA government represent the worst period of crisis with respect to production and human development in the post-green revolution era. The decisiveness with which the electorate threw the BJP out in 2004 reflected the utter bankruptcy of the party in government, and showed up its claim of "Shining India" to be a mockery of the vast masses of India's people.

The contours of what a BJP-led government headed by Narendra Modi would look like have emerged – an authoritarian government with a strong emphasis on a national security state; infiltration of the RSS into all institutions of the state; and communalization of the educational system and cultural institutions. This will be accompanied by a savage attack on welfare measures and the livelihood needs of the vast masses of the working people and the poor, in order to serve the interests of a big business-driven model of development.

In the course of the election campaign and midway through the polling process, it has become clear that the Congress and the UPA are losing ground steadily. In such a situation, the electoral battle to defeat the BJP and to implement suitable tactics after the election to prevent the BJP from coming to power are of crucial importance.

References

Communist Party of India (Marxist) (2005), *Political Resolution Adopted at the 18th Congress*, New Delhi, 6 to 11 April.

Jose, Vinod K. (2012), "The Emperor Uncrowned: The Rise of Narendra Modi," *Caravan*, 1 March.

Joshi, Purnima (2013), "Stratagem and Spoils," *Caravan*, July.

Karat, Prakash (1992), "BJP: A Reactionary Response", *The Marxist*, Vol. 10, No. 3, July–September.

Mukhopadhyay, Nilanjan (2013), *Narendra Modi: The Man, the Times*, New Delhi: Tranquebar Press.

Varadarajan, Siddharth (2014), "The Cult of Cronyism", *Seminar*, April; available at http://svaradarajan.com/2014/03/27/the-cult-of-cronyism/.

The Market Economy: Ideology and Reality[1]

C.T. Kurien

INTRODUCTION

Markets are among the oldest of human institutions and, arguably, the institution most commonly resorted to in day-to-day life. However, the celebration, if not the sanctification, of the market is a relatively new phenomenon, indeed just a few decades old. It is easy to identify two stages of this transformation.

It came to the forefront in the context of the emergence, towards the end of the First World War, of the state-dominated socialist economy in Russia, which fairly soon became the Union of Soviet Socialist Republics (USSR) or the Soviet Union. By the 1930s, the economic arrangements in the Soviet Union turned out to be distinctly different from the rest of the world, especially the United States of America (USA). For many American economists it appeared that while the capitalist economy of the United States was based on consumer preferences revealed through market prices, the socialist economy of the Soviet Union was dominated by decisions made by the state. In terms of production, for instance, capitalist producers had to respond to the demand of the consumers as reflected in market prices, while the state made production decisions in the socialist economy and distributed goods among consumers charging prices also determined by the state. The element of arbitrariness in economic decision-making that appeared to be the characteristic of the socialist economy did not appeal to economists in the United States and other capitalist economies, who were convinced of the logical nature of the capitalist system, closely identified with the working of the market and the price system. While there were certainly ideological overtones in this position, the discussions were largely academic in nature. An important academic contribution of this period was by Oskar Lange, the Polish mathematician and economist who spent much of the 1930s in the USA. In an essay entitled "On the Economic Theory of Socialism," Lange argued that a socialist state could use prices indicating the preferences of consumers and make production decisions accordingly, and that essentially it was a problem of finding solutions to a complex set of simultaneous equations.

The preference for a market economy took a definite ideological twist during the post-Second World War period, particularly from the 1950s to the 1980s, the Cold War era. Many American economists, political scientists and philosophers depicted American society (and societies of the rest of the "free world") as based on the will of the people expressed through free franchise ("democracy") in the political sphere and markets in the economic sphere. The opposite side was characterized as state-dominated dictatorships. This sanctification of the market economy as a symbol of freedom was expressed in such slogans as, "In the market economy the consumer is king." Typical of the popular writings of this period was *Free to Choose*, a book written by the Chicago University economist Milton Friedman (later a Nobel Prize winner) and his wife Rose Friedman.

The second stage of the celebration of the market economy is associated with the fall of the socialist economies, first in Eastern Europe and then, in the early years of the 1990s, in the Soviet Union itself. The fall of socialist economies was followed by the break-up of the USSR as well. The new economic order in these countries came to be depicted as "emerging market economies." With China too recognizing the market in the economic realm, though within the larger and politically controlled socialist framework, the propaganda on behalf of the market economy during these years had a triumphant note about it. This was further strengthened by opening up of many other parts of the world, including India in the 1990s, to rapidly moving global capital, and the approval that such opening up received from international institutions, particularly the International Monetary Fund (IMF) and the World Bank. That these movements, which were largely in the form of finance and financial markets, appeared to have internal arrangements to make necessary corrections, gave the market greater and louder support. It is somewhat ironic, though, that the multinational corporations that loudly champion the market economy have a large share of their economic decisions and transactions, including pricing, determined through non-market channels. The fact is that the championing of the market economy is clearly an ideological position, a central piece of the neoliberal creed, with little reference to the role and functioning of the market in real-life situations.

Academic Backing of Ideology

Frequently it is the case that ideology is a derivative of academic work, often based on isolated passages taken out of context and without a proper appreciation of the methodology that academics use in their work. Market ideology is no exception. Consider the way passages are invoked from the writings of Adam Smith to establish the claims made about the superiority of the market economy. Adam Smith, of course, was a great supporter of markets – of trade, to be more accurate. But it must be recalled that he was writing in the context of the restrictions on domestic trade that the mercantilists had propagated. He argued also that the market was necessary not only to sell what had been produced, but also to increase production and thus the wealth of the nation. An all-time favourite of market enthusiasts is his reference to the role of self-love in exchange: "It is not from the benevolence of the butcher, the brewer, or the baker that we expect our dinner, but their regard to their own interest. We address ourselves not to their humanity but to their self-love, and never talk to them of our necessities but of their advantage." However, sentences prior to it on the same page, so to say, are completely overlooked.

> In almost every other race of animals, each individual, when it is grown up to maturity, is entirely independent, and in its natural state has occasion for assistance of no other creature. *But man has almost constant occasion for the help of his brethren, and it is in vain for him to expect from his benevolence only.* He will be more likely to prevail if he can interest their self-love in his favour, and show them that it is for their own advantage to do for him what he requires of them. (Emphasis added)

If so, it is equally valid to claim that exchange is an expression of the mutual interdependence that is seen only among human beings.

As another economist subsequently expressed it: "We get our own purposes through a network of exchanges in which we are doing the things others want done, in order that we may get others to do what we ourselves want done." However, we do not understand exchange and markets by resorting to isolated texts. Fortunately, there is a whole exchange-centred theoretical tradition in economics championing the market economy, what is commonly known as the "neo-classical" school, which started in Europe in the nineteenth century and soon claimed "universal" validity as the *science* of economics. It is this school that now dominates the teaching of economics in what may be called the Anglo-American world (which includes India). Even those who are not professional economists will recognize it from one of its most familiar expositions via the diagram that purports to show how prices are determined by the intersection of a downward-sloping demand curve (representing the buyer, the consumer) and an upward-sloping supply curve (representing the seller, the producer), taking price on the vertical axis and quantity (bought and sold) on the horizontal axis in what is usually referred to as "the price–quantity diagram." The logical argument of the neo-classical school is, of course, more complex, and has been expounded by mathematicians both in the nineteenth and twentieth centuries.

In one sense, the neo-classical school emerged as providing a solution to one of the oldest problems to have engaged the attention of philosophers and, later, economists – the relationship between "use value" and exchange value. For long it had appeared that things that had high use value, such as water, had very little (or nil) exchange value, and vice versa. It was the treatment of this problem and its solution that gave rise to the neo-classical school. Its pioneers were three economists with a mathematical background, one from England and two from Europe. The English economist William Jevons wrote in 1870, in the Preface to his *The Theory of Political Economy*:

> All the physical sciences have their basis more or less obviously in the general principles of mechanics, so all branches and divisions of economic science must be pervaded by certain general principles. It is the investigation of such principles – to the tracing out of the mechanics of self-interest and utility, that this essay has been devoted.

If it appeared reasonable that at the margin the discrepancy between use value and exchange value would disappear, the "mechanics" of margin could be taken to other spheres as well – exchange, for instance. The exchange phenomenon could be thought of as a case where a utility or satisfaction-maximizing consumer and a profit-maximizing producer would reach equilibrium at the *margin*, which would simultaneously determine the quantity exchanged and the price. The precision that the procedure indicated seemed to be a revolutionary step, making economics a "scientific" discipline. It could be taken further. Karl Menger, the second of the pioneers of neo-classical economics, argued that production could be interpreted in the same manner. He stated that the means of production (including labour power) came to have economic significance only to the extent that they also yielded consumers' satisfaction, though only indirectly, by helping to produce things that consumers wanted. Consequently, wages too could be interpreted as equivalent to the marginal contribution of labour to production.

It took a while for economists to grasp the significance of the integration of the discipline that the marginal analysis claimed to have brought about. In the middle of the twentieth century, Joseph Schumpeter, one of the most outstanding economists of that period, claimed it to be quite revolutionary. He stated that the significance of the analysis was that the marginal utility principle brought the three divisions of economics – consumption, production and distribution, which so far had been treated in isolation as distinct topics – together under a single principle. "The whole of the organon of pure economics thus finds itself unified in the light of a single principle," he claimed, "in a sense in which it never had been before." What was striking about this unification was the primacy it gave to the consumer, who, through the expression of her or his choices in the market, was also making all other crucial economic decisions, including decisions as to what gets produced and how (the value of) output gets distributed among cooperating agents. The claim was that a market economy based on independent choices of individual consumers had a scientific basis to it.

Leon Walras, an engineer-turned-economist and the third among the neo-classical pioneers, gave a more systematic account of exchange activity. In his *Elements of Pure Economics*, he announced that his aim was to convert economics into a "physico-mathematical science" to demonstrate the working of the economic system. It is important to understand the method he adopted, partly because it is the strength of neo-classical economics, but also because it is the failure to grasp this method that leads to illicit policy recommendations, as will be shown later. Referring to the physical sciences, Walras stated: "From real-type concepts, these sciences abstract ideal-type concepts which they define, and then on the basis of these definitions they construct a priori the whole framework of their theorems and proofs. After that they go back to experience not to confirm but to apply their conclusions." Walras's attempt was to produce a science of "pure economics" similar in nature to geometry, which, though based on abstract concepts removed from real life, has very wide and fruitful applications in real life situations.

On this basis, Walras moved on to construct the pure science of economics, which, he claimed, was "the theory of the determination of prices under a hypothetical regime of perfectly free competition." And although the theory was expounded in terms of very high-level mathematics of his day, and, consequently, remained unrecognized for several years, Walras gave an exposition of it in simple prose:

> Let us imagine a market in which only consumers' goods and services are bought and sold. . . . Once the prices or the ratios of exchange of all these goods and services have been cried at random in terms of one of them selected as *numeraire*, each party to the exchange will offer at these prices those goods or services of which he thinks he has relatively too much, and he will demand those articles or services of which he has relatively too little for his consumption during a certain period of time. The quantities of each thing effectively demanded and offered having been determined in this way,

the prices of those things for which the demand exceeds the offer will rise, and the prices of those things of which the offer exceeds the demand will fall. New prices having now been cried, each party to the exchange will offer and demand new quantities. And again prices will rise or fall until the demand and the offer of each good and each service are equal. Then the prices will be current equilibrium prices and exchange will effectively take place.

Though the procedure might appear to be spontaneous, Walras brought in an auctioneer who did not participate in the bidding, but had the power to cancel all bids till equilibrium was reached. He then went on to show that production – the sale of productive forces by landlords, workers and capitalists to entrepreneurs – could also be analysed in this manner. The economy was nothing more than all these separate but interrelated and self-adjusting markets. This depiction of the economy as a simultaneously determined general equilibrium has been the crux of neo-classical analysis, on which more sophisticated and mathematically advanced work has been done from the mid-twentieth century and for which many of the scholars concerned received Nobel Prizes subsequently. However, the aura that the theory thus came to have at one time has been considerably eroded by more recent work.

But propagandists still maintain that it has been "scientifically" established that the self-adjusting market economy is the best economic order. Hence it may be helpful to take a closer look at some aspects of Walras's method. Walras started *Elements of Pure Economics* by stating that, in the broadest sense, economics was concerned with social wealth. He defined social wealth as all things material and immaterial that are scarce – i.e. useful on the one hand, and limited in quantity on the other. Useful things in limited quantity are appropriable. Appropriable things are exchangeable. Useful things limited in quantity are assigned value by exchange. Hence it was concluded that social wealth was the sum of value assigned to useful things limited in quantity through exchange. This was the universe (of discourse) with which Walras was primarily concerned. He recognized two other universes: one of production or industry, where the multiplication of useful things limited in quantity took place, and the universe of property, which dealt with the appropriation of such things. *He warned against the tendency to study all universes simultaneously and decided to leave out (abstract from) the universe of production and the universe of property, and to concentrate on the universe of exchange, which, according to him, had not received enough attention.* In other words, there is no one-to-one correspondence between a simplified theoretical model and the complex real-life situations it tries to analyse. It is the failure to recognize this distinction that leads to application of theoretical derivations directly into policy formulation in real-life situations. It results from the gulf that develops when academics who work on theory get isolated from real-life issues, and policy-makers and propagandists take conclusions from theoretical work directly into their sphere of activity. This is the most charitable explanation that can be given to the widespread phenomenon of selectively using conclusions from theoretical work as principles on which to base policies. The best remedy is to develop a procedure to understand real-life issues and institutions via an approach that may be described as *analytical description*. This is attempted in the next section.

The Market Economy: A Reality Check

To move to an understanding of how markets in real life function, a couple of observations about Walras's theory may be helpful. The first is to note that exchange as Walras depicts establishes only relative prices or exchange ratios. There is the suggestion that any one of the goods may be selected in terms of which relative prices can be converted into absolute prices. In real life, however, generalized exchange is possible only if there is a medium of exchange backed by a commonly recognized authority and hence is commonly accepted. That is the role that money performs in real life and the authority backing it is the state.

Secondly, the moneyless exchange that Walras expounds is basically barter, where owners of goods meet other owners of goods and a one-time exchange takes place that simultaneously determines the quantity exchanged and a rate of exchange that holds good only for that one instance. Markets, on the other hand, refer to multiple transactions, generally mediated through specialists in transactions, merchants. To put it differently, what Walras has expounded *is a theory of exchange, but not a theory of markets.* Markets are activities mediated through money and merchants, and the neglect of intermediation, therefore, makes Walras's analysis of limited relevance to real-life situations.

Once it is recognized that the market is essentially an institution of intermediation, it will be noted too that one of its main parties is rarely the producer but a seller, and that the second party need not be the consumer, but a buyer or customer who may soon play the role of a seller. The market must then be viewed as an interactive chain of sellers and buyers or customers. This understanding of the market has many significant implications.

The depiction of the market as an interactive chain was analytically brought out by Marx. Using C to stand for commodities and M for money,

Marx first drew a distinction between barter and generalized exchange. He represented barter as a C–C transaction, where two parties who are both owners of commodities enter into a bargain for exchanging a quantity of what one owns for what one desires. If the bargain results in an exchange, it will reflect a rate of exchange between the two commodities – but only for that transaction, one that is "extinguished" the moment it is over. Even if the same two parties transact the same two goods subsequently, it is not necessary that the previous exchange rate will prevail. In other words, unlike Walras, Marx did not hold that barter forms the basis for the emergence of a price system. Understood in this sense, barter is not a mere relic of the past. A great deal of barter takes place even today, not only between individuals but between countries as well (as, for instance, when a country exchanges copper for military ware). What is important to note is that both parties are simultaneously a seller and a buyer. Whether barter constitutes a "market" is questionable; it is more appropriately described as exchange of use values between two parties which calls for a "double coincidence" of needs.

If money and merchants are necessary for the functioning of real-life markets, it is important to understand the role that these two intermediaries play. Let us start with the merchant, the active intermediary. The merchant first buys a commodity either from a producer or a seller, perhaps stores it, and then sells it to another who may be, but need not be the final consumer, but a buyer who in turn may become a seller, i.e. another merchant. This set of relationships is best represented by going back to Marx. Marx depicted the process as M–C–M: the merchant first buys a commodity using money and then sells it for money. But since money is a quantity without qualitative features unlike the commodity C, the second M cannot be the same as the first one; it must show a *quantitative* difference, an increase represented by ΔM. Transactions involving the merchant, therefore, become M-C-M', with M' standing for M with ΔM added. To put it somewhat crudely, the merchant enters into exchange transactions to make money, more than what s/he starts out with. This is the case whether the merchant is the street vendor who brings vegetables and fruits to one's door, a corner shopkeeper, a departmental store, or even a huge global retail chain. It means that markets, merchants and money form a triad such that no one of the trio can be understood without the other two. Thus, while Walras and other theorists have the right to abstract from what they consider inessential (leaving out merchants from an exposition of the market, for instance), no one whose interest is in understanding how markets actually function can afford that luxury. The twentieth-century British economist John Hicks, in his *A Theory of Economic History*, emphatically states that it was specialization in trade by merchants that marked the beginning of the market economy.

Hence, it is important to understand the role of the merchant to get to know the working of the market and the nature of the market economy. A major function of a merchant is to store goods so that consumers do not have to spend time and effort to trace the producers of the goods they require. The merchant decides what to store from his knowledge of the requirements, as also the tastes and preferences, of potential buyers. In this sense, the merchant not only stores goods but information too. It will not be surprising, then, that the merchant uses the information that he has to his own advantage. In this we see something of a clash between neo-classical theory and real-life situations. A basic premise of neo-classical theory is that information is free, and is available equally to all participants in the system, producers as well as consumers. However, it does not take much effort to know that real-life economies, markets in particular, are characterized by *asymmetry of information.* It is one of the ironies of academic life that the economists who were awarded the Nobel Prize at the dawn of the present century were selected for discovering that asymmetry of information was indeed the characteristic of economic life, and that one of them received enlightenment during the period he spent in India!

Another recent theoretical finding to which Indian economists have made a major contribution is that real-life markets frequently are "interlocked," that is, not acting according to conventional theories of exchange, where the market for each good is treated as independent, in the sense that the buying and selling of each good must be treated as a function of its own price and nothing else. But look at buying and selling from the point of view of the merchant. She is in competition with others in the market, and will succeed only to the extent that one way or the other, she carves out a market of her own. Tying up different markets (getting farmers to buy fertilizers and to sell the output only to her, convincing them that she is offering a special deal, but without any of them knowing the details of her deals with others in the loop) is a standard strategy of merchants and is closely associated with asymmetry of information.

There is a further, related aspect of the strategy of merchants, and therefore a characteristic of real-life markets. It is well-known that markets tend to expand, and this has been recognized by classical writers such as Adam Smith and Karl Marx as well as contemporary writers like John Hicks, and can be seen to be related to the merchants' eagerness to make more money through trade. However, merchants will also be trying simultaneously to carve out markets of their own. There are different ways of achieving this objective. The familiar vegetable vendors may claim a particular street or a specified spot near a junction as their territory. The corner shopkeeper may cultivate clients by offering to have goods delivered at their residence or by allowing them to make payments once a month, instead of with each purchase. Big intermediaries have their own brand names that customers get used to. The idea is to get a set of attached customers, thereby making a protected market, something that provides an element of monopoly power. Product differentiation, real or visual, assisted by advertising plays an important role in this process. Real-life markets, therefore, have features of competition and monopoly, resulting in monopolistic competition, rather than the perfect, or at least free, competition that theoretical models assume. A major consequence of this process is that real-life markets always tend to expand (resulting from the relatively easy entry of new merchants who create new markets) and get differentiated or segmented (as a result of each merchant's effort to establish a protected market). While, as already mentioned above, the expansion of markets has been recognized from very early days, segmentation of markets has received recognition only in the immediate past. But the two have seldom been seen as happening simultaneously, resulting from the activities of merchants. A special kind of segmentation deserves some attention. It is a kind of natural segmentation based on the income (or purchasing power) of the customers. This is seen prominently in the case of hotels, where the segmentation is officially recognized by the "star" status, but is indeed very widespread in the spheres of entertainment, transportation, medical care and even education. This may be recognized as a vertical segmentation of markets.

A crucial aspect of markets, though not adequately appreciated, is that every market transaction is *a transfer of ownership*. It is obvious in the case of the vegetable seller: when you buy a vegetable, the ownership passes on to you. The same is true of all who sell, for the simple reason that only what is *owned* can be alienated. If so, the merchant can be thought of as one who specializes in transferring ownership, and the ΔM that he makes can be considered as this important service rendered. It also means that the market must be thought of as a place of constant juggling of ownership, perpetually in motion, never in a state of equilibrium!

It is important also to understand the function of money in relation to the market. No one will question the role that money plays as a means of payment, although theoreticians like Walras may claim that the basic role of money is to express *relative* values (for which any one of the goods in exchange may be selected). There was a period when precious metals such as gold or silver formed the basis of money, and so it was considered that the selected metal was used as money because of its intrinsic value. Paradoxical as it may appear, the most successful means of money for purposes of transaction is money that is intrinsically worthless, paper money, or even paperless money. It may appear strange that what is worthless or has no value in itself measures the worth of everything else. The fact is that what is worthless becomes the means to settle claims, ownership claims to be more explicit, because it is backed by authority. A piece of paper becomes money because it is guaranteed by the state (or its designated representative like the central bank): "I promise to pay the bearer the sum of . . .," which is seen on all currency notes. This is a fact that those who propagate the claim that the market functions on the basis of the "invisible hand" of self-interest overlook or deliberately hide. Or, if there is an invisible hand underlying the market, it is that of the state.

The financial market deserves special treatment especially because during the past three decades or so, it has been the most widely discussed real-life market (frequently referred to as "the Market") probably throughout the globe. Financial markets are closely related to banking, which not only handles credit, but also creates credit in the economy. The scope of finance is broader as it also includes stocks, the claims to ownership of companies or corporations. Finance as a separate category emerged in Europe and the United States in the early part of the twentieth century, institutionally known as investment banks which helped companies to raise funds for investment purposes. When companies issued shares, these banks also helped in selling such shares to the public. Subsequently, they started transactions in bonds issued by governments as well. But the phenomenal growth of finance is relatively new, going back to the early 1980s, again based on the operation of banks. When a bank makes a loan available to an individual or a company, it takes over an asset as collateral from the person or company to secure the loan. The rapid advance of finance is associated with the activity of investment banks to take over the collateral documents from banks, repackaging them (according to the interest receivable and duration primarily) and selling to those who have funds such "derivatives' named as collateralized debt obligations (CDOs). Soon CDOs of higher orders, such as CDO-squared, also appeared. Each one of these had a high degree of risk associated with it, but as long as there were individuals or institutions willing to purchase them and sell them, it was generally a profitable activity. Thus, finance became a profitable trading activity, a prestigious segment of real-life markets. It also appeared to be "self-regulating," with many individuals, corporations and institutions making profits (and becoming wealthy) through market operations, without any intervention from external agents such as the state. It has been estimated that in the United States, the ratio of financial assets to GDP (gross domestic product) was between 400 to 500 per cent immediately prior to the 1980s, but reached 900 per cent by the early 2000s. And, of course, it kept on rising till the collapse in 2008. It was not a coincidence that the revival of propaganda favouring the "free market" and the greater efficiency of the market economy happened during this period. Immediately following the crash of even some of the big concerns that claimed to be too big to fail, it became evident even to non-professionals that it was the quite visible hand of the state that bailed out the financial sector and prevented a calamity similar to that of the Great Depression of the 1930s. Apart from the unavoidable ups and downs that they caused, the financial markets are important because it is there that the role of intermediation and asymmetry of information come out most clearly.

In the discussion so far there has been no reference to the link between trade and production, although markets are usually considered as the link between the producer and the consumer. Historically, production and trade were possibly independent activities: the former local and the latter across territories. Production was either for consumption or on the basis of orders placed by those who desired a particular product. But with what may be described as large-scale (industrial) production, a new and close association between the producer and the trader has been established. Large-scale production, of course, is meant for the market. The producer, motivated by profit, realizes that profit only after the merchant (also motivated by profit) takes the product, finds the buyer and sells it. The common pursuit of profit leads to a mutuality in their relationship. In the early days of large-scale production, the producer probably had the upper hand. However, traders also have ways of scaling up their activity (recall that the early joint-stock companies were those of traders) and so there has been a changing scenario. Shrewd merchants had ways of marketing products made by small producers in their name, and thus capturing markets and growing big. We are now in a stage where the market is controlled by the big distributors, for instance, Walmart and Amazon and others globally, and Reliance, Spencers and similar big names in our country. The multinational corporations (MNCs) combined production and trade, but the trend currently appears to be for producers, distributors, bankers and others to focus their activities on the finance sector in spite of the problems recently experienced in that segment. What counts today is being big and being global (that is what finance does), with the assurance that the big will not be let down by the state – the Wall Street–Washington alliance or the Dalal Street–Delhi alliance!

Some Broader Issues

The ideological support that neo-classical economics provides to markets in the abstract and the reasons for its resurgence in the second half of the twentieth century have already been noted. The basis of this phenomenon was a series of studies done on general equilibrium during that period. These studies revived the Walrasian approach and built on it with greater mathematical rigour. Two scholars who had made significant contributions to these studies stated in one of their studies:

> The immediate common sense answer to the question, "What will an economy motivated by individual greed and controlled by a very large number of different agents look like," is probably: "There will be chaos." That quite a different answer has long claimed to be true and has indeed permeated the economic thinking of a large number of people who are in no way economists is itself a sufficient ground for investigating it seriously.

Following their studies in which they had also pointed out some major limitations of the general equilibrium theory, there was a lively debate about the validity and applicability of the theory. One of the issues that emerged is worth recalling.

Joan Robinson, the British economist whom many academics in India knew personally, compared general equilibrium analysis, especially of the Walrasian model, to a prisoner-of-war (POW) camp. The men are kept alive by official rations, but occasionally receive gift parcels from the Red Cross. The contents of the parcels are not tailored to the tastes of individual recipients, so that it is possible for each one to gain by swapping what he wants less for what he wants more. The camp official takes the role of the auctioneer and announces exchange ratios in terms of one of the goods picked from the parcels, and let the prisoners enter into exchange contracts. However, the contracts are valid only if at the announced prices the amount offered of each good is equal to the demand for it. If not, the entire contract is cancelled and the game starts again, and is played till the two conditions are simultaneously satisfied: viz., the announced prices lead to satisfactory contracts for all participants, and at these prices in all markets quantities supplied and demanded are matched.

The comparison of the "free" market economy with a POW camp experience may not be fair. But it brings out an important issue: the initial endowments of participants. Walras had recognized this, and took the commodities that the participants bring to the market as their endowments. Any endowment beyond that (property, for instance) he considered to be extraneous to the exercise with respect to the determination of prices. But some initial endowment for the survival of each of the participants was required for the model to become robust. In the revival of general equilibrium analysis in the second half of the twentieth century, this point was again examined as "the survival problem." One of the participants frankly stated that "the hardest part of the specification of the model is to make sure that each consumer can both survive and participate in the market, without anticipating in the postulates what specific prices will prevail in equilibrium." Among the alternatives that he put forward was what he had described as the "hard-boiled" one, "to assume instantaneous elimination by starvation of those whose resources prove insufficient for survival." Perhaps because it appeared to be too cruel, he settled for a softer alternative and stated that the model "would be found best suited for describing a society of self-sufficient farmers who do a little trading on the side." This confession calls into question the claim that neo-classical theory is applicable to problems of resource allocation in any part of the world. With special reference to India and its alleged problem of "surplus labour" it has been shown also that the critical issue is not the availability of resources as such, but their *distribution among the participants* – an issue that neo-classical theory has chosen to ignore.

These considerations have a bearing on a proper understanding of the nature of the market and of the market economy. Entry into the market is not "free," as is frequently made out by its apologists. Granted that resource power via demand is the driving force of the market, entry into the market is strictly limited to those who have something for which there is demand, i.e. something that they can sell. Most people enter the market with money that they have acquired by selling their services, for instance. In many situations, such as in our country, there are large numbers of people whose only resource, their labour power, is not in demand and hence they are *excluded* from the market. In the meanwhile, those who have money power use the market not only to get what they are able to command, but also to augment their money power further. It is becoming quite visible that market transactions and manipulations, especially in the financial markets, are quicker means of acquiring wealth than productive activity. The performance of the financial market is being accepted as the best index of wealth and welfare even at the national level. That such reliance on markets is leading to growing inequalities in wealth in practically all countries of the globe – the gulf between the haves and the have-nots – is now well-established. Those who propagate the ideology of the market economy either choose to ignore this fact or explain it away as the price to be paid for progress.

I am happy to join other contributors of this volume to honour N. Ram. I have known him for close to fifty years, first as a young cricket enthusiast. In the 1970s, I cooperated with him in bringing out *The Hindu*'s innovative "Open Page," which had, in its first issue, a discussion by a few economists on "Development: Where do we go from here and how?" Ram also invited me to become a regular contributor to *Frontline*, which I continue to be even today. In the 1990s, when Chennai experienced communal tensions, the late Sarvepalli Gopal, Ram and I took the initiative to start "Citizens for a Secular Society." Subsequently, the Nawab of Arcot, Ram and I formed "Harmony India," which still continues to be active. I have been a great admirer of Ram's passionate and principled commitments to secular values, freedom of the press and public issues in general. I wish him many more years of continued leadership in shaping public opinion in our country and beyond.

Note

1 This is a simplified and rearranged version of the Founder's Day Lecture delivered at the Madras Institute of Development Studies (MIDS), Chennai, on 18 April 2015.

A Critique of Economics as a Discipline
Prabhat Patnaik

Lack of objectivity, whether in journalistic reportage or in academic research, is commonly attributed to bad faith on the part of the practitioner concerned. There is, however, an additional powerful reason for it which affects even the most sincere and honest practitioners, and this has to do with the "discourse" within which they are trapped and which, for a variety of reasons (including, but not necessarily, ideological ones), draws conclusions about an *entire* universe while confining attention to only *a part of it*. The discipline of economics has been permeated by a lack of objectivity in this sense, and I can do no better in my tribute to Ram than to illustrate this phenomenon.

I

The discipline of economics of course has been much critiqued. There have been methodological objections to the founding of the discipline on the concept of an optimizing individual (individual consumer or individual wealth-holder or individual firm), i.e. to treating economics as a mere branch of "praxiology."[1] There have been objections to the ignoring of the concept of class, such as what classical political economy had dealt with, even though it *had* recognized "rational" behaviour on the part of the individual while treating that individual as belonging to a larger group. There have been objections to the acceptance on the part of the discipline of the premise that the system it studies, viz. capitalism, is always characterized by full capacity output (as in Ricardo) if not also full employment (as in the neo-classical system) – i.e. to the discipline's pervasive acceptance of Say's Law and hence the absence of any demand constraint, without which all welfare propositions regarding the functioning of markets, including those relating to the benefits of trade, would collapse. There have been criticisms more generally of its ignoring power relations in society, and thereby making an unsustainable distinction between the realm of the economic and the realm of the political, as if the latter, which is a key constituent of social power, did not have any economic implications.[2] And there have been criticisms of its complete ignoring of history, and of treating the categories that we observe as if they are immutable categories that emerged fully formed, like

Minerva from the head of Zeus, instead of being historically generated and hence being in different stages of formation in different societies.

The fact that I propose to produce a somewhat different critique of the discipline of economics here, distinct from all these criticisms, does not mean that I disagree with them; on the contrary, I believe that these criticisms are both powerful and weighty. But the critique I attempt here concerns an aspect of the discipline that scarcely ever gets discussed. *Economics, I argue below, focuses only on a part of the universe it purports to study, mistaking that part for the whole.*

II

The universe of the study of economics, as already mentioned, has always been, from the time of William Petty and Adam Smith until now, the capitalist system. True, the Marxian tradition, which takes political economy to be *a historical science*, sees its scope as being much wider: as a study of the laws governing production and distribution *under different social formations*, such as slavery, feudalism and capitalism, but not capitalism alone (Engels 1947). It views the discipline, for instance, as consisting of a political economy of feudalism and a political economy of slavery, in addition to the usual political economy of capitalism. But even though the subject matter of the discipline is much wider than is commonly supposed, the fact remains that the discipline as it has developed until now has been almost exclusively concerned with an analysis of capitalism. In discussing the discipline, therefore, I shall take capitalism as its subject matter. And here it is worth starting with the perception of Keynes.

In the last chapter of his *General Theory*, Keynes had remarked: "It is certain that the world will not much longer tolerate the unemployment which, apart from brief intervals of excitement, is associated – and in my opinion inevitably associated – with present-day capitalistic individualism" (Keynes 1949: 381). The unemployment that he was talking about is not the unemployment that exists when there is full utilization of the available equipment, or what is called "technological unemployment." Nor is it the unemployment that is captured by the Marxian concept of the "reserve army of labour" (which, though Goodwin [1967] defines it as the unemployment that exists when there is full capacity production, need not be so defined, and should refer, strictly speaking, to the level of unemployment at which what Joan Robinson [1956] had called the "inflationary barrier" comes into effect). What Keynes was talking about is unemployment over and above what constitutes the "reserve army of labour": it is associated with a deficiency of aggregate demand. It is what one would call today "Keynesian unemployment," which goes together with unutilized capacity as well. Keynes, in short, saw unemployment and unutilized capacity as the average state of affairs under capitalism.

But if, as stands to reason, investment is influenced by the degree of capacity utilization, then the existence of unutilized capacity as the average state of affairs under capitalism must mean low investment, and hence a state of quasi-stagnation.[3] Implicit in Keynes' perception, therefore, is a characterization of capitalism as a system which on average is mired in quasi-stagnation, broken occasionally by booms, which are "intervals of excitement" but necessarily brief and fragile, and hence collapse on their own.

This view of capitalism as a system characterized on average by quasi-stagnation contrasts, however, with what Keynes says elsewhere in his writings, such as "Economic Possibilities for Our Grandchildren" (1930) and his pathbreaking work, *The Economic Consequences of the Peace* (1919). In these writings he emphasizes the enormous development that the system brings about. In the first of these, in fact, he even visualizes the "economic problem" as we know it to have hitherto afflicted mankind, to disappear within a short span of time. How do we reconcile Keynes' view of capitalism as a system that is characterized on average by quasi-stagnation, with his recognition of the enormous potential for material development that it not only possesses but has actually displayed through its history?

The answer, in my view, lies in the fact that while Keynes sees the system *in its spontaneity* as being subject to a perennial state of quasi-stagnation on average, he sees its potential unfolding when there are some "external props" for it. In other words, Keynes sees capitalism as a system that needs "external props" to get out of the state of quasi-stagnation within which its *spontaneous working* traps it. For its dynamism, the system cannot do without "external props."

This is in fact the way Joseph Schumpeter (1952), a contemporary of Keynes, had interpreted him. Schumpeter had seen *The Economic Consequences of the Peace* as suggesting that the long period of late Victorian and Edwardian boom enjoyed by capitalism because of the external prop of "an expanding frontier" in the temperate regions of new white settlement was coming to an end, and that capitalism needed a new external prop which, as *General Theory* was to analytically demonstrate later, could only be provided by state intervention in demand management. Keynes' remark quoted above, about the world being unwilling to tolerate much longer the unemployment associated with capitalistic individualism, must then be seen as a reference to what capitalism looks like in the absence of "external props," such as was historically the case in the long inter-war period when Keynes was writing, and hence a desperate plea to adopt the external prop that he was recommending, viz. state intervention in demand management.

There are two important implications of Keynes' position that need to be emphasized. The first is that the "brief intervals of excitement" that are based on "euphoric expectations," and which constitute what these days are widely referred to as "bubbles," are not *an aberration in the functioning of financial markets*. They are not an *avoidable* feature of capitalism that arises only because of some mistakes or exceptional circumstances; they actually constitute the very *modus operandi* of the system. This is the way the system experiences booms, and if they are eliminated, then the booms too would get eliminated. The state of "quasi-stagnation," instead of being an *average* state of affairs of capitalism in its "spontaneity," would then become a *permanent* state of affairs where the economy would be stuck forever.

This is a point that is almost invariably lost sight of, especially in the context of the present (post-2008) crisis. Indeed, the idea of the housing "bubble" being a result of "mistakes" of the US Federal Reserve (Fed), of its chairman at the time, Alan Greenspan, or an outcome of the behaviour of banks consumed with excessive "greed" to the point where they started giving "sub-prime" loans, *in the absence of which the system would have performed satisfactorily*, has been very assiduously cultivated and imbibed. Hence, it is worth emphasizing that in the absence of such a "bubble" under the present economic dispensation, there would have been no boom in the first place (Patnaik 2010). *"Bubbles," to repeat, are the system's modus operandi.*

The Cambridge economist and Keynes' younger contemporary, Dennis Robertson, was well aware of this fact, but had a different suggestion to make: namely, that euphoric expectations, and the booms generated by them, should be curtailed deliberately through monetary policy so that the ensuing slump is prevented; i.e. that the aim of monetary policy should be to maintain a *stable though lower* level of employment rather than anything close to full employment. Reacting to Robertson's suggestion, Keynes (1949: 327) made three points. The first is that even if monetary policy tried to restrain the boom, it might not always succeed in the face of the euphoria. For instance, in his own words,

> the most enlightened monetary control might find itself in difficulties, faced with a boom of the 1929 type in America and armed with no other weapons than those possessed at the time by the Federal Reserve System; and none of the alternatives within its power might make much difference to the result.

The second point is that by *aiming at* a stable but low level of employment, "such an outlook seems to me to be dangerously and unnecessarily defeatist. It recommends, or at least assumes, for permanent acceptance too much that is defective in our economic system." And the third point is that even on its own, i.e. "ruling out major changes of policy affecting either the control of investment or the propensity to consume," the "quasi-stagnation" that would result from eliminating the boom would not necessarily entail any higher level of activity than the average state of "quasi-stagnation" through booms and slumps, i.e. when booms and slumps are not eliminated.

The second implication of Keynes' perception of capitalism is what particularly concerns us here, which is that capitalism is essentially an *incomplete system*, in the sense that it requires external props for functioning adequately. Keynes does not put it in these words, but it is clear from his remarks.

The terms "system" and "external props" which I have been using while interpreting Keynes need to be defined properly here. By the term "system" I mean a universe where there are workers, capitalists and a set of markets, for commodities, for labour power, for assets, and for direct and indirect claims upon assets (which is what financial markets amount to). It is this *isolated* capitalist system existing in its pristine purity, *which is the universe of study of the discipline of economics*, that is incomplete. What it needs is "external props" in the form, above all, of possibilities of encroachment into pre-capitalist sectors, including geographical expansion into these sectors, and of state expenditure. The capitalist state, in other words, is seen here as an external prop and not as a part of the economic system proper. True, a capitalist economy cannot exist without a capitalist state, which provides "law and order" and ensures that the "rules of the game" are followed; and for these activities, state expenditure needs to be undertaken, which in turn has to be financed by state taxation. *But any activity on the part of the state over and above this, i.e. any activity that stimulates consciously or unconsciously the level of aggregate demand, constitutes for the system an "external prop."* And my reading of Keynes is that he saw the system as always requiring such "external props" for its dynamism.

III

Michal Kalecki, who had independently discovered the "General Theory," was even more explicit about the necessity for external props. He of course did not talk of external props, but suggested a distinction between what Nicholas Kaldor (e.g. Kaldor–Mirrlees 1962) was later to call "exogenous" and "endogenous" stimuli. "Endogenous stimuli" are those stimuli for investment which arise *because the system has been growing*. The discipline of economics has recognized the operation of "endogenous stimuli" when it has postulated that investment is determined by the accelerator principle or by the capital stock adjustment principle, and so on. What investment behaviour postulated in this manner suggests is that when an economy is subject to growth, it continues to grow: investment occurs when output is increasing; in a growing economy investment too keeps growing, which in turn makes output grow and thereby sustains the growth process.

But precisely because growth here is predicated upon the fact that it has been already occurring, i.e. precisely because growth tends to be self-perpetuating, *the absence of growth too would be self-perpetuating*. If the economy for some reason is not growing, i.e. if it is stuck in a "stationary state," then there is no reason for anyone to undertake positive net investment, in which case the level of gross investment would be no higher than the replacement of capital stock, and hence the economy would continue to remain stuck in the "stationary state." Indeed Kalecki (1962) argued that with "endogenous stimuli" alone, the stable trend for a capitalist economy is a zero trend, i.e. a "stationary state." *What lifts a capitalist economy out of a "stationary state" is the existence of "exogenous stimuli" which cause some additional net investment over and above what "endogenous stimuli" alone would warrant*. In fact "exogenous stimuli" are defined as those stimuli that cause any additional investment over and above what the "endogenous stimuli" would warrant.[4]

Such exogenous stimuli, according to Kalecki, include – apart from state expenditure and incursions into pre-capitalist economies – "innovations" that generate investment because each entrepreneur wants to be the first to introduce it (Kalecki 1968). We do know from economic historians like Arthur Lewis (1978), however, that the introduction of innovations is not independent of market conditions, which is why during the Great Depression of the 1930s, a whole range of innovations remained unintroduced. Innovations, if they themselves depend upon the state of the market, i.e. if their introduction itself is predicated upon the prospects of an expanding market, cannot act as genuine "exogenous stimuli." They get introduced only when the market itself expands but not otherwise; and in such a case, they *cannot prevent the economy from settling into a stationary state*. They are, in other words, no different from "endogenous stimuli."

This idea has been theoretically developed by a host of writers from Josef Steindl (1952) to Joan Robinson (1956) to Baran and Sweezy (1966). The argument goes as follows: in markets dominated by oligopolists (which is true of most markets), where price has to be lowered to increase sales, the undertaking of additional investment for the introduction of an innovation can lead in actuality to a larger market share, and hence to a recouping of the additional investment (over and above what the "endogenous stimuli" would warrant), only if the entrepreneur introducing it can lower prices without retaliation from rivals. But the very nature of oligopoly implies that even those rivals who have not introduced the innovation have the capacity to lower prices to prevent losing their market share, and would do so, which means that a price war would be unleashed to the detriment of all. Since nobody would be interested in starting a price war, even those having access to the innovation would *not* increase investment over and above what the endogenous stimuli would warrant. The investment warranted by the endogenous stimuli would only take the *form* of the new process or product, but there would be no *additional* investment. And in such a case, innovations cease to be authentic "exogenous stimuli"; they cease to call forth any more investment than what the endogenous stimuli alone would warrant.

While this argument, endorsed alike by economic historians and economic theorists, has weight, there may be some innovations, especially those which, in the words of Baran and Sweezy, are "epoch-making innovations," such as the railways or the automobile, in whose case it might not apply. They would constitute genuine "exogenous stimuli," but only they and not the normal run of innovations. It is of course a moot point to what extent even epoch-making innovations constitute a genuine exception: the innovation of the automobile, which had occurred earlier, after all neither prevented the Great Depression of the 1930s nor caused a quick recovery from it; the recovery came only with the armaments drive in preparation for the Second World War. But let us accept the argument that epoch-making innovations constitute genuine exogenous stimuli. It follows then that *other than such epoch-making innovations*, it is only incursions into pre-capitalist markets and state expenditure that constitute the "external props" for capitalism. Or, put differently, capitalism cannot do without "external props" in the form of either "epoch-making innovations," which by their very nature are few and far between, or state expenditure, or incursions into pre-capitalist markets. *It is thus an incomplete system, in the sense that its dynamics come not from within ("endogenous stimuli") but from "external props" of the sort we have been discussing.*

Kalecki's own argument had a resemblance to the argument put forward by Rosa Luxemburg in 1914 in her work, *The Accumulation of Capital*. This is hardly surprising since, within the Marxist tradition, and contrary to the mainstream of the Marxist tradition, it was Rosa Luxemburg who had for the first time recognized the possibility, which was later to be theorized rigorously by Kalecki and Keynes as part of the Kaleckian–Keynesian revolution, of capitalism being characterized by a state of perennial demand deficiency, i.e. of capitalism being a demand-constrained system. In terms of the conceptual framework of the Marxist tradition, she had visualized the possibility of a state of permanent (*ex ante*) generalized overproduction. Indeed, Nikolai Bukharin (1972) had criticized Rosa Luxemburg precisely for suggesting that capitalism, left to its own devices, i.e. in its *spontaneity*, could be afflicted with permanent (*ex ante*) generalized overproduction, as opposed to the temporary generalized overproduction characteristic of periods of crisis. But what Rosa Luxemburg was saying in effect was an anticipation of the perception of Keynes with which I began this essay, namely, that (if we leave aside "external props" which the system in any case lacked during the inter-war period) capitalism is typically characterized on average by both unutilized capacity and involuntary unemployment.

The "incompleteness" of capitalism to which Luxemburg drew attention followed in her case, as it did in the case of Kalecki and Keynes, from recognition of the possibility of a demand constraint under capitalism. It is, in other words, not an independent ascription; nor is it something that follows from some assumption of a specific kind of investment behaviour. It is logically entailed in the very presumption that capitalism is a demand-constrained system. If the system can settle at any level of activity depending upon the state of aggregate demand, then, since the major determinant of aggregate demand is the level of investment itself (because income distribution and hence the magnitude of the "Keynesian multiplier" is independently given, and does not adjust to clear the market – as was, and would be, the case in socialist economies; Kalecki 1954), the behaviour of investment determines the dynamics of the system. And if investment responds to the growth of the market (and is not simply equal in magnitude to "full employment savings"), then it is obvious that in the absence of external props, the system would get stuck with quasi-stagnation or even a state of simple reproduction. The fact that this has not happened in history must then be attributable to the availability of such external props for the system.

The critique of economics as a discipline that I wish to advance in this essay, then, consists in the fact that it has been completely oblivious of the incompleteness of capitalism. It has treated capitalism as a complete system, which spontaneously overcomes any *ex ante* overproduction and perennially maintains full employment (or what virtually comes to the same thing, a "natural rate of unemployment"). It has, in other words, assiduously advanced a set of propositions without any scientific merit, such as: all markets including the labour market "clear", provided that the prices are sufficiently flexible; any observed non-clearance of markets is caused not by the nature of the market system but because prices are not sufficiently flexible; if labour market flexibility is introduced, then the result would be not a collapse of the monetary economy – with no "benchmark" money magnitudes to introduce inelastic price expectations into the system, without which there would be no stability[5] – but rather a perennial state of full employment; and so on. And it has advanced *logically untenable* concepts like the "real balance effect" (Patnaik 2008), invoking the authority of A.C. Pigou, though Pigou himself had disowned the so-called Pigou effect (Robinson 1966) to establish these propositions.

Treating capitalism as a complete system has often been buttressed through an appeal to historical facts which obviously show capitalism as having achieved enormous material advance. Such advance has been used to argue against the position that the spontaneous tendency of the system is on average a state of quasi-stagnation. But this constitutes a complete *non-sequitur* because the system has had access to external props historically.

My critique of economics as a discipline, therefore, amounts to the fact that it has closed its eyes to such external props, *to the phenomenon of imperialism, for instance*, and has therefore mistakenly taken only a part of the picture of the universe it studies as if it represents the entire universe. It has mistakenly believed that the capitalist system, consisting of workers, capitalists and a set of markets, is not ensconced within a larger universe which has provided it with the external props that are necessary for its dynamics.

What is more, every theoretical advance that could open the discipline to the totality of the universe it is supposed to be looking at has been systematically smothered by it. Leave aside Luxemburg and Kalecki, who never managed to attract much attention from mainstream economics anyway, even Keynes has been interpreted in such a way that the central message of his work remains obscured. While the dominant interpretation of Keynes – from the days of Franco Modigliani (1944) right up to Edmond Malinvaud (1977) and the monetarists (who happen to be orthodox Walrasians (Hahn 1984)) – has seen involuntary unemployment as resulting from the rigidity of money wages, even those who are not monetarists and are more sympathetic to Keynes have interpreted him in a completely misleading manner. Paul Krugman (2009), for instance, one of the more progressive Keynes-influenced economists in the United States at present, sees the message of Keynesianism as consisting in its recommendation that fiscal policy may become necessary in a slump. In other words, Keynesian economics is seen even by these Keynes-influenced economists essentially as the economics relevant for an economy caught in the "liquidity trap."

True, they would be opposed to a money wage cut on the grounds that it would cause "deflation" *à la* Irving Fisher (1933) and hence worsen the crisis; but leaving this aside, they would concede a possible logical route via which a positive effect on employment can occur from a money wage cut through a fall in the interest rate caused by a rise in money supply in terms of the wage unit, which of course could as well be brought about through monetary policy rather than a money wage cut. But here their objection to the economics that prescribes an increase in money supply in terms of the wage unit as the recipe for recovery would be that the interest rate might not get lowered in a crisis owing to the economy being caught in a "liquidity trap."

Keynesian economics, even on this sympathetic view, then gets reduced to a minor proposition: not that the capitalist system in its spontaneity is trapped in quasi-stagnation requiring "socialization of investment," as Keynes had suggested, but rather that situations may arise under capitalism from time to time when it gets caught in a "liquidity trap," and on such occasions, the use of fiscal instruments may become necessary. A totality of understanding of the capitalist system, such as what Keynes was advancing, is then presented merely as an argument in favour of a fiscal deficit under certain circumstances. And this obviously prevents the discipline from breaking out of its basic limitation mentioned earlier.

IV

But it may well be asked of me, what is the point of my critique? How does it matter whether we see capitalism as a complete or an incomplete system? What difference does it make? My answer to this question is that if we see capitalism as an incomplete system, then our focus of attention shifts to examining the kinds of external props it has used in the past or can use at present. Our inquiry, in short, takes a different turn altogether.

Keynesian economists like Alvin Hansen (1938) – and even Keynes himself, according to Schumpeter – had seen the "expanding frontier" in the temperate regions of new white settlement as providing the external prop for capitalism through much of the nineteenth century, right until the First World War. This perception, however, is not historically accurate. Even the investment stimulated by the "expanding frontier" would not have been possible without the colonial empire that Britain, the leading capitalist power of the time, possessed. Britain kept its markets open for the newly industrializing countries of the time, including in the "New World" and in continental Europe; if it had not done so and had adopted protectionist measures, then the Gold Standard would have become unsustainable and a "beggar-my-neighbour" policy all round would have set in much earlier than it did, undermining the long boom of the late Victorian and Edwardian era.

British goods, especially textiles, increasingly found a market in the colonies and in semi-colonies like China (Hobsbawm [1969] calls it a "flight to the colonial markets") *at the expense of local craft production*, unleashing a process of "deindustrialization" in the latter. The colonies in turn sold goods, mainly primary commodities, to continental Europe and the "New World," and through such triangular trade the British current account deficit vis-à-vis these latter economies, which were the newly industrializing economies of the time, was settled.

But this, by no means, was all. The colonies did not just settle Britain's current account deficit; their economic surplus was "drained" away *without any quid pro quo* by Britain, which used them for making capital exports to these very economies of continental Europe and the New World (Bagchi 1972). The export surplus of an economy like India vis-à-vis the latter, for instance, did not give India an iota of claim upon them; *it gave Britain claims upon them as a capital exporter* because Britain systematically appropriated this export surplus for itself as part of the process of "drain" emphasized by the Indian nationalist writers (U. Patnaik 2006). *The point, in short, is that the external prop available to capitalism in the entire period until the First World War was built upon the colonial system: the colonies of settlement created at the expense of local inhabitants in the New World, and the colonies of conquest, like India, which played a crucial role in the expansion of the frontier.* The picture was complex, and it differs from both what Rosa Luxemburg had visualized (which meant simply selling in colonial markets) and what Alvin Hansen had visualized (which meant simply exporting capital from Britain to the New World).

This entire edifice became unsustainable after the First World War. The reason for the end of that conjuncture was not just the "closing of the frontier" that Keynesian economists like Hansen emphasized, but also a change in the position of the colonies and semi-colonies which could no longer play the same role as before. Britain's Asian colonies and semi-colonies were encroached upon by Japan, whose relentless export drive undermined the pre-war arrangement for "triangular settlement," which in any case could not have lasted for ever (since the colonial markets would have got exhausted anyway). British attempts to enlist the support of the domestic bourgeoisies in countries like India against Japanese incursion required giving concessions to them in the form of protectionist policies; but these hardly improved matters from Britain's point of view. And the

World Agricultural Crisis which started in 1926, and sharply reduced the export earnings of Britain's colonies and semi-colonies, dealt a final blow to the arrangement (U. Patnaik 2014).

The inter-war period, therefore, was characterized by a situation where the earlier arrangement through which metropolitan capitalism could get an external prop for itself was not sustainable any longer, but no new arrangement could be put in its place. It was an interregnum when capitalism had no external props – which, in my view, constitutes an important explanation for the Great Depression.

The Depression, as already mentioned, came to an end with the preparation for the Second World War: sooner in the fascist countries which started arming themselves earlier, and later in the liberal capitalist countries when they started arming themselves in the run up to the war. And the post-war scenario was marked by a new external prop, namely, state spending, whether for welfare programmes under the aegis of social democracy as in Europe, or in the form of military expenditure as in the United States (whence the term "military Keynesianism").

Finance capital had always been opposed to state spending for a *higher level of activity*, though always favouring state spending *that benefited itself*. This is the reason why in Britain it had opposed Lloyd George's plan in 1929, of which Keynes was the real architect, for state spending on public works to alleviate unemployment. This also explains why, after the initial success of Roosevelt's New Deal, it put pressure, successfully, for a cut-back in public spending, which once more caused a recession in the US in 1937. But in the post-Second World War situation, when capitalism faced domestic working class militancy (Churchill's defeat in the British election was a symptom of this) within an overall ethos of a socialist threat, finance capital, which till then was still nation-based, hardly had any option other than to accept Keynesian demand management by the state. This, by providing a new external prop, unleashed a boom which was of an unprecedented magnitude, and is often referred to as the "Golden Age of Capitalism."

With globalization of finance, however, and hence the formation of an *international finance capital* in lieu of the various national finance capitals, things have changed. This international finance capital can dictate terms to the nation-states. They have little choice but to obey because of the fear of capital flight. "Sound finance," therefore, is once more in vogue (though the fiscal deficit is no longer supposed to be zero, but about 3 per cent of GDP). This in turn puts an end to state activism in demand management, and hence an end to the external prop that had sustained capitalism in the post-war period.

The fact that contemporary capitalism under the hegemony of international finance capital lacks any external props is a matter of great significance. What it means is that it would be characterized by high unemployment, unutilized capacity and quasi-stagnation, barring brief "intervals of excitement" (i.e. the formation of "bubbles"). To break the state of quasi-stagnation, capitalist states would go on making efforts to improve the "state of confidence" of the capitalists, by providing them with "inducements" of various kinds and generally increasing their class power. But since an increase in class power *per se* does not end quasi-stagnation (as investment is basically governed by the growth of markets, of which there are few prospects in the absence of any new external props), the increase in the class power of the capitalists would be a more or less continuous process that nonetheless proves futile for breaking out of stagnation.

This also has major political implications since the framework of democracy would become increasingly incompatible with such continuous growth in class power, leading to efforts on the part of finance capital to attenuate democracy in various ways. In short, capitalism in the contemporary era has come to an impasse which has many serious implications. But these cannot even be discussed by economists, because the discipline of economics to which they belong remains completely and blissfully oblivious of all this.

The idea of this paper was presented earlier at a panel discussion at Columbia University, and at a lecture at Goa University. I wish to thank Akeel Bilgrami, Carol Rovane and Akbar Noman of Columbia, and Silvia Noronha and Pranab Mukhopadhyay of Goa, for helpful discussions.

Notes

1 This issue is discussed in Lange (1963).
2 See Mitra (1977) for a criticism of the subject along these lines.
3 I am asserting this only in a general sense and not on the basis of any rigorous derivation from a model with an investment function. Such a model would be foreign to the spirit of Keynes' remark, and its absence does not invalidate my assertion. A rigorous discussion of these issues, though unrelated to Keynes' remark, may be found in P. Patnaik (1997).
4 For a fuller discussion of this issue, see P. Patnaik (1997).
5 See P. Patnaik (2008) for an elaboration of this argument.

REFERENCES

Bagchi, A.K. (1972), "Some International Foundations of Capitalist Growth and Underdevelopment," *Economic and Political Weekly*, Vol. 7, Nos. 31–33.

Baran, P.A. and P.M. Sweezy (1966), *Monopoly Capital*, New York: Monthly Review Press.

Bukharin, N.I. (1972), "Imperialism and the Accumulation of Capital," in K. Tarbuck, ed., *Imperialism and the Accumulation of Capital*, London: Allen Lane and the Penguin Press.

Engels, F. (1947), *Anti-Duhring*, Moscow: Progress Publishers.

Fisher, I. (1933), "The Debt-Deflation Theory of Great Depressions," *Econometrica*, 1 (4), October.

Goodwin, R.M. (1967), "A Growth Cycle," in C.H. Feinstin, ed., *Capitalism, Socialism and Steady Growth: Essays Presented to Maurice Dobb*, Cambridge: Cambridge University Press.

Hahn, F.H. (1984), *Equilibrium and Macroeconomics*, Oxford: Clarendon Press.

Hansen, A.H. (1938), *Full Recovery or Stagnation?* New York: Norton.

Hobsbawm, E.J. (1969), *Industry and Empire*, Harmondsworth: Penguin.

Kaldor, N. and J.A. Mirrlees (1962), "A New Model of Economic Growth," *Review of Economic Studies*, Vol. 29, No. 3, June.

Kalecki, M. (1954), *The Theory of Economic Dynamics*, London: George Allen and Unwin.

Kalecki, M. (1962), "Observations on the Theory of Growth," *Economic Journal*, Vol. 72, March.

Kalecki, M. (1968), "Trend and Business Cycle Reconsidered," *Economic Journal*, Vol. 78.

Keynes, J.M. (1919), *The Economic Consequences of the Peace*, London: Macmillan.

Keynes, J.M. ([1930] 1963), "Economic Possibilities for Our Grandchildren," in *Essays in Persuasion*, New York: Norton Library.

Keynes, J.M. (1949), *The General Theory of Employment, Interest and Money*, London: Macmillan.

Krugman, P. (2009), "How Did Economists Get It So Wrong?" *New York Times Magazine*, 2 September.

Lange, O. (1963), *Political Economy*, Volume 1, Warsaw: Pergamon Press.

Lewis, W.A. (1978), *Growth and Fluctuations 1870–1913*, London: George Allen and Unwin.

Luxemburg, R. ([1914] 1963), *Accumulation of Capital*, London: Routledge.

Malinvaud, E. (1977), *The Theory of Unemployment Reconsidered*, Oxford: Basil Blackwell.

Mitra, A. (1977), *Terms of Trade and Class Relations*, London: Cass.

Modigliani, F. (1944), "Liquidity Preference and the Theory of Interest and Money," *Econometrica*, Vol. 12.

Patnaik, P. (1997), *Accumulation and Stability under Capitalism*, Oxford: Clarendon Press.

Patnaik, P. (2008), *The Value of Money*, New Delhi: Tulika Books and New York: Columbia University Press, 2009.

Patnaik, P. (2010), "The Myth of the Subprime Crisis," available at www.networkdeas.org, viewed on 5 December 2015.

Patnaik, U. (2006), "The Free Lunch," in K.S. Jomo, ed., *Globalization under Hegemony*, Delhi: Oxford University Press.

Patnaik, U. (2014), "India in the World Economy, 1900 to 1935: The Inter-War Depression and Britain's Demise as World Capitalist Leader," *Social Scientist*, January–February.

Robinson, J. (1956), *The Accumulation of Capital*, London: Macmillan.

Robinson, J. (1966), *Economic Philsophy*, Harmondsworth: Penguin.

Schumpeter, J.A. (1952), "John Maynard Keynes," in *Ten Great Economists*, New York: Oxford University Press.

Steindl, J. (1952), *Maturity and Stagnation in American Capitalism*, Oxford: Basil Blackwell.

Gabriel Selvam: A Biography of Work

V.K. Ramachandran

Among the many things in which N. Ram was an early instructor (and I not good enough a learner) was on how to interview, take notes, edit copy, and present the results from conversation and observation.

NR was the first among us to meet Gabriel Selvam, and the description "upstanding young agricultural labourer" is his.

An Interview in Two Parts, 1977 and 2017

May 1977: Young Bonded Worker

G. Selvam (35) is an upstanding young agricultural labourer who has bonded himself as a *pannaiyal* (permanent farm servant) out of economic necessity. Selvam's family is of the Parayar scheduled caste.

A loan of Rs 100 taken over six years ago from CT, a petty usurer, led directly to his present condition as a farm servant. At that time, the loan was taken for subsistence needs and was perceived as a temporary expedient. On account of a 120 per cent interest rate, the loan of Rs 100 became a liability of Rs 220 over a year. The usurer pressed Selvam, then 31 years old, to sell his house in order to repay the loan. Selvam, refusing to abandon the family house site, went around asking for a way to work off his debt. An opportunity presented itself in the form of the landlord SCC. This landlord, who was looking for a young and strong farm servant, was willing to advance the money to clear the debt, provided Selvam attached himself as a farm servant for a remuneration of Rs 65 per month, plus one sheet, a dhoti, a shirt and a *thundu* (towel-cloth) a year.

Selvam took an advance of Rs 100 for going to work as a farm servant and used that to clear just under half of his debt. Then, after the first month of work, he took a loan of Rs 120 to clear the remaining amount. Since then, that is, for six years, Selvam has been working for well over thirteen hours a day. He worked at a salary of Rs 65 a month for four years. Two years ago, when paddy prices soared to nearly Rs 150 per 58-kilogram bag, the farm servants in the village asked their employers for a raise. Selvam was given a wage rise that was long overdue: in 1977 he was paid Rs 110 a month.

SCC, like some other big landlords in the village, has found it much to his advantage to hire a farm servant in this way. He has advanced small sums of money to Selvam over the years, sums always taken "temporarily," but with no real chance of the debtor repaying the debt and getting out of his present condition. Selvam makes it clear that he is not paid anything near the remuneration he should be getting for his work. "There is no choice," he says, "I can't leave my *mudalali* [employer, landlord] unless I can clear my debt of Rs 300. I would certainly like to leave."

In his childhood, Selvam was not as badly off as he is today. His father, Gabriel, was a poor or lower-middle peasant, cultivating surface-irrigated land that had been leased in from landlords of the village. His mother worked as a hired labourer. His father sent Selvam to school. Selvam studied in the Mission School in Gokilapuram, down the road from where he lives today, up to the fifth class. He completed the sixth class at the NMR School in Gokilapuram. He was a good student and his father sent him to Vatthalakundu, where he studied in the seventh and eighth classes, finishing when he was 16 years old. He stayed at a hostel at Vatthalakundu, and his father sent him Rs 20 a month. Selvam returned to the village after finishing the eighth class. He can read and write Tamil, and can still read some English.

Selvam's father tilled 6 *kuzhi* (3.6 acres) of surface-irrigated land belonging to landlord ST on *kuthagai* (fixed rent) for twenty years. He also worked 1.5 acres of groundwater-irrigated land belonging to SP, a landlord of Uthamapalayam. Selvam worked on the land leased in by the family. He married when he was 20 years old. His wife, Alphonse, is from a family of tenant cultivators from Pudupatti in Uthamapalayam *taluk*.

In about 1967, there was a sharp decline in the agriculture conducted by the family. The surface-irrigated land had poor soil and bad drainage, and standing water after rain affected the crop. The land was manured only for a single crop, one of the reasons for the yield being poor. The groundwater-irrigated land had a well with plenty of water, and a pulley and rope to draw the water with. But household cultivation was in decline, the family began to incur debt, and the age-old symbol of a peasant family heading towards destitution became apparent: the cattle they owned became thin and weak.

About the same time, eviction took place on a large scale in the village. Earlier, the paddy crops were the traditional *parunnel* and *samba* varieties; later, with the introduction of new seeds, yields were higher and agriculture became more profitable for the landlords. There was also fear among them, Selvam said, that the tenants would assert their right to cultivate the land. They brought pressure on the tenants to leave the land. Rents were raised, rack-rents were imposed on them. In some cases, landlords brought great pressure on them, offering the tenants small amounts of money to leave. The peasants were disunited, Selvam said, and out of fear, accepted the money and left the land.

Agricultural Wage Work
Selvam made it clear that big landlords can always bring pressure on agricultural labourers; as for agricultural labourers, there is little scope for their advance today. Opportunities for employment in some tasks have gone down since the arrival of tractors, Selvam said. The tractor has robbed those with ploughs and bullocks of ploughing work, and those with carts and bullocks of work in basal manuring. Even during threshing, the tractor has deprived agricultural labourers of employment. While earlier there would be four days' work at the threshing-floor and four bullocks would be needed to trample the grain for the second threshing, now the tractor can be driven over the sheaves to complete the task in less than an hour.

Unemployment is high and wages are poor – and women's wages have actually been brought down, from Rs 3 per day to Rs 2.50 per day. There was an agitation by Communists five years ago in southern villages of the Valley, Selvam recalls, when male workers won an increase in their grain wages from 4 measures per day to 5 measures, and female workers an increase to 3 measures for threshing. While wages in the village do not vary directly with the caste of the worker, discrimination against the scheduled castes, the overwhelming majority of whom are landless labourers, is deeply entrenched. Most of the farm servants in the village are Dalit.

Selvam has an extremely busy working year. During the 1976–77 agricultural year, he worked on both crops of paddy on surface-irrigated land, in different operations in the cultivation of irrigated *cholam*, *ragi*, tomato and banana on groundwater-irrigated land, and in *samai* on unirrigated land. In addition to agricultural work every day, he did domestic tasks at the landlord's house. Selvam's wife, Alphonse, laboured at agricultural operations for 57 days in 1976–77, and earned Rs 158.70 as wages. She seeded and cleaned tamarind for three days, for which she earned Rs 7.50.

Selvam's wage is lower than that of other farm servants in the village, some of whom are paid Rs 130 and Rs 140 by their landlord employers. But when Selvam asks for a wage increase, the landlord arrogantly insists: "I have already increased your wages. You used to get Rs 65, now you get 110." The standard that SCC uses, Selvam says, is not the wage paid to other farm servants in the village, but the Rs 65 pittance that Selvam himself used to receive before he was paid Rs 110 a month.

When Selvam is unwell, the landlord may give him a small amount of money to buy medicine, but he will not pay for treatment for Alphonse or the children when they fall ill. As for his home, Selvam cannot afford to erect a complete hut. When he gets a small amount of money, he adds a row of bricks to the hut. Some months ago, he bought a door-frame. Now, there is a door-frame, fixed with mud into a few rows of country-made brick, with no wall around it or roof above. The single room in the hut is 8 feet by 6 feet. "We do not know when this hut will be built," Alphonse said. "We lay a few bricks, and it may be a few months before we can add more bricks. It may take years to complete the hut in this manner."

With all this, Selvam must also face rudeness and admonition from the landlord, the loud arrogance of SCC as taskmaster of "his" farm servant. "Life is difficult for me," Selvam said. He sees his children at 5 in the morning (when he leaves for work), when the older children may be just beginning to wake up. It is seldom, and only in the slack season, that he comes home before they are asleep for the night. And the hours in between are filled with arduous, back-breaking labour that covers every task that an agricultural labourer in the village can perform.

I have seen Selvam, early in the morning, heaving farmyard manure on to a cart and, driving the cart to the paddy-field, unloading it in neat piles across the field. I have seen him, bare-chested, barefoot, and dressed in an old and torn *lungi*, with a soiled cloth on his head to protect him from the sun, walking with a hoe across his shoulder over the ridge east of the village on the road leading to SCC's groundwater-irrigated field in neighbouring Anamalaiyanpatti. I have seen him at the paddy-field, cutting and clearing water channels before the electricity comes on and irrigation water rushes up; and in the banana field, hacking at the tough young shoots that grow by the trees, cutting dry and withered leaves off the trees, and straightening tree-trunks with wooden props chopped and shaped by him. I have seen him, in the evenings, working in SCC's house, watering, feeding and washing the cattle, or chopping a tree-trunk for firewood for SCC's kitchen. I have seen him at the bus-stop in Uthamapalayam, straining to lift a motor pump, newly repaired, on to the carrier of a Gokilapuram-bound bus. Standing under a bus-shelter in Gokilapuram after 11 o'clock at night, I have heard the sound of a cart coming down the road from Anamalaiyanpatti. It is Selvam, urging the bullocks through pouring rain back to SCC's house. I have seen him after 11.30 at night, rain smudging the red mud that clings to his face and body, entering his hut and eating gruel and pickle by the weak light of an oil lamp, and preparing to catch some sleep before the next day of labour begins.

Selvam states clearly that it is not "loyalty" that keeps him with the landlord. It is his debt and the difficulty of finding alternative employment if he were to leave. "I have heard of the union of agricultural labourers in East Thanjavur. A union is needed, unity of agricultural labourers is needed. If there were a union in Gokilapuram, I would join it."

DECEMBER 2017: A WORKING LIFE

Selvam worked for a total of thirteen years with the landlord SCC. When he left, his monthly wage was a mere Rs 400 a month. He said that about 4,000 rupees were due to him and unpaid when he left SCC's employment.

Selvam worked fifteen years as a daily-wage worker after he left the employment of SCC. Three years after he left, his son Arokiyasami was married. Over the three years, Selvam spent one year as a worker in a cardamom estate in Parathodu in Kerala, owned by Vadivelu Goundiar of Pannaipuram. Alphonse worked as a wage labourer in the village all her working life, that is, until four years ago.

Ten years ago, Selvam began to work for Iswaran, brother of Bala-subramanian of the Kali Vilas landlord family. Iswaran is a retired college teacher. Selvam was hired at a wage of Rs 2,000 a month. Iswaran owns 10.8 acres of *thottam* land and 1.8 acres of *nanjai* land in the north of the village, on the banks of the Thamaraikulam irrigation tank, where he grows *nendran* banana and coconut.

Selvam goes to the field at 7 am every day, takes a break from about 11 to 2.30, and works again at the field till 6 pm. He takes care of the field, clears the channels for irrigation, works the locks of the pipes for drip irrigation, supervises and works with other wage workers at some operations (including planting and harvest), and weeds and cleans the fields. He also keeps the main trunks of the banana trees free of unwanted side-shoots, and applies fertilizer and undertakes all other plant protection tasks.

After three years with the landlord Iswaran, Selvam asked for a raise. His new wage was fixed at Rs 4,000 a month (the worker on the neighbouring field gets Rs 6,000 a month, he told us). The landlord agreed to henceforth account for Selvam's withdrawals against the new wage. Selvam is not paid his wage on a fixed day every month: he takes money for expenses – household expenses, festivals – from his employer "whenever I need it." His employer says he is keeping an account; Selvam trusts him and says that he, too, keeps track of how much he has taken from the landlord. Selvam estimates that he has credit of about Rs 10,000 with the landlord, but there is no formal account of Selvam's savings with him.

Four years ago, Alphonse developed a swelling on her right knee.

A doctor in Uthamapalayam gave her drugs and an injection, and the swelling "sank to her foot." Blood and pus were drained from the foot with a large syringe. Alphonse was discharged from the hospital, and told to spread an ointment on the wound. Selvam did this every day. But Alphonse began to scratch the itchy wound before it had healed completely. She eats betel leaf and nuts with lime, and the lime paste on her finger began to inflame the wound; it turned septic. Selvam took her in his son Shekhar's autorickshaw to Cumbum, where the doctor said that she needed emergency treatment at Theni. Alphonse was taken by ambulance to the Theni Government Medical College and Hospital, where the doctors advised emergency surgery. She had a second surgery, followed by a skin graft. In the post-operative ward, Selvam watched people on the other beds, and began to realise the importance of dressing Alphonse's wound correctly – that it was a task that needed an expert, something he could not do himself. He hired a person to change the bandage, at Rs 50 a day, for the three months they spent in the hospital.

Alphonse is back at home now. She can move a bit – to the sitting platform in front of the house, to change her clothes, to go to the bathroom; but not more than that. "We do not know how long she will survive. She has never done anyone any wrong. When she goes, it will be to heaven."

The Children
Arokiasamy (50), the oldest child of Selvam and Alphonse, works as a mason, and has a small business as a contractor for constructing small houses. His wife, Sumathi, has a tenth class school-leaving certificate, and works in the panchayat office as a data collector. They have two children: a son, Maniprathi (22), now a student at a polytechnic in Namakkal; and a daughter, Sunitha (21). Sunitha completed a BA degree and is now married. Her husband works on the staff of a tea estate owned by N. Ramakrishnan, former MLA from Cumbum.

Arokiamary (48), their only daughter, is now almost completely blind. She looks after her parents and brother, a much-loved carer in the home.

Shekhar (46) lives in Gokilapuram. He owns an autorickshaw, from which he earns an income of Rs 500 to Rs 1,000 a day. His wife, Thilakam, is a manual worker in agriculture and at non-agricultural tasks. Their children, Merlyn Marcia and Praveen, who are their grandparents' joy, study in class 1 and class 2 in the English-language medium section of the Savarimuthu Udayar Memorial Higher Secondary School, a reputed school in the neighbouring village of Rayappanpatti.

Vedamuthu (44) stays at home with his parents. He is a person with intellectual disabilities, and is unable to go regularly to work.

Xavier (41), the youngest son of the family, works at loading and unloading bags of rice at the government civil supplies godown in Uthamapalayam. His wife, Muthuarokiyam, and he are now residents of Uthamapalayam, where their children Akhilesh, Vimalesh and Pratibha go to school. Xavier earns Rs 600 a day, and an extra Rs 1,000 a month, for the manual work at the godown.

Forty Years On

Selvam and his family live today in the house whose initial construction costs led him into bondage in 1977. It is completed and expanded now: a neat, whitewashed structure that has the meagre furniture and appurtenances of a house that is still, after all, the house of a full-time rural manual worker. They were exploited and extremely poor – near-destitute – in 1977. Today, they are still poor, Selvam's wages are low, and he has no knowledge of how much of his earned wages are held by his employer. But he is no longer destitute, no longer in bondage, and no longer at the mercy of a harsh and cruel landlord of the old type.

They are better off now than they were in 1977 – "Oh yes, of course we are," Selvam says. "Our house is complete, and we never go hungry; we have special things to eat: egg curry twice a week, chicken on Sundays, fish once in about twenty days." Thanks to the public system for the distribution of cereal, there is enough rice for the family. The house has been electrified (Selvam says they received their electricity connection at the same time, conveniently, as their son Arokiasami's wedding.)

I have continued to meet Selvam over the years. I was associated with resurveys of Gokilapuram village in 1986 and 1999, and continue to be interested in changing agrarian relations in the village and region. I return to the Cumbum Valley regularly for tasks connected with the Gokilapuram Educational Trust, an organization of which the honoree of this volume is a founder trustee. Travel to the Valley gives me an opportunity to keep in touch with Selvam; as we grow older, we grow more conscious of the value of old friendships.

Selvam asks me if I remember the little kerosene lamp (of course I do – made of tin and with a flimsy glass chimney) that I used during our survey in 1977. I used it after dark during conversations and interviews in homes that had no electricity. "You gave it to me when you left the village after the survey," he says. After electricity came to the house, Selvam stored the lamp deep in a loft, where it remains today. He keeps it as a reminder of his friend – and of the days when they had only a single lamp for light in a half-constructed house.

After Snowden
Alan Rusbridger

For Ram, in admiration.

It is now nearly two years since Edward Snowden emerged from the obscurity of his backroom career as an electronic spy to tell the world about some of the things he had learned about the people and organization he worked for.[1]

It is a good moment to take stock. You may hate or love Mr Snowden, but few would deny that what he showed the world had a large number of very important implications. While there has been a deep and vigorous debate in many parts of the world in the past twenty months, the British discussion has been muted, often not very informed and certainly not very joined up. It is easier to reduce the debate to a simple polarity of "privacy versus security," or to throw around words like "treason," than it is to consider the way in which multiple issues collide and intersect.

And, of course, it is vital in the wake of atrocities in Paris and Sydney and Woolwich and Boston to work out what, if anything, has to change to deal effectively with problems western societies currently face. The attack on Charlie Hebdo in January 2015, in particular, encapsulated the argument for free speech as well as a desire for security.

But both are complicated arguments. How absolute is free speech? And what lessons can be learned from a case involving suspects who were, it seems, already on watch-lists – three or four known needles. Can you really make the leap from that incident to argue for the reintroduction of legislation – already rejected by parliament – to build an even bigger haystack?

In the wake of the hack attack on Sony, the world was crying out for better encryption for business, governments and individuals. But no sooner had the Hebdo attack happened, than political and intelligence leaders were complaining about strong encryption.

These are vital issues for the twenty-first century. There needs to be widespread and informed discussion. As that debate rippled around the world, I drew for myself a mind-map of the issues I felt Snowden had revealed to us. Some of them might have been very familiar to some. But for a general public – and for the people who have to make laws and balance public interests – I think much of it was quite new.

In this brief essay, I will very briefly ask a number of questions:

- What did Snowden do?
- What should the press do?
- What was the public interest?
- What should the state do?
- What should parliament do?

But before I ask those questions, let me touch on two little slices of history, both relevant to Snowden, and even the events in France.

In the month in which numerous political leaders descended on Paris to express solidarity over the defence of free speech, it is instructive to remember how that ever-precarious freedom was won. And to recognize that the fight for freedom of expression, which we rightly celebrated in Paris, was often difficult, and usually in the face of obstruction by governments and states.

The first is issue number 45 of *North Briton*, one of the most explosive and subversive texts ever published in London. John Wilkes is today considered one of the heroes of the fight for free speech and democracy anywhere in the world. As a person he was erratic, visionary, headstrong, provocative (against the Scots), racist (against the Scots) and licentious – imagine a combination of Charlie Hebdo, Edward Snowden, George Galloway, Julian Assange and John Stuart Mill. In April 1763, he published the notorious issue number 45 of his newspaper, one of the most provocative texts in Britain's long history of journalism. He was accused of treason, spied on, his papers seized and leaked by the state. Nearly fifty of his associates were arrested on general warrants, regardless of innocence or guilt.

Wilkes defended himself on grounds of civil liberties. In times of fear it is said that human rights should take a back seat, but Wilkes was living at a time of multiple and genuine threats to national security. (This was not so long after the Jacobite rising of 1745; we were engaged in a long war, and there was a genuine fear of riot and revolution.) The threat to the established order was far greater than today. In his appeal to Parliament, Wilkes made a calm argument that his rights, and those of the people arrested alongside him, had been grossly infringed. He asked his fellow Members of Parliament (MPs) to consider "whether (except in cases of High Treason) the papers of any English subject ought ever to be seiz'd, and whether . . . this is not deem'd to be a most odious method of fishing for evidence?" Wilkes eventually won. That we are free to report what MPs say at Westminster is due to him.

Fast forward just over two hundred years. America is at war in Vietnam. *The New York Times* begins to publish leaked extracts from top secret Defence Department documents outlining government policy on Vietnam. They had been leaked by the Edward Snowden of the day, a researcher working as a consultant to the Pentagon. National Security Adviser Al Haig said that it was "a devastating . . . security breach of the greatest magnitude of anything I've ever seen." The Nixon administration accused the newspaper of treason, damaging national security and violating the Espionage Act. The state tried to injunct *The New York Times* from further publication.

The case went to the Supreme Court, where the state argued that the paper had imperilled national security by revealing signal intelligence, the significance of which could not be understood except by intelligence experts. They cited the so-called mosaic theory – the idea that even apparently innocuous information could be harmful if pieced together by a knowledgeable observer.

But *The New York Times* won. Two judges considered the First Amendment to be an absolute affirmation of free speech. Another considered that the state could only intervene in circumstances of "direct, immediate, and irreparable damage to our nation or its people." Justice Black believed that "in revealing the workings of government that led to the Vietnam War, the newspapers did precisely that which the Founders hoped and trusted they would do."

The Pentagon Papers case was an important restatement of the US's First Amendment. It prevented future governments from seeking to prevent newspapers from publishing secrets – except in truly exceptional circumstances. And, as I will argue, it created a more mature working atmosphere in America than we have in Britain.

Daniel Ellsberg himself was acquitted of an offence under the Espionage Act after it was revealed that the American state had wire-tapped not only his lawyer, but also his psychiatrist. President Nixon took it badly: "The sonofabitching thief is made a national hero. . . . *The New York Times* gets a Pulitzer Prize for stealing documents. . . . They're trying to get us with thieves. What in the name of God have we come to?"

So, after those slivers of history, here are the questions:

What Did Edward Snowden Do?
I shall take it for granted that most readers will know approximately what has been published from the papers Edward Snowden leaked. But it is relevant to think about how he did it.

Like him or not, Snowden felt he had something important to tell the world. He had seen how *The New York Times* had been persuaded to sit on a story about illegal, warrantless wire-tapping in 2005 – claims of damage to national security again. He knew that the consequences for him, personally, of becoming a whistleblower of highly classified material could be severe. If he was going to put his own career and life on the line, he had to make sure it was not all wasted. There were three considerations at work in choosing with whom he would share the documents: (i) journalists he felt would understand and do justice to the material; (ii) a mixture of old and new media; (iii) a geographical spread.

Within a short time of the initial meeting with Glenn Greenwald and Ewen Macaskill from *The Guardian*, the material was spread across four countries in three continents. Two mainstream news organizations were involved from the start: *The Guardian* and *Washington Post*. It was always apparent that Greenwald, a former blogger working out of Rio de Janeiro, would publish on his own if *The Guardian* was suppressed. Laura Poitras, an independent filmmaker in Berlin, had her own network of friends and colleagues. In time, *The New York Times* and *Pro Publica* in New York had access to some of the material, as did newspapers such as *Der Spiegel* in Germany.

I mention this because it was not always apparent from the response of the British government that they fully appreciated the degree to which the material was out there. I think, in retrospect, some officials wondered what anyone hoped to achieve by destroying one copy of the documents in London. By taking *The Guardian* in Britain out of the equation, did people in Westminster and Whitehall hope to strike up a fruitful relationship with Greenwald in Rio?

What Should the Press Do?
Most journalists find little difficulty in answering this question. If a source gives you material of this nature, you certainly look at it. You handle it as responsibly as you can. You publish with extreme care. And – so long as you are convinced that there is a public interest in publication – you publish some of it. When I say "most journalists," I mean the overwhelming majority of editors, journalists, academics, and free speech thinkers and campaigners in most parts of the world.

There was a very small minority of journalists – some in this country – who thought differently. They boiled down into two camps. There was one camp – actually one journalist, Edward Lucas of *The Economist*, who said he would have marched Snowden down to the local police station. I don't think this is the official stance of his magazine, which grasped the significance of the material Snowden brought to light – especially the stories to do with the intelligence agencies' attempts to weaken aspects of encryption. But, also, any newspaper which hands its sources over to the police is not going to have any sources. There was a second camp, essentially summed up in an article by the former editor of *The Independent*, Chris Blackhurst, and it went like this: if the intelligence agencies say something will harm the national interest or national security, who am I to doubt them?

There are at least three possible answers to this. First, the national interest or national security cannot *only* be defined by the state. Secondly – as the examples of John Wilkes and Daniel Ellsberg show – what a government or intelligence agency defines as "harm" at a particular period in time can often seem dubious, or even comical, at another. Not long ago, we were told that the Wikileaks revelations were appallingly harmful. When Chelsea Manning came to trial, the prosecution produced little evidence of the sort of bloodcurdling harm that was claimed while they were being published. A senior British official I met recently waved his hand dismissively at Wikileaks: "Not that serious." Which absolutely *was not* what the British government was saying at the time. Thirdly, if a free press is to mean anything, then of course it must be free to make independent decisions about what to publish. If the state is the ultimate arbiter of what it considers should be allowed to be published, then the press is not free. But, of course, that is a different question from how to minimize or avoid harm. I shall come to that with the next question.

From the press point of view, everyone I knew at *The New York Times*, *Washington Post*, *Pro Publica* and *Guardian* – all extremely serious and ethical news organizations with huge experience of writing about national security – felt a responsibility to keep lines of communication open with the government and the agencies in order to minimize harm. Our *Guardian* colleagues in New York found this easier to do in the US than we did in the UK.

Whether or not the Snowden revelations did cause harm is difficult for any outsider to tell. I have been told on good authority that some of the Snowden revelations did impair some intelligence-gathering. I have equally been told – by a number of people on what I would consider equally good authority – that the *Guardian*'s journalism caused no harm. A senior member of the Obama administration told me he considered the *Guardian* had behaved responsibly.

In the end, an editor has to be guided by whether or not he or she believes there is a public interest in publishing. Anyone who believes in a free press must surely believe an editor has to have that right.

What Was the Public Interest?
Opponents of publication have, of course, minimized the public interest, or tried to shrink it to polarized alternatives: national security versus privacy, national security versus freedom of expression.

I noticed that President Obama was recently asked a question in such terms: surely the pendulum had to swing a little away from privacy to national security? And I noticed his answer: *That over the last six years threat streams have been fairly constant. We deal with them every day. The pendulum doesn't need to swing. We need a consistent framework. There needs to be a debate about laws. The discussion needs to involve the tech industry, who have responsibilities not only to security, but also to the customers who use their products, Meanwhile it is useful to have civil libertarians and others tapping us on the shoulder.* I wouldn't disagree with much of that.

I think there weren't just a *few* matters of public interest raised by Edward Snowden; I think there was a *huge number*. That was what I drew the map of issues to capture. You can see, in larger writing, the chapter headings – a very large number of issues affecting the press, civil liberties, security, the law, technology, telecommunications companies, encryption, privacy, confidentiality, international relations, the Cloud, the future of the web, consent oversight, the digital economy and so on. Each one of those is a vast and significant subject on which you could teach a university course or write a book.

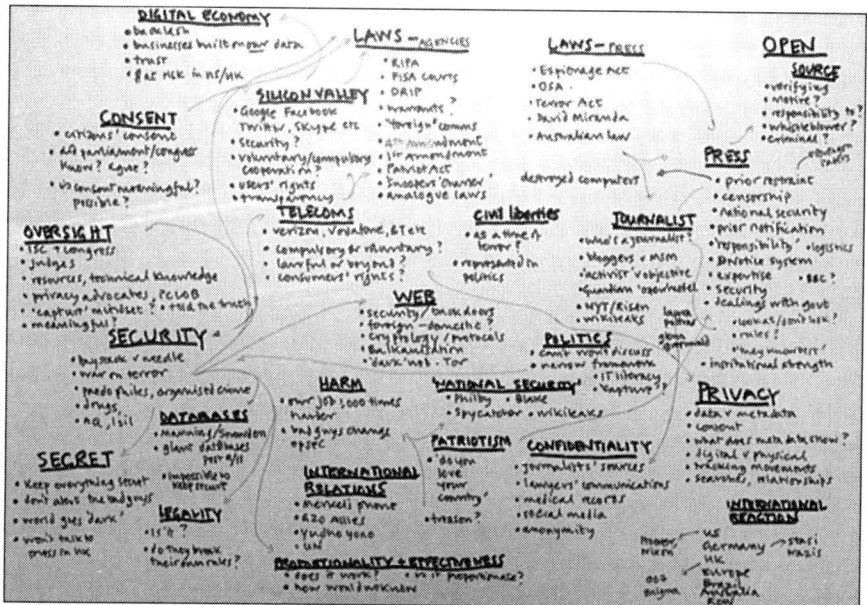

And then you can break them down further into sub-sections – each one of which could also be a book or a dissertation – and you begin to get a glimpse of the complexity of interwoven public interests that have been brought into something like daylight over the past eighteen months or so.

When you look at that map of issues, maybe you think a number of things:

1. It is very difficult to argue there is no public interest in what Snowden showed the world. There clearly was. And a great many people, from former presidents to business leaders to lawyers to tech entrepreneurs, have said so very openly.

2. There are *many* public interests, lots of which conflict with each other.

3. A good number of them are extremely complex. It would, for instance, be very difficult for one person to be an expert in the legal and technical and commercial issues involved in encryption – far less, be also aware of the swirling debates around human rights, digital economies and journalistic sources.

4. Who gets to hold the ring in reconciling these clashes and intersections of public interests, therefore, becomes rather crucial. Whether that is best done on our behalf by one committee of Parliament on Thursday afternoons becomes an important question in itself.

That leads on to the next question:

What Should the State Do?
It should, I hope, be apparent in Whitehall that two things have changed.

1. We are no longer living in a world in which it is possible, even if it were desirable, to prevent publication by traditional means. That much was surely becoming evident even in the late 1980s, with the hapless sight of a British Cabinet Secretary flying to Australia to try to stop the publication of Peter Wright's memoirs. Breaking up computer discs in a London basement might make someone feel better in Whitehall, but it had no effect at all on publication, which continued in New York, Washington, Rio, Berlin and elsewhere.

2. The mentality of the 1911 Official Secrets Act – a measure introduced in some panic before the First World War and whose influence lingered on for generations – has to change. I know we are allowed to know who the head of MI5 is, these days. But the agencies still work in a world in which they struggle to know how to deal with the press, far less allow – and openly participate in – the sort of argument that now has to take place about security and civil liberties.

In relation to their dealings with the press, there is one narrow but important question about what to do when the next such leak happens. Some people want the DA (Defence Advisory) Notice scrapped. Some, it is said, would like jail sentences of up to ten years for editors. Whether this would change the behaviour of editors, I rather doubt. And if it did – if newspapers were intimidated into refusing to handle secret material in future – Whitehall would have a far greater problem of not dealing with mainstream media outlets but with whistleblowers who would self-publish, or working with bloggers or new media players who would not dream of being part of any organized system of what they would view as censorship.

I came to have great respect for the people who operate the DA Notice system, and would be sorry to see it go if the alternative was more restrictive. But I would urge something more open and more like the way our colleagues in the New York office of *The Guardian* were able to work. In America, of course, the Pentagon Papers judgement is crucial, in that any editor knows he or she can approach the Department of Defence or the White House knowing that this will not provoke the threat of an injunction. The opposite is the case in Britain.

For much of the time, the GCHQ's (Government Communications Headquarters) general policy was to offer no comment at all on any document (this, I have to say, has changed in recent weeks). In contrast, when dealing with the US National Security Agency (NSA), it was common for our editors to be connected with experts in the agency who would go through documents paragraph by paragraph, flagging areas about which they had anxieties. I don't say we always agreed where to draw the line, but many of those direct conversations were of great help in getting our bearings. In all we had contact with more than a hundred officials on both sides of the Atlantic while publishing the stories.

Of course, everyone accepts that some things are better kept secret. But the new world is different from the old world. The old world was much more about clandestine targeting of suspects. Now the demand is that entire populations should make their communications available for collection, inspection and analysis. That is a profound shift, involving very powerful technology companies – never mind voiceless individuals.

We are asked to believe that the state always had the power to open letters. But think back to the eighteenth-century view that there was something odious about the state seizing and storing papers. It is no accident that the nation which best understands what Snowden is saying is Germany.

To give one, very current, example closer to home. For centuries, institutions, callings and professions have considered the confidentiality of communications to be sacred. I am thinking of the law, medicine, the church, parliamentarians and journalists, and their oath, or obligation, to clients, or patients, or sources, or constituents, or communicants.

But a Home Office consultation document – the deadline for entering objections closes tomorrow – has codified that in future, the state will not feel bound by these conventions or promises or practices. The Home Office wants the police to feel free to authorize themselves to access the phone and email records of journalists and priests and lawyers and doctors – and even MPs.

British journalists have recently woken up to the fact that the police have been using terror legislation to work out who their sources are, despite the fact that what they are writing about had no connection at all with terror. If sources feel they can quite easily be identified by the electronic trail involved in talking on the phone, or sending an email, or meeting someone at a traceable location, there won't be many sources in future. Journalism – which relies on unauthorized sources for much that is good and valuable – would be changed for ever in this country. That is not something to sneak in through paragraphs 3.72 to 3.74 in an obscure Home Office consultation document. It is a subject of the utmost importance to society. Which is why pretty much every significant editor in the country has written to Theresa May protesting at it. She did, in the end, concede that the approval of a judge would be needed. But we learned much about the official mind-set in the process.

Which leads to the final question:

What Is the Role of Parliament?
Parliament is where we currently expect these clashing public interests to be resolved. In America there has been a Presidential report, alongside another by the Privacy and Civil Liberties Oversight Board, and numerous congressional debates. The same is true in Germany. In Europe, politicians actually requested to hear from Snowden himself.

In the UK there has been little apart from the RUSI (Royal United Services Institute) inquiry suggested by Nick Clegg. A flick at the issue from the Home Affairs Committee. A debate in Westminster Hall – quite a bit of which was taken up with whether The *Guardian* should be prosecuted. There was considerable resentment in the House of Lords last summer at the way they felt bounced into renewing existing surveillance powers, with no notice and minimal debate.

The Intelligence and Security Committee, with a budget of £1.3 million, is charged with overseeing a security operation with a budget of £1.7 billion and growing. In addition to that oversight it is also looking into its own role post-Snowden, as well as allegations about British involvement in the torture of terror suspects – a vast issue forensically dealt with in the US. The Chair of the Intelligence and Security Committee occasionally pops up on radio when there are terror outrages or demands for greater powers. It is not always clear from his tone whether he regards himself as a regulator or advocate on behalf of the agencies he oversees.

I want to end with the remarks of Richard Barratt, a counter-terrorism chief at both MI5 and MI6, who has spent more than ten years looking at Al Qaeda for the UN. He was a guest on the BBC's "Hardtalk," and was asked whether he supported the calls for ever-wider surveillance powers in the wake of the Paris killings. Like President Obama, he wanted a clear focus on civil liberties as well as effective security. We should, he said, be concentrating on what we are fighting for – not just what we are fighting against.

He meant the preservation – and even the evolution – of our civil liberties. John Wilkes would have been proud.

Note

1 This piece was written in April 2015. – *Editor*

The Zero Hunger Challenge
M.S. Swaminathan

―――

INTRODUCTION

I have the good fortune of knowing N. Ram for over forty years now. I first met him when he was in the United States representing The Hindu Group of newspapers. Over the years our friendship has grown, and my admiration for his wonderful qualities of head and heart has also grown. Ram has brought his journalistic talents to the fight for causes that are important for the evolution of a just, egalitarian and secular democracy. He has never been afraid of fighting for causes that are important for maintaining and enriching diversity and pluralism among the people of our country. He has considered social and gender equity as fundamental to achieve a progressive nation of which we can be proud.

Ram has fought for causes that are related to probity and honesty in public life. Thus he took up the cause of corruption, as exemplified in the Bofors deal, with courage and conviction. Unravelling the sources of corruption in defence purchases has been a major contribution by him to the strengthening of honesty and integrity in governance. He has given his time freely to causes that promote ethics in journalism, and has fought the evil of paid news. Thus, he has been serving as a role model for fellow-journalists, who respect and revere him for his principled stand on issues of national importance.

Above all, Ram is a humanist. He is generous in his hospitality, and in assisting friends and colleagues. When I mentioned to him, in 1989, the proposal for establishing the M.S. Swaminathan Research Foundation (MSSRF) at Chennai, based on a pro-nature, pro-poor, pro-woman and pro-livelihood orientation to technology development and dissemination, he generously gave time to help the institution in every possible manner, including getting land from the government. Ram is one of the leading advocates of scientific temper in the country, and in this respect he emulates the example of Jawaharlal Nehru. Knowing that the media play an important role in taking science to society, he helped to establish a Media Resource Centre at MSSRF with a generous endowment from The Hindu Group. He has also been serving as a Trustee as well as Chairman of the Ethics Committee of the Board of MSSRF for over twelve years, and has played a key role in shaping the work of the institution and in taking the benefits of science to rural and tribal families. He worked with Sashi Kumar to establish the Asian College of Journalism.

Ram is a compassionate person with a deep concern for the economically and socially underprivileged sections of society. He is also a protagonist of the need for taking the benefits of modern technology to rural women and men. Thus, he has given active support to the Village Knowledge Centre programme as well as the Biovillage programme of MSSRF. He is a champion of the fight against hunger, and is convinced that nutrition security is basic to human security. For example, he believes that the best vaccine against tuberculosis is nutrition. He is very concerned about malnutrition in pregnant mothers since nearly every fifth child born in the country is characterized by low birth weight. Therefore, in an article dedicated to the remarkable life and work of Ram, I wish to refer to a few areas relevant to his role which are currently in progress at the MSSRF, of which he is a distinguished Trustee.

The Challenge of Science, and Sustainable Food and Nutrition Security

Ram has been fighting against the coexistence of grain mountains and hungry millions. In 2015, the UN Millennium Development Goals gave way to the UN Sustainable Development Decade. Sustainable development involves concurrent attention to environmental and economic sustainability as well as social and gender equity. The concept of the former King of Bhutan, of Gross National Happiness (GNH), should appropriately be an important component of the sustainable development indicators. An area of great importance is the achievement of the goal of Zero Hunger by 2025. Price volatility indicates that the future will belong to nations with grains and not guns. Therefore, every effort should be made to enhance the productivity and production of major crops, and efficient implementation of the National Food Security Act (2013) which makes availability of food a legal right.

In recent years, the political will and associated action for eliminating poverty-induced chronic hunger have shown signs of strengthening. Mr Lula da Silva, former President of Brazil, introduced the bold concept of "Zero Hunger" over a decade ago. This programme has led to a substantial drop in the number of children, women and men going to bed hungry in Brazil. In 2013, Mr Ban Ki-moon, Secretary General of United Nations, launched a Zero Hunger Programme with the following five components and a time frame of 2015 to 2025:

1. Zero stunted children of less than 2 years of age
2. 100 per cent access to adequate food all the year round
3. All food systems are sustainable
4. 100 per cent increase in smallholder productivity and income
5. Zero loss or waste of food.

Hunger and Malnutrition

In spite of the various steps taken from time to time to address the problems of hunger and poverty, we have not been able to achieve the UN Millennium Development Goal of reducing the extent of prevalence of hunger by half by 2015. According to the National Family Health Survey 3 (NFHS 3), 45 per cent of children in India under 3 years of age were stunted and undernourished. The long-term effects of early malnutrition include cognitive and physical growth deficits across multiple generations, and reduction in immunity to infections and childhood vaccines. Another measure is the Global Hunger Index calculated by the International Food Policy Research Institute (IFPRI). This index is based on three components: undernourishment, or the proportion of undernourished people as a percentage of the population (reflecting the share of the population with insufficient calorie intake); child underweight, or the proportion of children under the age of 5 who are underweight (that is, have low weight for their age, reflecting wasting, stunted growth, or both), which is a widely used indicator of child undernutrition; and child mortality or the mortality rate of children under the age of 5 (partially reflecting the fatal synergy of inadequate food intake and unhealthy environments). In 2014, India ranked 55 among 76 countries on the Global Hunger Index.[1] Obviously, we have not fulfilled Mahatma Gandhi's hope that we will be a nation without hunger, since, to quote him (mentioned in his speech at Noakhali in 1946) "To the hungry, God is bread."

The scenario in India is also referred to as the South Asian enigma. The region has witnessed extraordinary economic growth, yet levels of undernutrition remain high. Two out of five (40 per cent) children in South Asia are stunted (UNICEF 2013). Lack of economic growth is not the primary reason for the persistence of hunger. Major factors are inadequate purchasing power, and the absence of synergy and convergence among the food and non-food components of nutritional security.

Science Policy for Food and Nutrition Security

I would like to briefly summarize some of the steps we need to take to achieve the Zero Hunger target by 2025. Two guest editorials I wrote in

Table 1 *Output of major crops in India and world rank, 2013* in metric tonnes

Commodity group	Total production and India's rank in world food production
Foodgrain	265.0 (III)
Rice	106.5 (II)
Wheat	95.6 (II)
Pulses	19.5 (I)
Oilseeds	32.7 (V)
Fruit and Vegetables	280.0 (II)

Science give a summary of the strategy for achieving Zero Hunger in India (Swaminathan 2009 and 2014). As shown in Table 1, India ranks high in the production of major crops. In addition, we produce over 140 million tonnes of milk and thereby have become the world's number one milk producer. Thus there is no reason for the prevalence of undernutrition and malnutrition in the country.

At the outset, poverty-induced undernutrition or inadequate consumption of calories is the most important food security challenge in our country. In cereal-based diets, undernutrition is often the mother of malnutrition. Nevertheless, while developing a strategy for achieving a hunger-free India, we should pay concurrent attention to overcoming the following three major forms of hunger.

1. Undernutrition, caused by inadequate consumption of calories (most widely prevalent)
2. Protein hunger, caused by insufficient consumption of pulses, milk, egg or other protein-rich diets
3. Hidden hunger, caused by deficiency in the diet of micronutrients such as iron, iodine, zinc, Vitamin A, Vitamin B12, Vitamin D, etc.

Addressing Undernutrition: Green Revolution and Evergreen Revolution
The technologies associated with the green revolution in wheat and rice contributed to overcoming undernutrition. The effects of different reduced height (*Rht*) alleles on wheat plant height provided an opportunity to tailor plant architecture to suit high soil fertility conditions. The green revolution was possible only because of a symphony approach resulting from synergy between scientific skill, political will and farmers' toil. Indira Gandhi released a special stamp titled "Wheat Revolution" in 1968 to mark the achievement of Indian farmers and scientists in making as much progress

in wheat production in four years (1964–68) as during the preceding 4,000 years.

In the late 1960s I observed that our farmers, particularly in the Punjab, started using more fertilizers and groundwater, which could result in long-term ecological harm. Therefore, I made the following statement in my presidential address at the Science Congress held in Varanasi in January 1968:

> Intensive cultivation of land without conservation of soil fertility and soil structure would lead ultimately to the springing up of deserts. Irrigation without arrangements for drainage would result in soils getting alkaline or saline. Indiscriminate use of pesticides, fungicides and herbicides could cause adverse changes in biological balance as well as lead to an increase in the incidence of cancer and other diseases, through the toxic residues present in the grains or other edible parts. Unscientific tapping of underground water would lead to the rapid exhaustion of this wonderful capital resource left to us through ages of natural farming. The rapid replacement of numerous locally adapted varieties with one or two high-yielding strains in large contiguous areas would result in the spread of serious diseases capable of wiping out entire crops, as happened prior to the Irish potato famine of 1845 and the Bengal rice famine of 1942. Therefore, the initiation of exploitative agriculture without a proper understanding of the various consequences of every one of the changes introduced into traditional agriculture and without first building up a proper scientific and training base to sustain it, may only lead us into an era of agricultural disaster in the long run, rather than to an era of agricultural prosperity.

I coined the term "evergreen revolution" (this was first published by N. Ram in *The Hindu*) to emphasize the need for integrating ecological principles in technology development and dissemination. For example, the world requires 50 per cent more rice in 2030 than it did in 2004, grown on approximately 30 per cent less arable land than today. Securing "food for all and forever" will be possible only if the evergreen revolution pathway, which involves increasing productivity in perpetuity without ecological harm, is adopted. There has been a growing appreciation of my concept of an evergreen revolution, as the following quotations from Professor E.O. Wilson and President Obama would indicate.

> The problem before us is how to feed billions of new mouths over the next several decades and save the rest of life at the same time, without being trapped in a Faustian bargain that threatens freedom and security. No one knows the

exact solution to this dilemma. Most scientists and economists who have studied both sides of it agree that the benefits outweigh the risks. *The benefits must come from Evergreen Revolution.* (Wilson 2002; emphasis added)

Together, we can strengthen agriculture. Cooperation between Indian and American researchers and scientists sparked the Green Revolution. Today, India is a leader in using technology to empower farmers, like those I met yesterday who get free updates on market and weather conditions on their cell phones. And the United States is a leader in agricultural productivity and research. Now, as farmers and rural areas face the effects of climate change and drought, we will work together to spark a second, more sustainable Evergreen Revolution. (President Barack Obama, 2010)

Overcoming Protein Hunger
Thanks to the growth of the cooperative movement, scientifically mentored by the late Dr V. Kurien, our country is now producing over 140 million tonnes of milk, which represents the largest production of milk in the world. Similarly, we now produce over 270 million tonnes of fruit and vegetables. Egg and fish production have also gone up substantially. Only in the case of pulses production is the country short, by 2 to 3 million tonnes. Fortunately, the United Nations has declared 2016 as the International Year of Pulses. The M.S. Swaminathan Research Foundation (MSSRF) has been promoting the concept of "pulses panchayats." For example, the *panchayat* of Edaiyappatti village of Tamil Nadu has converted itself into a pulses panchayat. We need urgent steps to increase production and consumption of pulses in our country.

The Horticulture Mission can help to provide horticultural remedies for nutritional maladies. It will be advisable for the Horticulture Mission to associate with home science colleges or nutrition departments in every state in designing farming systems that are nutrition-sensitive. With support from the DFID (UK Department of International Development), MSSRF coordinates a multi-country, multi-institutional project titled "Leveraging Agriculture for Nutrition in South Asia." I have developed a methodology for designing farming systems in order to address the nutritional needs of the area, known as Farming System for Nutrition (FSN), which is now being implemented in several parts of the country. Some of the opportunities available for introducing horticultural remedies for nutritional maladies are indicated below (Das, Bhavani and Swaminathan 2014).

Existing kitchen gardens should be redesigned to make them "nutrition gardens". Also, at every panchayat level a few men and women should

Table 2 *Horticultural remedy for nutritional malady: crops for specific deficiencies*

Nutritional malady	Horticultural remedy
Protein	Broccoli, spinach, banana, strawberry, watermelon
Calcium	Almond, broccoli, Chinese cabbage, kale, orange
Iron	Dark leafy greens
Vitamin A	Asparagus, cabbage, carrot, lettuce, mango, sweet potato
Thiamin	Green leafy vegetables, asparagus, avocado, broccoli, cabbage
Riboflavin	Mushroom, plantain, spinach, apple, tamarind
Niacin	Asparagus, broccoli, mushroom, peanut
Vitamin C	Grapefruit, guava, lemon, sweet potato, tomato, watermelon
Total Folate	Asparagus, broccoli, lettuce, spinach, strawberry, beet
Free Folic Acid	Dark leafy vegetables

be identified who can become Community Hunger Fighters. Such Community Hunger Fighters can be trained to master the science and art of leveraging agriculture for nutrition. Empowerment of local communities with knowledge on malnutrition problems prevailing in their areas, and methods of overcoming them, will be the most effective and least-cost method of concurrently addressing calorie deprivation, protein hunger and hidden hunger.

Overcoming Hidden Hunger
Hidden hunger is becoming a serious problem due to lack of a balanced diet. Again, a food-based approach to solve this problem will be better than a drug- or tablet-based approach. This involves strengthening the science of biofortification. Biofortification can be achieved through the following methods.

1. Consumption of naturally occurring biofortified plants like *moringa*, sweet potato, pomegranate, nutri-millets, fruit and vegetables, as well as milk, eggs and other forms of animal protein.
2. Cultivation and consumption of biofortified varieties selected by breeding and selection, such as iron-rich pearl millet and zinc-rich rice.
3. Cultivation and consumption of genetically biofortified crops, like golden rice and iron-rich rice.

High priority should go to naturally occurring biofortified crops rich in micronutrients, such as *moringa*, breadfruit, pomegranate and sweet potato. Such naturally biofortified crops should be introduced in farming systems. Secondly, plant breeders can add the dimension of nutrition in their breeding programmes. For example, *bajra* (pearl millet) has been enriched with iron in a joint programme of the International Crop Research Institute for Semi-Arid Tropics (ICRISAT) and Nirmal Seeds. Biofortified crops developed by selection or breeding are also becoming available for the following nutrients under the "Harvest Plus" programme of the Consultative Group on International Agricultural Research (CGIAR): pearl millet – iron (zinc); rice – zinc; wheat – zinc; cassava – Provitamin A; beans – iron (zinc); and maize – Provitamin A.

The third approach is genetic modification of the kind achieved in the case of rice. Let me turn to the golden rice project. Vitamin A deficiency is responsible for about 2 million deaths, 500,000 cases of irreversible blindness and millions of cases of xerophthalmia annually. Children and pregnant women are at highest risk. To prevent clinical Vitamin A deficiency in developing countries, chemically synthesized Vitamin A supplements have been distributed periodically among deficient populations. This has been shown to be an efficient and generally safe strategy. However, supplementation programmes with periodic mass distribution have been difficult to sustain because of high transaction costs.

As many children in countries where there is a dietary deficiency in Vitamin A rely on rice as a staple food, genetic modification to make rice produce the Vitamin A precursor, beta-carotene, is seen as a simple and less expensive alternative to vitamin supplements, or an increase in the consumption of green vegetables or animal products.

The rice plant can naturally create beta-carotene within its leaves, where it is involved in photosynthesis. However, the plant does not normally produce the pigment in the endosperm, where photosynthesis does not take place. In 1992, Ingo Potrykus of the Swiss Federal Institute of Technology and Peter Beyer of the University of Freiburg started a project to genetically engineer rice plants to produce beta-carotene in the endosperm. "Golden rice," named for its yellow colour due to the beta-carotene present in the grain, was created by transforming rice with only two beta-carotene biosynthesis genes: psy (phytoene synthase) from daffodil (*Narcissus pseudonarcissus*), and crtI (carotene desaturase) from the soil bacterium *Erwinia uredovora*. The psy and crtI genes were transferred into the rice nuclear genome and placed under the control of an endosperm-specific promoter (endosperm-specific Glutelin [Gt1] promoter), so that they are only expressed in the endosperm. The original golden rice was named SGR1, and under greenhouse conditions it generated 1.6 micrograms/gram of carotenoids. In 2005, a team of researchers at a biotechnology company, Syngenta, created a variety of golden rice named "golden rice 2" (Paine *et al.* 2005). They joined the phytoene synthase gene from maize with crtI from the original golden rice. Golden rice 2 produces twenty-three times more carotenoids than golden rice, and preferentially accumulates beta-carotene. To receive the recommended dietary allowance, it is estimated that 144 grams of the most high-yielding strain would have to be consumed. Bioavailability of the carotene from golden rice has been established, and found to be an effective source of Vitamin A for humans.

To digress a bit, we can replace a purely drug-based approach for the treatment of diseases such as tuberculosis, HIV/AIDS and leprosy with a food-cum-drug-based approach.[2] After many years, agriculture, nutrition and health are coming together, thereby helping to treat hunger in a holistic manner. It is obvious that nutrition plays a pivotal role in increasing the effectiveness of drugs (as was recommended by the Committee on Leprosy eradication, chaired by me; GOI 1982).

Role of Genetic Engineering
It is 62 years since the beginning of the new genetics based on the discovery of the double helix structure of the DNA molecule by Watson, Crick and Wilkins. It is also thirty-two years since the production of transgenic plants started, thanks to the work of Marc Von Montagu, Jeff Shell, Mary Dell Chilton and several others. The first patent for a living organism went to Dr Anand Chakraborty, who developed, through recombinant DNA technology, an organism for cleaning up oil spills. Since then, bioremediation has become an important tool for promoting environmental hygiene, including cleaning up oil spills. The science of molecular genetics has been applied with great benefit in the fields of medicine, industry, environment and agriculture. In the case of medicine, the public have been experiencing several beneficial fall-outs, such as new vaccines, insulin and genetic medicine. The major concern in medical genetics is one of ethics, as for example the application of recombinant DNA technology for reproductive cloning.

Therapeutic cloning, on the other hand, has been welcomed. In the case of environmental biotechnology, there is great interest in bioremediation methodologies since there is growing pollution of ground and river water. In food and agricultural biotechnology there are public concerns about biosafety, environmental safety, biodiversity loss, and human and farm animal health.

In the case of technologies which carry both benefits and possible risks, it is important to have regulatory mechanisms which can help to analyse risks and benefits in an impartial, transparent and professionally competent manner. This is why the Government of India introduced in 2013 in Parliament, a Biotechnology Regulatory Authority Bill. Unfortunately, the validity of this Bill from the point of view of debate and decision has expired with the conclusion of the term of the previous Lok Sabha. This gives the Indian Council of Agricultural Research (ICAR), Department of Biotechnology, Indian Council of Medical Research (ICMR), the Council for Scientific and Industrial Research (CSIR), University Grants Commission (UGC), Ministry of Environment and Forests, and other agencies a wonderful opportunity to go through the text of the Bill once again, taking into account the numerous comments, criticisms and suggestions which have been received, and get a new Bill prepared for introduction in the current Parliament. While it may take time to set-up a Parliament-approved National Biotechnology and Biosafety Regulatory Authority, guidelines for safe field testing should be developed. Enforcement of procedures for the release of genetically modified organisms (GMOs) for commercial cultivation may take time, but field testing under well-defined safeguards should go on. There are numerous GM varieties in the breeders' assembly line, and they should be tested in the field without further delay. Meanwhile, procedures for their release can be finalized through appropriate discussion and legislation. Field testing with due safeguards can be done in the farms of agricultural universities.

An Agricultural Biotechnology Committee which I chaired in 2003, and which submitted its report early in 2004, had recommended both a Parliament-approved regulatory agency and the necessary infrastructure for conducting all-India coordinated trials with GMOs. Such an all-India coordinated trial, to be organised by the ICAR, should have as its coordinator an eminent biosafety expert. The necessary precautions, such as the needed isolation as well as demonstration of the importance of refuge, should be undertaken under this coordinated project. More than ten years have passed since this recommendation was made and we should lose no further time in implementing it. We should put in place a trial and safety assessment system which answers the concerns of anti-GMO experts and environmental organizations. *The present moratorium on field trials with recombinant DNA material serves as a serious handicap as well as a disincentive in harnessing the benefits of the wide array of transgenic material currently available with various public and private sector research organizations and universities.* Many of the GMOs in the breeders' assembly line have excellent qualities for resistance to biotic and abiotic stresses, as well as improved nutritional properties. Much of this work has been done in institutions committed to public good. Also, much of the work has been done by brilliant young scientists who are getting discouraged because of the lack of a clear official signal on the future of genetic modification in agricultural research.

While urgent steps are needed for putting in place a widely accepted regulatory system, full advantage should be taken of the molecular marker-assisted selection procedures of breeding. Many of the desired goals can be achieved through marker-assisted breeding. Varieties developed through marker-assisted selection are accepted for organic certification. Agriculture is a state subject, and it is very important that the state agricultural universities and state departments of agriculture are involved in the design and implementation of the field trials. *It takes nearly ten years for a new variety to be ready for cultivation by farmers. Therefore speed is of the essence in organizing field trials and gathering reliable data on risks and benefits.*

Return from investments in biotechnology research is high. Public sector institutions should accord priority to the development of high-yielding climate-smart and disease-resistant varieties, while obviously the private sector will prefer to produce hybrids whose seeds will have to be brought every year by farmers. Public and private sectors should develop a joint strategy which will help to ensure the inclusiveness of access to improved technologies among all farmers, small or large. Public sector R&D institutions should give high priority to the breeding of varieties which can help farmers minimize climate and market risks. Also, seed companies should provide to small farmers insurance policies that will save them from total monetary loss in seasons characterized by drought or other natural calamities beyond the control of farmers.

There is need for pan-political support for promoting safe and responsible genetic engineering research. Every research institution should have a project selection committee which will examine carefully whether recombinant DNA technology is necessary to achieve the desired breeding goal. In many cases, marker-assisted selection would be adequate for developing a variety with the necessary characters. Recombinant DNA technology should be resorted to only when there is no other way of achieving the desired objective.

The report of the Parliamentary Committee headed by Shri Basudeb Acharya (2012) has to be carefully studied, and the suggestion of the Committee that we should set up a Biosafety Regulatory Authority on the Norwegian model should be examined for appropriate action and adoption.

National Food Security Act

The National Food Security Act (2013) of India is designed to convert the right to food into a legal obligation. This Act contains several interesting features, such as the adoption of a life cycle approach to food entitlements, special attention to the first 1,000 days of a child's life, recognition of the eldest woman in the household as the head of the household from the point of view of receiving entitlements, and enlargement of the food basket to include millets like *ragi* and other minor millets in the public distribution system. The National Food Security Act will help to overcome undernutrition and thereby lay the foundation for achieving the Zero Hunger target. The Act will help to provide not only wheat and rice, but also a whole range of what I call "climate-smart nutricereals," at a very low cost. This in turn will help to halt genetic erosion among what are known as "orphan crops." It is of historic interest that a country which was leading a "ship to mouth" existence fifty years ago is now the first country in the world where the legal right to food is enshrined in a Parliament-approved legislation.

The National Food Security Act of 2013 mandates the government to procure wheat, rice and nutri-millets (often called coarse cereals). Such procurement at remunerative prices is the pathway for stimulating interest among farmers to produce more. India is also just beginning to uncover the potential of agribusiness, diversification, marketing and exports, as well as increasing value addition to food production. The country is exploring whether, with proper protection for the poor and the vulnerable, commercial agriculture can be a catalyst for economic development. Also, climate change, manifested in adverse alterations in temperature, precipitation and sea level, will add to the problems of farmers and farming.

What steps should we take to ensure sustainable advances in agricultural productivity and production so that undernutrition can become a problem of the past? In my view, we should attend to six key areas to safeguard the stability and sustainability of agricultural production in our country.

First, we should ensure that soil health is not only conserved but improved continuously (I elaborate on this point in a later section).

Secondly, irrigation security will have to be ensured through integrated attention to harnessing rain water, river and other surface waters, ground water, treated waste water and sea water. Rain water harvesting at the farm level should be made mandatory all over the country. Sea water constitutes 97 per cent of the world's water resources, and we should promote sea water farming based on sylvi-aqua farms along the coast, as is being done by MSSRF.

Thirdly, technology and inputs need to be tailored to the agro-ecological and socio-economic conditions in which farmers work. Technology is the prime mover of change, and technology upgradation via the introduction of biotechnology, information technology and agricultural mechanization is essential to attract and retain youth in farming.

Fourthly, farmers should receive appropriate credit and insurance support. Credit should be made available at 4 per cent per annum, or even lower interest rates, as recommended by the National Commission on Farmers (NCF). Insurance procedures should promote group insurance on an agro-ecological basis. The government should promote an Indian single market, so that agricultural commodities can move across state frontiers without hurdle.

Fifthly, assured and remunerative marketing ultimately holds the key to economically viable agriculture. Procurement at a minimum support price (MSP) is the greatest incentive to farm families. The MSP should be C2 (total cost of production) plus 50 per cent, as recommended by the National Commission on Farmers. WTO (World Trade Organization) regulations may come in the way of providing our small farmers prices which can help to keep them above the poverty line. Fortunately, our government has taken the stand at WTO negotiations that in the case of countries like India, where over 50 per cent of the population depend for their livelihood on crop and animal husbandry, fisheries and agro-forestry, sustainable food and livelihood security should be the basis of pricing policies, since this is in no way trade-distorting. Policies for achieving the Zero Hunger target should not be considered as violations of WTO rules.

Sixthly, high priority should be accorded to saving precious grain through improved agronomic practices, including management of the triple alliance of weeds, pests and pathogens. The Food and Agriculture Organization (FAO) estimates that nearly 1.3 billion tonnes of food are either wasted during the post-harvest phase or lost during the production phase. We should also establish safe and modern storage at three levels: first, on the farm itself; secondly, at the procurement centres; and thirdly, in a national food security storage grid. We should create at least at fifty different locations in our country, with priority being given to remote, hill and tribal areas, ultra-modern storage structures, each capable of holding about 1 million tonnes of foodgrains and other commodities to be used in the public distribution system. Thus, we should have foodgrain stocks of 50 million tonnes at any one time, preserved in safe storage. This will be prudent in an era of climate change, expanding population, diminishing per capita land and water resources, and high price volatility.

Finally, there is need to give the power and economy of scale to small holders. This can be in the form of cooperatives, which have been very effective in the dairy sector, or producer companies. Group farming through self-help groups can also be promoted. Today, the small farmer in India has neither the holding capacity nor the bargaining power to ensure that he gets a reasonable price for his produce. Also, some kind of group cooperation is essential to promote ecologically sustainable production measures like integrated pest management, scientific water management and improved post-harvest management.

Climate Change

The Fifth Assessment Report (AR5) of the Intergovernmental Panel on Climate Change (IPCC) finds beyond reasonable doubt that the earth's climate is warming. Temperature projections for South Asia indicate that by the mid-twenty-first century, temperature rise may exceed 3°C over higher latitudes under the high emission scenario. The frequency of hot days in South Asia is likely to increase further in the future. Rainfall projections for South Asia indicate the occurrence of more rainfall at higher latitudes by the mid-twenty-first century under the high emission scenario. Observations also show that there have been more extreme rainfall events and fewer weak rainfall events in the central Indian region. Global mean sea level will continue to rise during the twenty-first century. The magnitude of sea level rise is likely to be in the range of 26–55 centimetres. This trend significantly increases the risks for South Asia's coastal settlements, as well as for coastal economies, cultures and ecosystems, particularly if combined with changes in cyclone frequency or intensity. Low-lying, densely populated coastal areas in South Asia, including in India and Bangladesh, will be at increased risk of storm surges, putting many millions of people at risk.

The IPCC finds that on a global level, climate change could affect food security by the mid-twenty-first century, and that most of those who are food-insecure will continue to be in South Asia, where there are currently roughly 300 million undernourished people. This will be exacerbated by declining agricultural productivity in the region. The key risks identified for South Asia include water and food shortages. The tropical and sub-tropical regions of India are projected to be vulnerable to increasing temperature and CO_2 levels, with a decline in rice yield of as much as 23 per cent by 2080.

Rice, a key staple crop in the region, is most vulnerable in the northern part of South Asia. In the Indo-Gangetic plains, which produce 90 million tonnes of wheat a year (about 14–15 per cent of global production), projections indicate a substantial fall in yields by the mid-twenty-first century, unless there is a shift to different crop varieties and management practices. The decline in productivity could lead to higher food prices and living costs, malnutrition, and worsened rural poverty. This may result in a net increase of 15 per cent in poverty in South Asia by the year 2030.

The IPCC AR5 suggests that if countries adopt scientific crop management measures, they can avoid losses ranging from 15 to 18 per cent of current yields. Even when effective adaptation occurs, local food systems are still likely to experience negative yields as a result of local temperature increases of about 2°C. Reduced dry season flows together with a rise in sea levels will increase salt water intrusion into many South Asian deltas, compound existing threats, and negatively impact both capture fisheries and aquaculture production.

An Example of Climate Change Adaptation
It is a known fact that the state of Andhra Pradesh is vulnerable to both droughts and floods. The M.S. Swaminathan Research Foundation has been working with the rural and farming communities of Andhra Pradesh for several years now. Climate adaptation-related initiatives with a focus on semi-arid agriculture and water, and the mangrove conservation programme, have yielded good outcomes and insights. One of the key initiatives undertaken under the climate adaptation programme is to build capacities at the local level to manage climate risks. A mini agro-meteorological facility was set up at project sites to record real-time data on precipitation, temperature and humidity. This information was disseminated through a network of Village Knowledge Centres on a daily basis. Select people were trained to record and interpret these data, which helped in the practice of weather-based farming. Over a period of five years, the farmers developed their own rules of thumb to manage climate risks associated with specific agricultural activities. The project helped bring a scientific outlook to existing local adaptation practices. It highlighted the need for location-specific adaptation measures, and for participatory research and knowledge management. Following the success of this project, a cadre of Climate Risk Managers from select places across states were trained in the art and science of climate risk management.

Based on the Andhra Pradesh experience, I suggest the following plan for adaptation.

1. A good starting point for effective adaptation is to map the vulnerabilities (both biophysical and social) of the region. A vulnerability atlas showing area-specific vulnerabilities can be produced.
2. Climate risk management at the local level is critical. Building local capacities is central to promoting good adaptation measures. Every *panchayat* should have a climate risk manager to provide critical weather information and suggest possible remedies to address problems.

3. Providing right information at the right time is critical to manage risks. Hence, climate information service provision should be central to adaptation-related planning.
4. Identifying and promoting appropriate catalytic technologies, climate-related awareness among the public and social mobilization are important elements for the success of adaptation.
5. Extension agencies should be provided with appropriate training to understand climate-related impacts and effectively advise communities to manage their agricultural activities.

Soil Health and Achieving the Zero Hunger Challenge

Long ago, Aristotle described the soil as the stomach of a plant. Nearly 90 per cent of the world's food supply comes from crops or animals reared on the soil. According to the FAO, our soils are in danger because of expanding cities, deforestation, unsustainable use, pollution, overgrazing and climate change. Thus the current rate of soil degradation endangers our capacity to achieve a balance between human numbers and the human capacity to produce food. The United Nations had therefore designated 2015 as the International Year of Soils. The focal theme for the year was "Healthy Soils for a Healthy Life." Every nation should try to promote effective policies and action for the sustainable management of soil resources. In India, we will have to produce at least 50 per cent more food by 2030 from diminishing per capita land resources and expanding biotic and abiotic stresses including climate change. There is hence no time to relax on the soil health conservation movement.

We should now establish in every *panchayat* a Soil Health Conservation and Amelioration Centre which will provide farmers with Soil Health Cards, and help them to not only maintain but enhance soil health. We have an excellent National Soil Survey and Land Use Planning Institution at Nagpur under the umbrella of the Indian Council of Agriculture Research. Soil survey data are useful at the watershed, irrigation command area and farm levels for a variety of purposes, such as crop planning and rainfed agriculture, depth and frequency of irrigation in command areas, and drainage arrangements. The National Bureau of Soil Survey and Land Use Planning has developed methodologies for relating soil survey data to the choice of cropping and farming systems. The wealth of soil information available in soil survey reports and maps must be communicated to the farmers. Every Village Knowledge Centre should have adequate information on the strengths and weaknesses of the soil resources of the village, and of methods of optimizing agricultural production based on efficient soil management.

In particular, the organic matter content of tropical soils is low, and building up soil organic matter is an urgent task. Organic farming helps to improve soil physics, soil microbiology and soil nutrient status at the same time. Chemical agriculture, on the other hand, only attends to the nutrient status (like NPK) of the soil. Soil health literacy is important for emphasizing the multiple roles of soil in terms of ecological, livelihood and food security.

Well-managed soils also help to improve water management. In the heavy black soils of Madhya Pradesh, two crops can be taken provided a ridge and furrow method of planting is adopted. The furrow serves the purpose of inter-row water harvesting. Thus, a good crop like soybean can be raised on the ridges during the *kharif* season, and another crop like wheat or corn or maize can be raised in the furrows during the *rabi* season. Land use decisions are also water use decisions. Therefore, land use planning is exceedingly important both for irrigation water security and food security.

On 31 December 2014, the Government of India promulgated an ordinance to amend some provisions of the land acquisition law brought to Parliament by the earlier government. The amendments are designed to ensure the Right to Fair Compensation and Transparency in Land Acquisition, Rehabilitation and Resettlement. The National Commission on Farmers had emphasized that serious steps should be taken to prevent the diversion of good farm land for non-farm purposes such as the establishment of special economic zones (SEZ). We had proposed that like the SEZ, there should be special agriculture zones (SAZ). While SEZ allocates land for economic activity, SAZ should conserve good farm land for agriculture. For example, I had suggested that the Indira Gandhi Canal area of Rajasthan, the Kuttanad below sea level farming system of Kerala and similar important agricultural sites should not be allowed to be diverted for non-agricultural use. I welcome the initiative of the ICAR to prepare a soil map of India based on an extensive database on soils, their area and characteristics, to enable grouping them based on soil taxonomy. This soil map could be used as the basis for identifying SAZ, which will serve as guardians of our food and livelihood security systems in the coming decades.

It is to be hoped that the amended system of land acquisition will take into account the need not only for fair compensation to farmers, but also the need to conserve land for raising food and other crops that we need for human health security and for achieving the Zero Hunger challenge.

Power of Public Good Research

Public good research in agriculture is designed to promote risk-minimizing agronomy, and also the ease of adoption by small and marginal farmers. For example, public good research institutions concentrate on the development of varieties rather than hybrids, since in the case of hybrids, the farmer has to buy the seed every year from the company. In contrast, farmers can keep their own seeds of good varieties of wheat, rice, maize and other crops. We should not underestimate the power of public good research in contrast to profit-maximizing private sector research. I shall try to illustrate this from two recent examples, one dealing with Basmati rice and the other with semi-dwarf wheat varieties.

Basmati is appropriately referred to as the queen of rice, and has been cultivated for centuries in the foothills of the Himalayas. Because of its cooking quality, it is valued highly in national and international markets. Pakistan also grows Basmati rice. After the advent of high-yielding varieties of rice possessing genes for semi-dwarf character, Basmati rice was given less importance due to its tall stature and low yield potential (about 1 tonne per hectare). It was to overcome this difficulty that the Indian Agricultural Research Institute (IARI) started developing semi-dwarf Basmati strains which could respond well to fertilizer and irrigation water application. Their work, which began nearly forty years ago, has now resulted in outstanding varieties like Pusa Basmati 1121, which has helped to increase foreign exchange earnings. In 2015, IARI released another variety, Pusa Basmati 1509, which matures in 120 days and has dwarf stature, sturdy stem, non-lodging and non-shattering habit, and yields about 5 tonnes per hectare. Because of its early maturity, Pusa Basmati 1509 has become very popular among farmers adopting a rice–wheat rotation. No wonder, there is enormous demand for the seeds of this variety, which now occupies a major portion of the Basmati area. This is a good example of the power of public-good research, with a sharp focus on increasing the productivity and profitability of small holdings.

IARI has also been developing and releasing wheat varieties which help to increase production and productivity of this crop. Starting with semi-dwarf wheat varieties like Kalyan Sona and Sonalika in the 1960s (these are selections made from the material sent by Dr Norman Borlaug), the Pusa wheats, as well as those bred by scientists of the Punjab Agricultural University and other agricultural universities and institutions, have transformed our wheat scenario. From about 7 million tonnes in 1947, wheat production has now reached about 96 million tonnes. The aim is to produce within the next twenty years, 150 million tonnes of wheat from 30 million hectares. This will be possible, considering the fact that our wheat breeders are continuously producing outstanding new strains. A recent example is HD 2967, developed by the wheat breeders of IARI. This variety now occupies about 6 million hectares in north India and contributes 35 million tonnes of output. It is resistant to major pests and diseases, and yields on an average more than 4 tonnes per hectare. It is only this kind of research that can help us to achieve an evergreen revolution leading to the enhancement of productivity in perpetuity without ecological harm.

While the benefits of wheat and rice research both to farmers and to the country have been phenomenal, the actual expenditure on such research has been only a few crores per year. Thus, the return from investment in public good research is exceedingly impressive. This is why the National Commission on Farmers has laid emphasis on adequate support for research and training at our national research institutions and agriculture universities. This is the best investment the country can make in the interest of sustainable food security, thereby making possible the implementation of the provisions of the National Food Security Act.

Among the facilities needed for strengthening public good research are translational research centres which can convert laboratory findings into field application. We also need facilities for taking more than one crop per year, such as green houses and growth chambers. In the case of wheat, accelerated work became possible after a centre was established at Wellington in the Nilgiri hills, where a summer crop of wheat can be taken. This is also possible in the Lahul and Spiti Valley region of Himachal Pradesh. In the case of rice, IARI and the Tamil Nadu Agriculture University have established an off-season multiplication centre at Aduthurai in Thanjavur district of Tamil Nadu. This again helps to purchase time in breeding. We need to augment such facilities so that we will be able to meet the new challenges arising from climate change and global warming. There is no time to relax on the food production front. Translational research centres, which can help to convert scientific discovery into field application, are also urgently needed. Every ICAR institution and agricultural university should have a translational research wing, so that the gap between discovery and application can be minimized or even eliminated.

Conclusion

Keeping in mind N. Ram's deep concerns in relation to the persistence of hunger and poverty, I have dealt at length with issues relating to the elimination of hunger in our country. All the national and international reports dealing with the prevalence of hunger and malnutrition indicate that India is the home for the largest number of malnourished children, women and men. On the other hand, our hard-working farmers produce over 270 million tonnes of foodgrain, 300 million tonnes of fruit and vegetables, and 140 million tonnes of milk. If there is equity in the distribution of food and the other components for a balanced diet, hunger can be eliminated in our country. The best tribute we can pay to Ram is to work for the cause of achieving the Zero Hunger challenge proposed by the UN Secretary General. In all such endeavours, I am confident that Ram will extend the full support of his powerful pen, and persuasive voice and wisdom.

Notes

1. The 2017 Global Hunger Index ranks India as 100 out of 119 countries.
2. According to Dr Soumya Swaminathan, good nutrition is the best "vaccine" against tuberculosis (personal communication).

References

Das, Prasun Kumar, R.V. Bhavani and M.S. Swaminathan (2014), "A Farming System Model to Leverage Agriculture for Nutritional Outcomes," *Agricultural Research* Vol. 3, No. 3, September, pp. 193–203.

Government of India (1982), *Report of the Working Group on the Eradication of Leprosy* (Chairman: M.S. Swaminathan), Ministry of Health and Family Welfare, Government of India, New Delhi.

Obama, Barack (2010), "Remarks by the President to the Joint Session of the Indian Parliament in New Delhi, India," available at http://obamawhitehouse.archives.gov/the-press-office/2010/11/08/remarks-president-joint-session-indian-parliament-new-delhi-india, viewed on 17 October 2017.

Paine, J.A., C.A. Shipton, S. Chaggar, R.M. Howells, M.J. Kennedy, G. Vernon, S.Y. Wright, E. Hinchliffe, J.L. Adams, A.L. Silverstone and R. Drake (2005), "A New Version of Golden Rice with Increased Pro-vitamin A Content," *Nature Biotechnology*, Vol. 23, pp. 482–87.

Swaminathan, M.S. (2009), "Gene Banks for a Warming Planet," *Science*, Vol. 325, 31 July.

Swaminathan, M.S. (2014), "Zero Hunger," *Science,* Vol. 345, 1 August.

Wilson, E.O. (2002), *The Future of Life*, London: Vintage Books.

How the Present Reads the Past
Romila Thapar

For N. Ram: Friend and Editor

My first meeting with N. Ram was before he became the editor of the newspaper and the magazine that I was later to associate with him – *The Hindu* and *Frontline*. He had applied to do research in modern history at the Centre for Historical Studies in the Jawaharlal Nehru University. So we interviewed him – as we did all those applying to do research – and were glad to have him as a research student, looking forward to his being at the Centre. We thought that he might go in for an academic career, but he eventually became an active participant in the editing of the family newspaper and the magazine.

His politics were to the Left and we wondered if this would become evident on his having a say in editorial policy. *The Hindu* in those days was seen as a newspaper commanding authority but with a base largely in south India. Its readership in Delhi at that time was more limited. But it gradually gathered an impressive readership when it came to be recognized as a serious and reliable paper with a greater proportion of in-depth news and analysis than the usual north India-based newspapers. Later, with Ram as editor-in-chief, it took a big leap to join the forefront of Indian national dailies. *Frontline* moved gradually from what was thought to be a predictably Left position to a somewhat more open arena for discussion of current issues, and, in this process, expanded its perspective from a more political magazine to one covering a larger variety of subjects – some of current interest and some more general.

The 1960s and 1970s were decades which saw the continuation of lively debates on the shape and form that we wished Indian society to have. The Nehruvian concept was not one of a static state, as its detractors hold it to be in present times, because with each major debate there were adjustments and modifications. It was conceded that secularism was an essential component of democracy, although the debates on secularism did not probe the implications for a secular India in sufficient depth. There were many occasions when the colonial interpretations of the Indian reality were examined, with the suggestion that where they were erroneous they should be set aside. This exercise should have been carried out more extensively than was done at the time, and it is one that many ex-colonies need to do.

These discussions touched on many aspects of life and were reflected in the diverse scope of various publications of the time, more especially in magazines such as *Economic and Political Weekly* and *Seminar*. These maintained a serious level of discussion on contemporary issues, and invited contributions from academics and from journalists who had established reputations as specialists in particular fields of study. Some of these authors also contributed to *Frontline*. They ranged from being liberal and left-of-centre liberal to markedly left. The ideological position was flexible, depending on who was writing the article, but of course the choice of contributors gave the magazine its ideological flavour.

It was in magazines such as these, of which there were others too, that ideas related to the social sciences were first floated, sometimes prior to being worked into a more research-based thesis for specialized journals. The central question that dominated our thinking, and was often also the crux of debates among economists and political scientists in particular, focused on the kind of society that we envisaged for India as an independent nation. On this hinged the question of governance and how best to move without too much friction from being a colony to becoming a nation. Inevitably this required at least two other perspectives that had earlier been omitted. One was some knowledge of the social structure of society since familiarity with the economy was not sufficient. This introduced the sociologist and social anthropologist into the discussion. The other was the perspective on whether society as an entity had evolved from earlier forms. This brought in the historian. The bare bones of what were to become extensive studies in the social sciences were now gaining visibility and finding a readership. *The Hindu*, some decades ago, was among the first of newspapers to carry long interviews with historians, ancient and modern, the purpose of which in part was to explain to the public the ways in which the study of history was changing. The focus was on the kinds of new questions that historians were asking. This was an effective way of encouraging communication between the researcher and the general reader, an activity that still needs far more attention than we give it.

These were the kinds of issues around which many conversations revolved, particularly among academics and serious journalists who had thought about them. Such conversations were thought of as having some significance not only as the voice of citizens, but also because these opinions did matter to the makers of policies. Sometimes such views were incorporated into policies and sometimes not, but at any rate there was an awareness of the opinions of those beyond the practitioners of governance. This was an ambience quite different from today, characterized as our systems now are by a general absence of thinking policies through to their logical or likely conclusion. The dialogue between academics and opinion makers was in earlier times regarded as expected and useful. It was important to conveying new ways of thought to the wider public.

It was in this context that I initially got to know Ram. He was among the few editors who were sensitive to the question of how the present reads the past. There was therefore the need for a serious understanding of the early past to recognize when it was being misread in support, for instance, of present-day politics, as it commonly was. As has been frequently pointed out, these were not just interpretations in understanding the early past; but to a far greater extent they were attempts at reading the past so that it could be used to legitimize the extremist policies and activities of religious right-wing organizations – the presence of which has grown exponentially. Ram was clued into the debates that were challenging the colonial interpretations of history. The focus of these tended to be more on pre-modern history since that was where the colonial interpretation had focused.

It was also in the 1970s and 1980s that the *Hindutva* version of history was presented to the public as the authentic history of pre-modern India. Historians had the choice either of isolating themselves and writing on relatively obscure subjects, or else of questioning the so-called authentic, indigenous history. Those concerned about the academic quality of the discipline had inevitably to protect this quality, both through their own research and by pointing to the fallacies of the popular versions where they were fallacious.

It was during the 1980s that I began to visit Chennai more frequently than before. I gradually came to know Ram as an affectionate and dependable friend with his generously welcoming hospitality. Initially when I gave some lectures for Prakriti, I stayed elsewhere. But it soon became an established practice that I would stay at Ram's home irrespective of who had invited me. This always brought unexpected forays into local life, most of which kindled new and pleasurable interests. On one occasion we spent an evening with the Nawab of Arcot, which gave me a glimpse of a very different Chennai from the one I was familiar with. On another occasion I was transfixed by R.K. Narayan's view of the world as he held forth to the two of us. Or else there was always a surprise visitor at any time of day – a writer, a journalist, an artist, a musician, even a politician, all leading up to fascinating conversations. I gradually realized that Ram is actually an institution in Chennai. When Mariam became a part of Ram's home my pleasure was doubled, since my closest friends in college in Delhi had been her two aunts, and I felt an immediate bond.

In an odd kind of way our friendship took a new turn when I shifted from a PC to a Mac! Ram was familiar not only with the Mac but all the gadgetry that went with it. And since I am double left-handed with computers I shared his enthusiasm but not his ease with the gadgets. The greatest joy was when he patiently taught me how to load some of his fine collection of music CDs on to my computer. This was a real bonus.

Inevitably, and over the years, Ram and I discussed history. His primary interest was of course in modern history, especially in contemporary events and their context. But he followed the debates that were current about issues in earlier history, in part because so much of historical interpretation impinges on activities in our own times. These conversations would occasionally end up with my writing an article on the subject for *Frontline* or *The Hindu*. The public, Ram said, could only become aware of why there were these controversies if the issues were explained in publications accessible to the public. Many historians were, and are, appalled by the obviously superficial arguments of those whose writing of history was intended solely to propagate the *Hindutva* ideology, and their attempts to denigrate what historians wrote from a reasoned and critical perspective. The historical writing of the latter was, and is, consistently dismissed by *Hindutva* supporters as being "Marxist," which for them was merely an abusive term! None of them showed any understanding of what is meant by a Marxist analysis of history. So the established Marxist historians often found themselves in strange company.

The attacks on our writing of history had begun earlier but came to the forefront during the period of the Janata government with Morarji Desai as Prime Minister (1977–79). An anonymous note was sent to him stating that the textbooks in History written by some of us for Middle and High School should be banned as they were anti-national. The demand was made by the *Sangh Parivar* all through the years since then and it still continues, except that now the demand is that all our books should also be burnt! This initial debate over the validity of the textbooks that we wrote raged for three years, with articles for and against various positions in the Sunday papers. Articles in *The Hindu* were prominent in this debate. The then Education Minister, Pratap Chandra Chunder, appointed a committee of a dozen historians to assess the books. They were cleared unequivocally by all except one, whose objection was that school teachers would find it difficult to teach from them. But soon after this the government fell and the books remained in use.

In the 1980s the issue of the Babri Masjid gained momentum, culminating in the destruction of the mosque in December 1992. The historicity of Rama had been asserted and an exact spot located as the *janmabhoomi* (place of birth) of Rama. It was asserted that the mosque had been built on this location where a temple to Rama had stood, which temple had been torn down in order to construct the mosque. The historicity of Rama, important as it is or may be to devotees of Rama, is of less concern to historians. Barring the popular story of Rama, there is no other evidence referring to him as a historical figure, as there is, for instance, for the Buddha, Mahavira, and for Christ and Mohammad. But the question of the temple was a challenge to historians as the evidence for such a temple is lacking.

As historians we objected to these statements being called historical facts. We made a distinction between belief and history. Whereas those who wished to believe that this was the birth-place of Rama and that a temple had been located on that exact spot would obviously do so, this belief could not be taken as history as the required evidence was not forthcoming. So far there is no definitive evidence to support the existence of such a temple, neither from text nor from excavation. There is after all a fundamental difference between faith and history as some of us kept pointing out. We were not opposed to faith since people believe what they wish to, but they cannot insist on their belief replacing historical fact.

The leaders of the Bharatiya Janata Party (BJP) had used an additional argument to justify tearing down the Babri Masjid, a protected heritage monument of the sixteenth century. This was their statement: that this act avenged the raid of Mahmud of Ghazni on the Somanatha temple which had instantaneously created a trauma among the Hindus of India against the Muslims. But, as I tried to show in a detailed study of this and subsequent events at Somanatha (a summary of which was published in *Frontline*), only the chronicles of various Sultans and other Turko-Persian narratives wax eloquent about the destruction of the temple. They do so amidst a welter of confusion as to the identity of the idol that was destroyed (although other sources suggest it was a *lingam*). The temple would have been desecrated in such a raid but Hindu sources make no mention about the destruction of the temple. Powerful Hindu kingdoms, contemporaries of Mahmud, such as the Cholas, the Chalukyas and the Palas, do not mention Mahmud or any ensuing trauma. The first reference to the raid having given rise to a Hindu trauma against the Muslims was made in a debate in the House of Commons in 1842, eight centuries after the event.

The subject of Hindu–Muslim antagonism that was to become the bedrock of the two-nation theory quoted in explanations for the Partition of India in 1947, was manipulated by various Hindu and Muslim political groups involved in the politics of the twentieth century. This has its roots in the first modern history of India written by James Mill in 1818–23, and the theory was repeated in subsequent colonial histories. The idea is embedded in the colonial view of the Indian past, and was appropriated by both Hindu and Muslim religious nationalisms in their bid to create Islamic and Hindu nations in the subcontinent. It is central to the current theories of the politics of religious identities, faithfully following the directives of the colonial readings of Indian history.

This was not the only version of history that had its ancestry in colonial interpretations. Another idea, not entirely disconnected from the above, was formulated in the writings of Orientalist scholarship and particularly in the views of Max Mueller, and this was also axiomatic to the colonial view of the Indian past. This was initially projected as the theory of Aryan race but was later modified as the Aryan foundation of Hindu/Indian culture.

These themes were central to the *Hindutva* version of Indian history as encapsulated in the concepts of *pitribhumi* (place of his ancestors) and *punyabhumi* (place of origin of his religion), enunciated in the 1930s by V.D. Savarkar. So with reference to origins it was necessary to prove an unbroken descent of the Hindus from the Aryans, and this required them to be indigenous to the subcontinent. This would also make Hinduism not only the oldest continuous religion of India, giving its practitioners primacy in contemporary India, but also the only religion among the religions followed in India that originated in India. The Aryans have to be indigenous because the roots of Hinduism cannot be outside India.

Some decades ago it had been argued that "the Aryans" (i.e. "the Aryan-speaking peoples" as they should correctly be called) had entered north-western India as invaders, destroyed the Harappan cities and settled in the area. Sir Mortimer Wheeler, writing on the decline of the Harappan cities in the 1950s, had summed it up in his much-quoted remark: "Indra stands accused." But by the 1960s this theory had been disproved. In my address to the Indian History Congress in 1969, I had stated categorically that there was no such invasion. Further that the Aryans probably came as migrants slowly and over a period of time, and settled amidst the existing population. What I was saying reflected the received opinion among serious Vedic scholars and historians, an opinion that many still hold.

However Aryan enthusiasts – whether of the *Hindutva* ideology or others – hotly contest this view, irrespective of how familiar they may or may not be with the study of the subject. No distinction is made between the two historical processes of invasion and migration, and they are treated as identical. That they cannot be treated as identical is obvious since the impact of each is different. To put it at its simplest, invasion results in an imposed culture that is integrated through governance, whereas migration brings about a gradual interface shading into the existing cultures, affecting kinship, language, belief systems. Both processes bring new cultural idioms, but of different kinds and varying degrees.

In their enthusiasm to describe the Aryans as indigenous, there is now an insistence that even the Harappans were Aryans. Since the Harappan pictograms have not been deciphered and we do not know what language they spoke, the evidence to support this identity is lacking. But this theory presents many other problems related to the dissimilarities between the Harappan and Vedic societies.

Currently the accepted chronology is that the Harappan cities preceded the composition of the *Rigveda*. Some enthusiasts argue, however, that the *Rigveda* should be taken as pre-Harappan and therefore dated to 4000 BC. Or better still, they claim that the Harappans were Aryans and could therefore have been the authors of the *Rigveda*. This conflicts seriously with the linguistic data generally used in attempting a chronology for the Vedic texts.

The geography of the Harappan culture extended from Badakshan in the Pamirs to the north, and south to Oman (in Arabia) and southern Gujarat, and from Baluchistan in the west to the foothills of the Punjab in the east. The geography known to the *Rigveda* is limited to the northern part of this area, going from the borderlands to the Doab. So was there a migration from here into the Ganga plains and then southwards into the peninsula? Or were all the people inhabiting these lands to be called Aryans? This would also be problematic.

There is some evidence to indicate that the Harappans had trade connections with Mesopotamia and possibly supplied copper – hence the Harappan settlements at copper mines in Oman – and lapis lazuli from the Pamirs. None of this finds mention in the *Rigveda*. Mesopotamian texts speak of the land and people of Meluhha to the east with which they traded. This is generally identified with the Indus cities. There are no references to this in the *Rigveda*. Some scholars have linked Meluhha to *mleccha*, mentioned in the later Vedic corpus – but the latter refers to those that do not share the culture and language of the Aryans, and are of low status. If Meluhha is identified with the Harappans, then this would not suggest that the Harappans were Aryans.

In recent years a proposed change in the name of the Indus Civilization is doing the rounds, namely, that it be called the Indus–Sarasvati Civilization or better, the Sarasvati–Sindhu (Hindu) Civilization. This of course gives it an immediate Vedic Hindu label. The argument is that a larger number of Harappan sites are located on the banks of a now dried-up river which geologists refer to as the Hakra–Ghaggar, but which some today would like to identify with the river Sarasvati mentioned in the *Rigveda*. It is said to have been a monsoon-based river flowing parallel to the Satlej and the Indus, and debouching into the Rann of Kutch. Its upper reaches are thought to have been captured by the Yamuna and the Satlej because of a tectonic shift, and this resulted in its drying up from the Hissar area onwards.

There are problems with the use of the new title. The evolution of an urban civilization is not derived from the number of pre-urban sites but from the nature of such sites. What is expected is evidence of an evolution of agro-pastoral groups becoming farmers and then evolving into urban settlements. This change is clearly shown in the archaeology of Baluchistan and the North-West, and has been the explanation for the urbanization of cities close to the Indus. Such a parallel exercise has so far not been carried out for the sites in the Hakra–Ghaggar area. If the sites on the Hakra–Ghaggar are to be referred to in the title, then it should more correctly be called the Indus–Hakra civilization. But even the sites that have been identified close to the dry bed of the Hakra are just south of the confluence of the present-day Satlej with the Indus. They are therefore part of the Indus plain.

Where does the Sarasvati come in? It is first mentioned in the *Rigveda*. In the famous *nadistuti* or hymn in praise of the rivers, the pre-eminent river is the Sindhu/Indus and not the Sarasvati. The latter is mentioned together with the other five rivers of the Punjab as well as the Ganga and the Yamuna. The hymn therefore refers to the time after the Yamuna and the Satlej had "stolen" the waters of the Hakra–Ghaggar. Nor is there mention of the more westerly part of the Hakra just south of the confluence of the Satlej and Indus. The Ghaggar to the east of this, which is what some identify with the Sarasvati of the *Rigveda*, had only a small connection with the early Harappan cultures and cannot be regarded as the epicentre of the civilization. Since the geological change took place in the early second millennium BC, the name Sarasvati may have been given to the Ghaggar – or what remained of the Hakra–Ghaggar – and chronologically, this would be dated to the post-Harappan period.

What we really need is a detailed geological and geomorphological study of the area where the Hakra–Ghaggar is thought to have flowed, together with the palaeo-channels and river channels, as also a study of the changing river courses across the undivided Punjab and the Doab. Once this information is established and, hopefully, ordered chronologically, only then should parallels from archaeology and, subsequently, the data from texts, be introduced. At the moment the evidence from scientific sources is still contradictory, and this calls for further investigation. But can the construction of a mythology wait that long?

Historians have pointed out that the Harappan and the Vedic societies were dissimilar and cannot be equated. The Harappan was a sophisticated urban society and the Vedic an agro-pastoral society unfamiliar with urban institutions. This unfamiliarity marks a substantial difference. Attempts are being made to search for artefacts that may clinch the argument of a common culture but these have not yielded any convincing results.

Among these has been the vexed question of the presence of the horse. The horse was central to Vedic culture in many ways. It was used in herding, in drawing chariots, as fast transportation, and quite centrally among animals in rituals, as in the famous *ashvamedha* sacrifice. The horse is conspicuously absent in the Harappan cities and is not depicted on seals, where other familiar animals find a place. A very small number of bones have been found in excavations that some have identified as horse bones, but others have disputed this and identified them as the bones of the onager, the wild ass. The breeding of horses was more common in Central Asia, and in West Asia the horse arrives in the second millennium BC. Interestingly, the earliest undisputed presence of the horse in India comes from a culture unconnected with the Harappan or the Vedic, namely, the Megalithic culture of peninsular India dated to the post-Harappan period.

However, in order to prove that the horse was a common feature of Harappan culture, which would then make it Aryan, a couple of enthusiasts – N.S. Rajaram and Natwar Jha – claimed that they had discovered a Harappan seal depicting a horse. The image of an animal on a broken Harappan seal was altered through using a computer to make it look like a horse and then claim it as such. The claim was said to prove that the horse was known to the Harappans and therefore they were Aryans. Two American scholars – S. Farmer and M. Witzel – analysed it carefully and were able to expose it as a fraud. The broken seal actually depicted the hind parts of a bovine, subsequently made to look like a horse. Where other editors were hesitant to publish this exposé, Ram recognized the importance of what was now being referred to as the "Piltdown horse." He published it in *Frontline*, together with comments by various historians and archaeologists. The *Frontline* issue, appropriately called "Horseplay in Harappa," has now become a collector's item! Needless to say, those of us who commented on what had been done are now among the main targets of attack from the supporters of those who made the claim.

Abuse and acrimony against the critics of the above claim pour in daily, especially on the social media. There is little realization that the question of the identity and history of "the Aryan" requires a definition of the term that has been extensively used in Indian sources in various contexts, and that therefore its definition has changed through history. Furthermore, a study of both the term itself and the implied concept of Aryan demands some specialization in a variety of disciplines, which, when co-related, may then provide an answer. It is a complex study and would now be better served by a coordinate of investigators from various disciplines. In the nineteenth century, one needed to know only the Sanskrit language and some philology to investigate the term. But that was more than a century ago and since then knowledge has moved on. Today, this study demands combined expertise in various fields that have approached it in diverse ways before it can be knit together. It has to meet requirements in Vedic Sanskrit, which is not the same as the Classical Sanskrit taught in most universities; in linguistics pertaining to both Aryan and non-Aryan languages, given the presence of non-Aryan elements in the language of the *Rigveda*; in the archaeological distribution of various cultures and the reconstruction of the societies that the material cultures suggest; in geological and geomorphological studies, to ascertain changing river courses that are crucial to the arguments about the Satlej and the Hakra rivers, and the identity of the Sarasvati; and most recently in genetics, to ascertain population composition and possible migrations, and in which studies it is often forgotten that "Aryan" is a language label and not a genetic label. There are now many scholars working in one or more of these fields.

In each of these there can be, and are, contradictions or agreements of a scholarly nature. Where there are disagreements they do not resort to abusing the other but examine the arguments. In genetic studies alone there are many theories about the Indian population that have a bearing on how we see caste and "the Aryan." Some results maintain that the upper castes are related to the European; others that all castes have an identical gene flow and there is no intervention from outside; or that there is a distinction between groups identified as castes that show mixing from elsewhere; and others identified as tribes that are indigenous. It makes sense therefore to construct hypotheses of what may have happened, but to test each in the context of the evidence and to be aware of factors influencing the evidence. The seriousness of a particular hypothesis depends on the evidence it uses for its construction. We often forget that knowledge advances through questioning and critical analysis, and not through merely repeating statements.

But to insist on the validity of only one theory to the exclusion of all others on the basis at best of debatable evidence, makes one suspicious that the purpose is not to analyse and understand the past but to use the theory for purposes of the present. To observe this connection it might be useful to go back a little into historiography, to see how and why the history of India was written the way it was.

Contemporary nations across the world that were earlier colonies of European powers have inevitably inherited a construction of their history as authored by colonial scholarship. Some have questioned this construction, as historians did in the last half-century, but some in India have continued to think along colonial lines – as I hope to show. We should keep in mind that on the one hand, colonial scholarship gave attention to the existing institutions of the indigenous culture although interpreted through a colonial perspective, but on the other hand and to a greater extent, its intention was to use the past to facilitate the working out of colonial policy. Success in doing this required changing the economy of the colony to adjust it to the requirements of the colonizer even if it meant impoverishing the colony; to reformulating the structure of the society of the colony through mapping castes in new ways; and through combining multiple religious sects into large bodies of monolithic communities identified by religion – Hinduism, Islam, Christianity, Sikhism and so on.

This was the most serious disjuncture experienced by Indian society in its history. Prior to this, two thousand years ago and later, there had been invasions by Shakas, Kushans, Hunas, Arabs, Turks and Mughals. This did mean governance by people who, at the level of the new elite, were initially less familiar with the local scene. Their intervention was not to restructure the systems but rather to let them continue, although of course adjusting them to their own advantage if so required. Such adjustments worked within the parameters of the society and economy as it functioned in India. Wealth was not drained away to distant parts, caste was not reoriented but adapted to new functions, and new religious sects mushroomed all over as before. These changes were not a disjuncture, nor were new attempts made to write the history of the land in a way that legitimized the act of disjuncture.

I have already referred to two axioms that infused colonial thinking in the initial writing of Indian history. These played a crucial role in the ensuing political ideologies of the transition of the colony to becoming nations. The theory of the Hindu and the Muslim being innately hostile to each other, and the latter oppressing and enslaving the former, allowed colonial historians to say that the arrival of the British liberated the enslaved Hindus. Such mythologies took root and continue to be narrated in the oft-repeated phrase that Indians have been slaves for a thousand years, a phrase that in historical terms is meaningless. Colonial rule is, as I have argued, a disjuncture not experienced before in history. In colonial reckoning the Hindus, being in larger numbers, are the majority community, and the Muslims and others, the minorities. The second axiom that in part drew from this was that the civilization of India was Hindu, its religion was Hinduism and its language was Sanskrit, and that the foundation of this civilization was its Aryan culture. These theories were at the core of colonial historiography, and although there were others, these two were central to Indian politics and have remained so.

History is an essential requirement of nationalism. Eric Hobsbawm described it appropriately when he said that history is to nationalism what the poppy is to the heroin addict. History provides an identity since it is always a history written from the perspective of those who are the ideologues of the particular nationalism, and it has to be a shared history which creates the bond between various groups aspiring towards becoming a nation or at least demonstrating their cohesion as a group. The ideology of nationalism that was influential among Indian historians had to contend with these two axioms that gained political currency from among others less pertinent to the politics of nationalism. But these required more incisive and analytic investigation of a kind that was as yet less familiar to the study of history generally.

Indian anti-colonial nationalism was aware of the need for a secular perspective. This it tried to maintain, but did not succeed entirely – in part because of the limited definition of secularism as being merely the coexistence of all religions, the so-called Indian definition of secularism. This was clearly inadequate without an insistence that all religions had to be of equal status. And this in turn was difficult to assert if it was also maintained that one was the religion of the majority community and the others of the minorities. This automatically introduced inequality. The notion of majority and minority communities was a notion inherited from colonialism yet it was by now so ingrained that it was not even questioned.

As a counter to anti-colonial nationalism there developed in the early twentieth century religious nationalisms of an extreme kind. Taking their cue from the colonial interpretation of the Indian past, the Muslim League drew on Muslim aspirations that culminated in the demand for a state; the Hindu Mahasabha was its Hindu counterpart. At the barest level and setting aside more complex reasons, both were attracted to the two-nation theory and inevitably ended up supporting the idea of establishing two states based on religious identities – Islamic and Hindu. One came into being, the other may yet be averted.

Anti-colonial nationalism was no longer required after 1947. The colonial enemy had been exorcised, it was said. But actually this was not the case. One of the more interesting aspects of new nation-states established from ex-colonies is the degree to which they are still rooted in colonial ideas and institutions. Governments of the post-colonial period do not challenge colonial laws or the construction of identities that draw strength from colonial constructions. Authoritarianism is useful. But when there is a clash between colonial ways of looking at the nation and democratic definitions of nationhood, then the identities have to be reassessed. This is in a sense being illustrated in our times.

When the colonial power is no longer present, the nation cannot legitimize the hierarchy of power among various contesting groups. Democratic functioning demands equality. Even where the defined majority is the dominant group, it has to ensure its dominance. Anti-colonial nationalism had envisioned a secular nation as the natural outcome of a society that existed on the basis of multiple cultures and religions, and as was required of a democracy. But ideas of a Hindu *rashtra* as a counterpart to an Islamic state were taking shape. What was required was a monolithic Hindu religion geared to mobilizing Hindus towards a political goal. *Hindutva*, as distinct from Hinduism, was projected to play this role. Its role was and is distinctly different from that of the religion, Hinduism, and the two should not be confused.

What is interesting is the continuing colonial imprint on this ideology. The territory of Hindu *rashtra* was that of British India, presumably because for those times it was seen as fixed, although of course these boundaries changed radically in the next half-century. This was nothing new as boundaries have always changed in every century. But the Hindu *rashtra* had to be a definitively defined territory since other matters hinged on this definition.

The Hindu was defined as one whose *pitribhoomi*/the place of his ancestors and *punyabhoomi*/the place of origin of his religion were both within this territory. This excludes Parsis, Jews, Muslims and Christians, since their religions originated in areas outside these boundaries. There was a need for well-defined boundaries rather than the vague notions of a *Jambudvipa* or *Bharatavarsha* or *Aryavarta*. These would not have done, despite being the names used for territories in ancient Indian texts. It also explains why the Aryans have to necessarily be indigenous to India, both because of ancestry and religion. According to this argument the Hindus alone would qualify on both counts and therefore they have the right to primacy as Indian citizens.

The assumptions of what the Aryan represents are also tied to colonial ideas. In pre-colonial history the term *arya* was used in the Vedic corpus but essentially as an identity underlining those that were to be respected, incorporating a pattern of culture drawing on language, custom, belief systems. Subsequently these became less important, barring language, and *arya* became a qualifier used with reference to royalty, Buddhist monks, respected citizens and such like irrespective of their origins.

Colonial writers gave currency to the Aryans as a people and a race, and in Europe there was an association with superiority as well. These ideas were picked up in two movements that were influential in India. The Theosophists endorsed them and especially Col. Olcott, who was the first to state that the Aryans were indigenous to India and were responsible for taking civilization to the west – a theory now held by *Hindutva*. For a while the Theosophists were close to the Arya Samaj in north India but this did not last for long. Dayanand Sarasvati, the founder of the Arya Samaj, argued that the Aryans came from Tibet. For him the superiority of their religion lay in the fact that it did not demand the worship of icons and instead focused on ideas of belief and ethics.

In the late nineteenth century "race science" became the explanation for many problems of historical origins in Europe. Racial identities became popular explanations for social institutions of the past, and for both including and excluding groups. The Aryans were said to be racially superior. It was argued that the original Aryans from Central Asia split into two branches, with one going west to Europe and the other settling in Iran and India. This led to theories of kinship. The British and the upper-caste Indians were described by some as parted cousins, now meeting through the accident of colonial rule. A contrary view, that of Jyotiba Phule, questioned this but this was set aside by scholars. Phule had argued that the Aryans were *brahmanas* who came from outside India and used caste to oppress the people of India. Where many views were and are being projected, each has its own agenda.

Nineteenth-century fantasies about Indian culture and history as interpreted by prevalent colonial opinion or by European Romanticism continue to prevail in the public mind. Historical fantasies do not die easily, more so because there is something so comforting about a simplified, glorious past that is unproblematic; and especially so when the present is competitive, harsh and uncertain. So if everyone was Aryan, then there would be no problems of origins and identity – at least seemingly. How would one then explain the necessity for caste, or the existence of inequalities in wealth, or the need for diversity in religious beliefs? The simplicity of the

Hindutva version of history has obvious attractions. There is no need to meticulously assess the veracity of the evidence that is being quoted and to discard that which is unviable no matter how attractive it may be; there were no social contradictions since every man and woman knew his and her place in the world and lived accordingly and harmoniously; all religious diversities were ultimately a manifestation of the same single belief. All the history that one requires, we are told, is contained in the *Mahabharata, Ramayana* and the *Puranas,* and all one has to do is to read them to become a historian. That one has to be trained in the use of diverse sources and in the use of critical reasoning is irrelevant to the making up of this history.

Many years ago I wrote that the question of the origins and identity of the Aryans was the biggest red herring to be dragged across the path of early Indian history, and I continue to think so. There are many far more significant questions that we are still grappling with. For instance, how do we understand the emergence of Harappan urbanization and the details of its functioning? What was the nature of the Harappan state, and how did the cities control both their agricultural hinterland and the extensive trade networks that enabled the production and export of goods to Mesopotamia? Was there a trade in copper and lapis lazuli? Why did the cities decline given that they were not invaded? Were elements of the Harappa culture internalized in subsequent cultures?

This introduces the need to study urban centres in the complexity of their ecological environment, their demographic complexion and their cultural outreach; and their commercial activities that gave them an economic viability as urban centres and which were essential to an urban existence; and the differences in the structure of their societies as suggested by the variation in living conditions; and the reading of what we believe were their religious observances and mythologies, that we can only be more certain about after the Harappan pictograms are deciphered. In insisting on calling them Aryans we impose a language on them – Indo-Aryan – that so far has been of no help whatsoever in reading the pictograms, and we impose a belief system on them for which the evidence has yet to be found. By making them the authors of the Vedic corpus we deny them their urban culture.

In the subsequent period the story becomes more complex as there is more archaeological evidence from other parts of the subcontinent and the texts of the Vedic corpus. There is no evidence of urban centres from the decline of the Harappan cities in about 1700 BC until the emergence of towns in Magadha in about the sixth century BC, and steps towards urbanism elsewhere at around that time. It is a millennium that saw a variety of small settlements but no towns. This is the period generally projected as the archaeological counterpart to the Vedic culture as epitomized in the Painted Grey Ware culture of the North-West. But the more persistent presence is that of the extensive Black and Red Ware cultures spread over northern India. And the even more assertive presence is that of the various megalithic cultures in the peninsula and especially in the southern parts, with their elaborate graves and habitation sites. These seem to have no connection with the Vedic corpus.

What happened, then, with Harappan urbanism? Did it also fade out with the city-dwellers? Was urbanism not feasible in the environment where these post-Harappan cultures existed? A new technology was introduced at this stage with the introduction of iron gradually superseding that of copper and bronze. How was the new technology introduced and adapted? Who controlled it, and did this control affect the dominance or otherwise of the various contemporary cultures? But clearly this single technology in itself was not sufficient to bring about urbanism in these and other areas. These are among the more fundamental historical questions that some have tried to answer but much remains to be researched. Interestingly, when this second urbanization happens it remains a continuous process occurring from region to region and there is no break of a millennium.

The continuous and extensive human activity during the period of the non-urban millennium, the period generally associated with the composition of the Vedic corpus, points to the existence of many cultures, to their dispersal and their juxtaposition at some places. Should we not see this as a period of the mixing and merging of cultures involving language, custom and belief systems? Should we still continue to see the Vedic culture as a self-contained, insulated culture of a small segment of society, or should we recognize that although it was treated as such by its authors it was in fact located in the midst of many other cultures, strands from which went into its making? Should we not concede that it changed in the process of accommodating variant cultures? And if it did, then how did it change?

This might explain the context of what are said to be non-Aryan linguistic elements in Vedic Sanskrit, or the presence of some *brahmanas* whose mothers seem to have been non-Aryan *dasis*. This would not detract from the quality of Vedic thought and intellectual enterprise but would expand on the factors that went into its making and make it less exclusive. Like the earlier Harappa culture that had knit together many cultural strands, Vedic culture would also be seen as one example constituted in what was to become the Indian pattern of culture formation – namely, the amalgamation of diverse patterns of living and believing.

This might make us move beyond being confined to thinking of the history of the subcontinent in terms of the north and the south or Aryans and Dravidians, and other such dualistic, limited categories, many of which are now out-of-date. If we map cultures that are juxtaposed, we have to ask: what were their relations with each other, what were the agencies through which they were interconnected, and how did these agencies and interconnections change at different times? Cultures do not leap over long geographical distances, so the study of closer interconnections becomes imperative and tells us much about cultural changes.

My intention in giving the historical background to a couple of current public debates that claim to use history in contemporary politics is to point out that the present uses the past in many ways. Sometimes it is just to bolster political aspirations. The arguments made by historians are to validate their readings of events and situations that occurred in the past. But others are known to sometimes turn to history to justify actions in the present. Both the historian and the public have to comprehend the meaning of a historical statement as an understanding of the past. But they cannot ignore the possibility of that statement being used for a different purpose in the present. The historian has to be vigilant both about how the past is being interpreted and about the way it is being used in the present. It is for this reason that the debating of questions, whether of history or other areas of knowledge, is essential; and that the level of the debate must draw on adequate reliable evidence, and be based on logical and reasoned argument. One is deeply appreciative of an editor such as Ram, who has provided space for such debate.

Working with N. Ram

Ram at 70

John Cherian

I first came to know about Ram after enrolling as a student in the Jawaharlal Nehru University (JNU), in the early 1970s. As an active member of the Students Federation of India (SFI) at the time, I heard of Ram's politics and his activism during his student days in Madras. I remember meeting him for the first time along with a very young V.K. Ramachandran in Bombay's Shanmukhananda Hall in the mid-1970s. Both of them were there to attend the all-India conference of the Centre of Indian Trade Unions (CITU). At the time I never suspected that Ram would, in the near future, play a key role in my career in journalism.

After completing my PhD in the late 1970s, having no great interest in academics, I strayed into the world of journalism. Some of my contemporaries from JNU, like Appan Menon and Manoj Joshi, were already in the print media: both Appan and Manoj worked for *The Hindu* when G. Kasturi was the Editor of the newspaper, but it was Ram who had facilitated their entry there. When Appan passed away unexpectedly, Ram came all the way to Delhi to spend a day with the bereaved family. Appan at the time was no longer an employee of *The Hindu*. I remember Ram giving a moving speech at the memorial meeting for Appan that was held at the India International Centre, New Delhi. He helped us in setting up the Appan Memorial Trust. The Trust gives an annual award to print journalists specializing in international affairs.

After Ram became the Editor of *Frontline*, he was looking for a journalist with expertise in international affairs to write for the magazine. Luckily, I managed to fit the bill. Ram has always valued expertise in specialized fields. After he formally took over editorship, *Frontline* gave considerable emphasis to world affairs, though reporting on national affairs became its forte. In those days, the Indian media used to pay very little attention to international affairs. Ram decided to devote an entire section of the magazine to reportage on international affairs. In fact, *Frontline* became compulsory reading for those aspiring for a place in the civil services. Ram as Editor encouraged us to write on diverse topics. The politics of Latin America and Africa, generally ignored by the rest of the Indian media, were highlighted in the pages of *Frontline*. Thanks to Ram, I tell my friends, I have the kind of job I always aspired for – to write extensively on international affairs and on subjects that are seldom touched upon in the Indian media.

Ram never discouraged us from taking a generally anti-establishment view on issues relating to foreign policy and defence – holy cows for most of the media. *Frontline* was the first national magazine to take a stand against the India–America nuclear deal when others in the mainstream media were toasting the deal. When the national media went jingoistic over Pakistan following the terror attack on the Parliament and after the terror attacks in Mumbai, *Frontline* opted to stay on the side of caution and common sense, and urged the continuation of bilateral talks with Pakistan.

Frontline has consistently argued for improved relations between India and China. The magazine's in-depth coverage of the Tibetan issue was due to Ram's keen personal interest in the subject. In one of the stand-out issues of *Frontline* with Tibet on the cover, I remember Ram writing all the articles pertaining to the cover story.

On issues relating to communalism, *Frontline* under Ram's stewardship was a trailblazer. The issue featuring the demolition of the Babri Masjid has become a collector's item. His encouragement of long-form journalism has made *Frontline* one of the few magazines of its kind worldwide, for magazines having a similar format have vanished or withered away all across the world. Ram's careful nurturing of the magazine and of its in-house talent has made *Frontline* what it is today.

Ram himself is a champion of progressive causes, and his world view was reflected in the pages of *Frontline*. The anti-apartheid struggle in South Africa in particular and the liberation struggle in the wider region were widely chronicled in the pages of *Frontline*. Whenever South Africa is mentioned, Ram talks about his visit to Robben Island where Nelson Mandela was incarcerated.

We were encouraged to travel on assignments to places where few Indian journalists ventured to go. Thanks to the editorial policy conceptualized by Ram, *Frontline* became a magazine that was taken seriously by many opinion makers around the world for its progressive take on issues. Many diplomats based in Delhi depend on *Frontline*'s reportage while analysing the politics of the country. At the launch of the redesigned *Frontline* in Delhi in October 2012, the hall was packed with ambassadors, politicians and academics.

I have had the pleasure of travelling with Ram on media trips to several countries. The first such visit was to Cuba in 1994. The country was going through a "special period." The Cuban economy was under tremendous pressure due to the combined effects of the American blockade and the collapse of the Soviet Union. Friends of Cuba worldwide had got together and organized a "Solidarity with Cuba" movement. The India chapter sent a ship full of essential supplies, including grain and medicine, to Cuba. Fidel Castro spoke for more than two hours, holding the audience spellbound. Ram, as is his wont, was busy taking copious notes. Young journalists who have travelled with Ram on official assignments all talk about him sharing notes and going out of his way to be helpful.

In Havana, I remember that Ram was particularly excited to visit the house in which Ernest Hemingway resided and the bar he frequented in the last years of his life. We had a particularly memorable encounter with Gregorio Fuentes, credited by many as the model for Hemingway's protagonist Santiago in the classic novel, *Old Man and the Sea*. Fuentes was a fisherman and the first mate of Hemingway's boat, *The Pilar*.

A trip to Iran with Ram was memorable. Besides Teheran, we visited the beautiful cities of Isfahan and Shiraz. In Teheran, we visited the offices of the *Teheran Daily*. During the discussions we had, I casually mentioned that *Frontline* had done a cover story that was supportive of the Hezbollah in Lebanon. The story was done after the Israeli invasion of Lebanon in 2006. The next day, there was a headline in the paper implying that *The Hindu* supports the Hezbollah whereas it had not taken such a position. Ram at the time was Editor-in-Chief of *The Hindu*. He just smiled when he saw the front page story in the leading Iranian daily.

Wherever Ram goes, he takes a lot of photographs, which he immediately downloads on to his computer. He should bring out a book of these photographs. Considering the places he has visited, such a book will be a treasure trove. And, as many can vouch, he takes good photographs. Our last trip together was in 2014 to Tibet. Ram was excited to be in Lhasa and once again climb up the steep steps of the Potala Palace. It was probably the third or fourth time he was doing so. We were together on a bumpy twelve-hour bus ride from Lhasa to southern Tibet. There were no toilets to speak of on the way and the temperature was below freezing point. After the arduous trip, Ram looked much fresher and energetic than me.

The Thinking Intellectual as Editor

P. Jacob and Suresh Nambath

"Let them come," he said. We had just told him that the Tamil Nadu police were coming to The Hindu Group's office premises in Chennai to arrest three directors of the company and two senior journalists. And, all panic dissolved in the face of his quiet resoluteness.

The date was 7 November 2003. Earlier in the day, the Tamil Nadu Assembly had sentenced the Publisher, Editor, Executive Editor and two senior journalists of *The Hindu* to fifteen days of simple imprisonment for breach of privilege of the House. About thirty minutes after the Assembly passed its order in the evening, police jeeps carrying about two dozen policemen, some of them in riot gear, arrived at Kasturi Buildings. A short while later the Editor-in-Chief, N. Ram, came out and asked one of the officers why they were there. When he further asked on what authority they had entered the premises, they turned tail. But the police action was repeated a little later. Officers of the company then escorted them to the newsroom of *The Hindu*, where Mr Ram met a couple of senior police officers. He handled the situation calmly, courageously, in an unflappable manner.

Indeed, in the days and weeks that followed, it was Mr Ram, who had taken over as Editor-in-Chief of The Hindu Group of publications on 27 June 2003 – after having been the Editor of *Frontline* and of *The Sportstar* since 1991, and still earlier the Associate Editor of *The Hindu* – who handled well the period of tumult that the newspaper group faced on account of the vindictive approach of the then state government. That typified the man. He had the knack of infusing confidence in the rest of the team. He was always in charge of the situation, and the institution was clearly in safe hands.

During the period from June 2003 until January 2012, when he stepped down as Editor-in-Chief (and eventually became Chairman of the Board of Directors of Kasturi & Sons Ltd, the company that owns the newspaper group), Mr Ram presided over a number of advances and initiatives. The newspaper notched up its first million net-paid circulation in 2004–05; all the publications of the group went through comprehensive redesign exercises, in the case of *The Hindu* the first on such a scale in its history, led by Mario Garcia; the newspaper introduced the institution of the Readers' Editor; a Code of Editorial Values was formulated and set down. . . .

At the same time, he was not into change for the sake of it. "If it ain't broke, don't fix it," he would say. Changes he did make, but these were brought about over time, and with a steady hand – almost imperceptibly. By the time he stepped down as Editor-in-Chief, he certainly left the newspaper group in good shape. The vision he brought to the table was striking and has stood the newspaper group in good stead.

Great newspapers are as rigorous in the reporting of facts as they are free in the expression of their opinions. And they need great editors for this very purpose: the commitment to truth-telling, to factuality and accuracy in reports have to be combined with a fearless expression of views, a readiness to perform the critical function, the watchdog role in a society that is subject to pulls and pressures from different sides.

For *The Hindu*, Mr Ram fulfilled this role over several decades, especially during his period as Editor-in-Chief. Two things were accomplished at the same time: ending editorializing on the news pages, and featuring sharper editorials and analysis on the opinion pages. The news pages were not allowed as a platform for reporters to parade their views, irrespective of whether the views were in or out of line with the newspaper's own editorial stand. And the opinion pages were opened up to fulfil the newspaper's critical role, acting in the public interest on a variety of issues of import, nudging the government toward progressive programmes and, when necessary, policy correctives.

Mr Ram effectively played the role of a public intellectual, not only through the pages of the newspaper, but also as a public persona on public platforms and other media. On several occasions he was able to intercede in public affairs, changing the discourse and actions of the public sphere through editorials in the newspaper and addresses at events organized by civil society.

His office was always open to all those who wished to see him – politicians of all shades, bureaucrats with complaints, and journalists with doubts or grievances. His own political views did not stop him from receiving visitors from across the spectrum. Both Praveen Togadia and Prakash Karat were received in his office.

As a public intellectual, he has never shied away from taking sides; indeed, he believed taking sides was integral to performing his role as the Editor of a free and independent newspaper. Depending on the issues, and in the public interest, the newspaper under his stewardship adopted either constructive cooperation or an adversarial approach toward the establishment.

Earlier in time, back from Washington where he was on assignment as *The Hindu*'s United States correspondent (1980–82), as he passionately conceptualized and gave shape to *Frontline*, he was in his element. He was hands-on with the work from October of 1984, during a period that witnessed such churn in the Indian polity. He would plan the content, even edit and revise much of the copy by hand, and spend hours on the production floor. It was such a pleasure for juniors, a learning experience, to watch him and assist him.

A great editor in every sense of the term – that is what Mr Ram has been. Not only is he a highly skilled and careful writer, but he is a quintessential editor to whom respecting the creative pride of a given writer whose work you edit is invariably as important as improving the copy. And he does this down to the smallest comma, with remarkable attention to detail for an intellectual who you would assume would tend to stop worrying about the occasional typo and missed punctuation. At an earlier point he would do this pen on paper; today he does it with keyboard and mouse. In his writing and editing he is a perfectionist with attention to detail of a high order.

He was relatively slow to take to the computer, and an old and trusted manual typewriter was what he used up until the early 1990s. But when he took to it, he really took to it. By the first decade of this millennium, there was hardly a computing device or system that he was unfamiliar with. It seems almost an obsession with him today to remain updated on this front.

Quick and sharp, perceptive in his decisions, he had the ability to judge his staff for their strengths as well as weaknesses. He was a good mentor – also a tough trainer. He would easily see through manoeuvres and games. He made choices on postings with due deliberation, and once they were in place, gave them the professional respect they deserved. Mr Ram is hands-on to a significant extent but not a micro-manager. As Editor-in-Chief, he was invariably available well beyond midnight when needed for consultations.

He paid a lot of attention to *The Hindu*'s editorials: he would choose the topics and writers for the day with care. While he disapproved of long meetings, the manner in which he conducted the daily editorial meetings in the forenoon was a tutorial in journalism. As a tough taskmaster, he would insist on the writers delivering strictly to deadline; he rewrote relentlessly where needed, setting the bar high.

He was kind and considerate at an individual level: there are innumerable instances that readily come to mind. There was a sense of fairness and balance and equanimity about him. He has always been accessible, but doesn't suffer fools easily.

He could articulate his views very well. He has been a very good and sought-after public speaker who can put across his ideas in measured prose.

He found his mettle as Editor-in-Chief. In everything he did and said in that role, one saw his sense of responsibility as a custodian of the legacy of a great institution.

The greatest takeaway from watching and working with him? A sensitivity to the ordinary person's life concerns, to the plight of the deprived.

Working with N. Ram

Parvathi Menon

N. Ram, as those who have worked with him as news reporters will endorse, was in every sense a reporter's editor. A journalist before and after he became an editor, he gave confidence and a sense of purpose to his team. He made quick and usually unerring judgments on the wheat and chaff of emerging news, whether it was for the daily newspaper, *The Hindu* (always his first love, I believe), or for the less hurried, news-and-analysis perspective of the fortnightly *Frontline*, a magazine that I worked for as a reporter for the better part of my journalistic career. His sense of the news agenda and its priorities for the short and long term were conveyed, always, in clear directives with a minimum of explanatory fuss.

Confidence and clarity are qualities that the best editors possess. Ram's practical editorial capabilities however rested on something more. As a practising journalist first, later as Editor of *The Hindu* and *Frontline*, and then as Editor-in-Chief of the whole stable of the Hindu Group's publications, Ram's vision for journalism took inspiration from a long international tradition of public purpose journalism, a tradition in India that, historically speaking, included within its fold those sections of the Indian press – *The Hindu* included – that were a part of the freedom struggle. The legacy of that enlightened, intellectual tradition of journalism is many-sided, but perhaps its central tenet is that journalism is an instrument of reason that weighs in for progressive change in a society. Ram developed these ideas into a theory of the media, and its function and role in Indian democracy – on which he wrote and spoke extensively while continuously refining his understanding. For his reporters, and for readers of *The Hindu*, he distilled this vision in a one-page editorial comment entitled "Yesterday, Today, Tomorrow," when he took over as the Editor of the daily in 2002. The "*Panchasheel*" of journalism that he delineated rests on five central characteristics that newspapers must strive for, namely: truth-telling; freedom and independence; justice; humaneness; and contributing to the social good. This is today part of the vision statement of *The Hindu*.

For those who worked with him in *The Hindu*, *Frontline* and other publications in the company's stable, the Ram era was memorable, and for many, even perhaps personally transformative. For me this goes back to my entry into The *Hindu*, in 1986. Ram had returned from the US, where he had spent three years as *The Hindu*'s Washington correspondent, and re-joined the newspaper in Chennai (then Madras) as its Executive Editor. I had just finished a PhD in History from the Aligarh Muslim University, and was not very clear about what I wanted to do. Teaching, perhaps in the same university, was one option, but for personal reasons I wanted to be in the south. I had as a student contributed to *Frontline*, but journalism was not what I had done a PhD for. Or at least that is what I thought until I got an offer from Ram to work in The *Hindu* – but on rather intriguing terms, as part of an "experiment" as he called it. He made offers to several social scientists like me who had just completed their PhDs to work in the newspaper as senior researchers on an experimental basis for a year. We were encouraged to write for a popular readership drawing from our areas of research expertise. At the end of the year the two sides – the management and the new recruits – would assess whether the experiment was worthwhile for both.

Specialized journalism was not unknown in those days, but it was most common in technology and business writing. Here too, specialists usually grew into their roles and attained expertise learning on the job. To find a productive role for a clutch of specialists-come-lately to provide context to news and commentary in the deadline-driven enterprise that is a daily newspaper was an experiment for the editors. For the said group – who came from disciplines like history, economics, political science and, in one case, even medicine – it was an even bigger experiment. Having spent five years or thereabouts pursuing narrow academic specialties, to be told to manufacture content in a day was alarming and initially un-doable, but in time it produced some enduring pieces of long-form journalism – even though these were terribly delayed by journalistic standards. I remember here my friend and colleague Bala (G. Balachandran), a doctorate in economics with previous training as a physicist, with brilliant insights into issues like science policy, whom Ram appointed as *The Hindu*'s first Development Correspondent. Bala's first contribution was an entire supplement.

At the end of the year some of us stayed and some left; but the idea that daily journalism in its many functions and roles needed specialist contextualization was to stay. Years later, when Ram began promoting the case for journalism education and its importance for Indian journalism – which led to the establishment, with Sashi Kumar, of the Asian College of Journalism in Chennai – this idea was integrated into the one-year journalism course curriculum. "Key issues in journalism," a series of lectures by area specialists, is a compulsory component of the course; so is "Covering deprivation," a compulsory module that was the result of yet another important strand of Ram's blueprint for public purpose journalism.

Journalists at *Frontline* and *The Hindu* in Ram's time were to become familiar with his style of working – his intense engagement at any point of time with one story, issue or investigation that he would pursue doggedly, and put all his resources to unravelling and understanding until he was on top of it. These phases of single-minded and concentrated pursuit of a story were jokingly referred to as "the current bee in Ram's bonnet." A news story would become the entry point to a bigger and more complex story-canvas that Ram, with other journalists on the story, would probe exhaustively. A report on corruption and commission agents in the purchase of Bofors guns for the Indian army would lead to an explosive story that became a landmark in investigative journalism into official corruption. A tragic accident involving a busload of child workers on a new year's morning as they were being driven to work in a fireworks factory in Tamil Nadu became the start of a long investigation into child labour, its causes and solutions. A crime report on the police in Bangalore busting a "kidney racket" led to a sustained and comprehensive journalistic exposé led by Ram on organ donation, its practice, its legal and ethical dimensions, and the role of medical practitioners, state governments, donors and recipients of organs. With Pokhran II, the nuclear test conducted by the Atal Bihari Vajpayee government in 1998, India's nuclear weaponization programme became the focus of Ram's attention. *Frontline*, which he was heading at that time, followed the national debate on it closely.

Journalists who have worked with Ram on any one of his story obsessions, I believe, remember the experience as tough but exhilarating. He was a demanding taskmaster and would call you, sometimes several times a day, for precise and clear updates on the progress of the story and the shape of the report you were to file. In the meantime he would be in knowledge-gathering mode, reading background, consulting the experts, and batting ideas around with colleagues, friends and sources. News stories, commentary and editorials followed. Often it was a speaking engagement, a seminar or a public debate that he would use to draw insights and conclusions from the story.

There must have been dozens of these intense engagements over the years with Ram at the helm in which different sets of journalists participated. The trashings and the praise, the intensive learnings and the hard work, the excitement at the forward push of a story, will be remembered and mentally slotted by them as special moments in their journalistic careers.

For me as a historian, the brief Ram gave me when I first joined, of writing on issues of history, was like opening a door on to a terrain of new possibilities. I entered journalism at a time when a new phase of Indian politics was emerging in which history – a history in this case based on myth and hearsay, and with little or no basis in evidence – had become the handmaiden of a new, dangerously sectarian and indigenist vision for the republic of India. For example, take the "history" that was floated in the 1990s of the fifteenth-century Babri Masjid – a mosque built in the reign of the Mughal emperor Babar, which was torn down by mobs owing allegiance to the Bharatiya Janata Party on 6 December 1992. The historical idea that gripped the masses was based on the premise that the mythical figure of Ram, the protagonist of the *Ramayana* venerated in India as a god, was a historical figure born at the exact spot where the Babri Masjid was constructed, and that Muslim zealots had built the mosque to obliterate all traces of his history. Every element in this theory is false, but it gathered steam as ideas tend to do when riding on the back of a political movement that offers the promise of change to a society steeped in social and economic backwardness and inequity.

How can the truth-telling and the social good elements of journalism be applied in reporting such "history"? Some of the answers to this question came to me not as any sudden revelation, but with continuous reporting in my career on issues of history – whether this was reporting on the historical bases of political movements, or writing about historical monuments, or even when profiling historians and their work. Reporting history, I now think, demands to be taught as a sub-specialization in journalism schools, just as reporting science or reporting the arts are taught. This is especially important for journalists who work in societies where the challenge of new forms of identity politics and sub-nationalisms threatens reason and progressive change.

Ideally, but not always, a journalist who reports history must have had a sound degree in history, especially the methodological basis of history, which, as the historian Irfan Habib once noted, is akin in many ways to investigative journalism but conducted with "a long view." The ability to look at historical sources, decide what is of relevance to the story but without burdening the average reader with mountains of boring data, connecting it to contemporary concerns, learning to quickly access sources of expert knowledge and information, checking for new research on the subject, judging authenticity, sticking to a word limit, and working to a deadline are skills that can and should be taught and learnt.

As I retire from a long and interesting career in journalism, there is much to thank Ram for. *The Hindu* in particular and journalism in India in general have been enriched by his presence – and that is surely the best tribute to him.

Freedom to Function

Prabhakara S. Motnahalli

My association with N. Ram (NR) began when I joined *The Hindu* in June 1983 as the paper's North East India correspondent in Guwahati. Mr G. Kasturi was then the Editor and NR was the Associate editor.

Then in my forty-seventh year, I was a member of the editorial staff of *Economic and Political Weekly*, Mumbai (then Bombay), having joined *EPW* in December 1975. When I received a telephone call (I think it was NR who called, or to whom I was connected) some time in May 1983, enquiring if I would be interested in joining *The Hindu* as its correspondent in Guwahati, my immediate reaction was surprise, delight and, even more so, relief. I was then in dire straits, homeless and living in seedy paying guest accommodations and dormitories maintained by churches and charities – a most depressing experience after having been fortunate (no small luck this, in Bombay) over the previous seven years living alone as a dependable caretaker in independent flats of two friends living away from Bombay, six years in Gamdevi and a year in Bandra. My luck had however recently run out, and I do not even want to think of the four or five months in Bombay before the call came from Chennai (then Madras).

To cut a long story short, I made the trip to Madras after discussing the prospect of returning to Guwahati with Krishna Raj, Editor of *EPW*, and met Mr G. Kasturi with NR sitting in, in what was clearly some sort of an interview that lasted for about half an hour. I had a feeling even during the interview that the decision had been made to recruit me, as indeed turned out to be the case. Less than a month after I returned to Bombay to wind up what had been a nomadic, *EPW* office-centric existence, I was back in Guwahati, like a homing bird that had briefly lost its bearings – immensely enriched by the experience of nearly eight years of life and work with *EPW* in Bombay, and immensely happy to be back in familiar territory.

Though I had been a journalist for eight years before joining *The Hindu*, I knew very little of daily newspaper journalism. I knew of the paper, of course, having been a more or less regular reader since my days in Dharwad (1959–61), and had been reading it professionally after I joined *EPW* in 1975. I did not know anyone working for the paper, certainly neither Mr Kasturi nor NR, though I was familiar with NR's name and had followed his reports from Washington. After the meeting with the Editor, NR took me round the office and introduced me to Mr K. Narayanan (KN), the News

Editor, informing him about my joining the paper as its North East India correspondent and left me with him. Much of the rest of the day I spent with KN, who briefed me about how the paper functioned, its history and personalities, how the issue was brought out, explaining, with the assistance of a representational sketch, the journey made by the copy received from a correspondent, from its raw state to the final product as it passed though various desks and machines, till its finished appearance in print. This last bit I was keen to know. He also took me to the office canteen and the printing press. I do not remember the details now, but I think I spent two more days in Madras, spending the whole day in the office mostly with KN, and familiariszing myself with persons and processes, marvelling at the canteen where one could eat a bellyful of food for less than a rupee – not that I was allowed to spend anything, for the friends I was making took care of such things. I also accompanied NR one evening to meet P. Sundarayya, the veteran communist leader who was under medical care at the Apollo Hospital, and shared breakfast with NR at his home, meeting his wife and young daughter.

The Guwahati I returned to in June 1983 was a very different Guwahati than I had left in December 1975, not to speak of the Guwahati I first saw in February 1962. During my earlier sojourn when I was teaching at Guwahati University (February 1962 to December 1975), it was only by courtesy that I could claim to be a resident of Guwahati, since I lived on the university campus seven miles to the west of the city. Returning twenty-one years later, I rented a house in the heart of the city, bought basic furniture and became a true resident.

NR had suggested before I left Madras that my first copy as *The Hindu*'s correspondent should be a longish analytical report on the "current political situation" in Assam. This was no bromide. I had realised even as the call from Madras came that the paper which till then did not have a full-time resident correspondent in the state was keen to have one now, for reasons obvious. The state and society of Assam, politically always in a bit of ferment, had been for the past three or four years in the grip of an agitation launched by the All Assam Students' Union (AASU) along with an umbrella organization called All Assam Gana Sangram Parishad (AAGSP) created by AASU with the stated objective to secure the removal of foreign nationals illegally residing in the state. The issue has deep historical roots going back to the period before the country's Partition; some would argue that these historical roots go back to the facts and circumstances of the "annexation/ integration" of Assam into British India, later Independent India.

The proximate cause for the agitation was the discovery that the electoral rolls of Mangaldai Lok Sabha constituency, that had fallen vacant following the death of the sitting member necessitating a by-election in 1979, had been compromised by the inclusion of the names of "suspected foreign nationals." The stand of AASU and its allies was that the by-election would not be allowed to be held till the names of "suspected foreign nationals" were deleted from the electoral rolls. This grew, over the years, into a larger demand covering all "suspected foreign nationals," that came to be known as three "D"s: Detection of suspected foreign nationals, Deletion of the names of such suspects from the electoral rolls, and Deportation (to where and how, it was never clear) of those thus detected.

However, by the time I returned to Guwahati as *The Hindu*'s correspondent, the issue of the Mangaldai Lok Sabha by-election had been overtaken by far more contentious issues: the aftermath of the forcing through in the face of violent "popular" resistance, on the stated grounds of "constitutional compulsions," of elections in February 1983 to the 126 seats in the state assembly. In the face of resistance to holding the elections and calls for boycott of polls, the outcome was a farce – a heavily bloodstained farce at that.

Literature on these issues is vast, contentious and controversial, natural as with most reading of past history and increasingly even of contemporary history. I was to some extent familiar with the issues, having been writing on such matters even when I was teaching at Guwahati University. My task now as a full-time journalist was to report and analyse these issues, in the immediate context of what came to be known, inaccurately in the media but then such is the nature of the beast, as the "anti-foreigner agitation" in Assam. I duly wrote the required article that was carried on the paper's Edit Page over two successive issues.

I had little to do with NR or indeed any other senior editorial persons in respect of my work after I formally joined the paper and started reporting. My sole contact was the News Editor to whom I marked my copy; and it was the News Editor who gave me instructions and directions on what the paper required from me.

However, I used to meet NR as well as the Editor, the News Editor and other senior editorial personnel whenever I visited Chennai on work, or while on my way to Bengaluru to attend to occasional rites of passage: a death or a marriage in the family of my nieces and a nephew, the only family I had. On such occasions the office generously enabled me make a mini *Bharat darshan* (Guwahati–Chennai–Bengaluru–Mumbai–Kolkata–Guwahati) tour, all by air and at office expense, of places where I had strong personal and professional links.

This is not the place to write about my years as *The Hindu*'s correspondent in Assam and the rest of North East India, and in South Africa where I lived for eight years (1994–2002) before returning to Guwahati and retiring. I did learn, though, after I retired as a full-time employee and settled down in Guwahati, that NR had taken the initiative to have a full-time resident correspondent of the paper, and in a serendipitous coincidence, the choice had fallen on me.

Further, early in 1994 when after over a decade of active reporting from the north-east region I yearned for a change, and deeply desired to work in the newly liberated South Africa, it was NR who spoke to Mr Ravi, then Editor of *The Hindu* (NR was then in charge of *Frontline* and other publications), and enabled my move to South Africa, where I lived and worked for nearly eight years, metaphorically the apogee of my journalistic career.

Indeed, refusing to accept my wish to "fully retire" on my return from South Africa, NR, still formally with *Frontline*, once again took the initiative to have me engaged as "an editorial consultant" on a generous retainer. During this period of "editorial consultancy," when NR became Editor-in-Chief of *The Hindu*, I had the unusual experience of being "summoned" to Chennai, the frightening word not at all appropriate to describe the two celebratory functions I attended: in September 2003 to mark the 125th anniversary of the founding of *The Hindu*, and in March 2006 for the re-launch of the redesigned *Frontline*. I also took part in the two-day consultative conference on the "redesigning" of *The Hindu* held at a resort in Mahabalipuram. I am mentioning these things for in May 2006 I had completed seventy years and had formally written to NR requesting to be relieved from the position of "editorial consultant"; but as was his wont, he did not respond to my formal written request; instead, a fresh notification of the annual renewal of the "engagement" as editorial consultant followed.

In retrospect, I am glad NR refused to countenance my request to "fully retire." It was during these years that I wrote substantially both in *The Hindu* and *Frontline* on developments in the north-east region outside Assam, in particular in Manipur, which I visited several times. Twenty-nine out of the forty-one essays that a publisher selected for inclusion in a book were written when I was an "editorial consultant."

Yes, I have reason to be grateful for the faith and confidence that NR and the Editors before him reposed in me, allowing me full freedom to function. I have other reasons, too, for being grateful to NR. He was always solicitous and helpful when persons he knew as friends or colleagues or fellow-workers fell ill. I had an inkling of this aspect of his personality when I accompanied him, probably the very evening of my interview for *The Hindu* job, to see an ailing P. Sundarayya, as I have mentioned earlier. When, late in 2006, I was diagnosed as having prostate cancer and informed the office of my decision to have surgery, NR suggested that I should travel to Chennai where he would be of help to ensure the best possible treatment at the Madras Cancer Hospital, whose head he knew well.

But then, I have never believed in seeking specialized medical assistance, having in three earlier cases of surgery (neurofibromatosis, gastritis and gall bladder) sought medical assistance locally available – Bengaluru in the first instance, and Guwahati in the other two. Prostrate cancer surgery, too, I got done in a Guwahati hospital. However, post surgery, NR arranged for consultations with the head of the Cancer Hospital in Adyar (Dr Shanta), who and whose assistants were satisfied with what had been done in Guwahati.

I am recording these little details for NR also had the capacity to be unobtrusive in offering help.

Finally, a word or two about the man. As I have noted earlier, I never worked at the office in Chennai, the Chennai office being merely a place where I renewed old friendships and always looked forward to eating at the canteen. However, during the three months between returning from Cape Town and going home in Guwahati, I had about three months to wait: for my booked luggage which I had to clear at the Madras port; and to complete the paperwork relating to my formal disengagement from *The Hindu,* meaning collecting the provident fund money and the like. During this period I resided in the Royapettah Woodlands, within walking distance of the Chennai office where I spent the whole day. I had the chance to see NR at work during this period every evening when he would walk into the newsroom and look over the "work in progress," as it were, for about an hour or two. It was then I realized what was meant by the expression, "hands on editor," used to describe NR by his colleagues in the office: active, but not peremptorily obtrusive. It has been a privilege to know him as a friend, and as a colleague, for over a quarter of a century (1983–2010).

There Is No Other Ram

Nirmal Shekar[1]

When my friend and senior from college (Madras Christian College) emailed me requesting me to write a piece on the theme "Working with N. Ram" for a collection of essays, I was at once thrilled and apprehensive. What do I say about an extraordinary media personality with whom I had worked for thirty-five long years at *The Hindu* and *Sportstar* – reporting directly to him as Sports Editor of *The Hindu* and Editor of *Sportstar* for nine out of those thirty-five years?

When an insider is asked to write about a high-achieving public intellectual and consistently truth-telling editor of Ram's stature, readers are always eager to get a glimpse of the man behind the public figure – in this case, "the other Ram." In the event, it might be a little disappointing to readers if I told them that while there are many fascinating aspects to Ram's extraordinary personality, mostly what you saw and heard in public was what the man really was. He has no secret "other" side that I, or anybody else who has worked with him, can throw light on.

Then, a few days after V.K. Ramachandran's email arrived, it struck me out of the blue. There is indeed an N. Ram that only those who have worked closely with him as journalists will know of. To get an idea of the unique persona of this exceptional human being, we need to do a thought experiment. Consider the life and times of the man, an editor *par excellence* who always spoke truth to power, while wiping clean memories of the core humanistic/journalistic values to which Ram has devoted his entire life. It might sound counter-intuitive, but you need to do something unconventional to get to the truth when you are dealing with a man quite as special as Ram.

For once you do this, an astonishing truth reveals itself to you. Even without any reference to many of the superlative qualities that most of us have deemed absolutely essential to get to the heart of his place in the world in which we live, Ram is right up there with the greatest of the greats as an editor. This is simply because, word for word, sentence for sentence, day after day after day in the trenches of today's 24/7 journalism, Ram is one of the finest editors – if not the single finest in modern times – of as authentic and independent an English-language newspaper as India has ever had.

Such a confident assessment coming from a mere Sports Editor might seem a bit of an over-reach. But for almost three-and-a-half decades I have had innumerable – and cherished – opportunities to watch him at work and to meaningfully participate in editorial discussions that went way beyond the narrow boundaries of sport. There are others more qualified than I am to write about things other than sports which are close to Ram's heart. But when he spoke on a subject – politics, history, science, anthropology, you name it – you immediately became aware that his sheer range of interests and depth of knowledge are mind-boggling. As an aesthete, too, his tastes are first-rate.

Although as a lover of sports, and particularly of cricket, he took a special interest in what hacks from my tribe filled our pages with on a daily basis, his sagacity and sheer breadth of knowledge – accommodated in a brain that had little room for any sense of superiority or condescension – converted even the most self-absorbed and naive among us into humble journalists who would always be willing to dig deeper and deeper for the truth, and present it in the right context to the readers.

When I joined the *The Hindu* and *The Sportstar* (the name of the magazine had the definite article then) as a cub reporter, I often struggled to meet the demands made by Ram, for they were nothing like what had been asked of me as a journalist until then. But what he was doing was merely easing my way into one of the most important sections of a newspaper that has always been praised for its top-notch sports coverage.

Ram could have very easily found me a misfit. But he displayed immense patience and monumental talent to help me through my early grind – which, looking back now after all these years, was no grind at all. It was a great opportunity to work alongside one of the finest and most resourceful young editors (Ram was then an Associate Editor at the newspaper) working at Kasturi and Sons Limited.

Never once did Ram give the impression that he believed he was god's gift to journalism. He was no raging egoist at or near the top of the ladder barking orders at us. He could get down to the level of the ordinary reporter or sub-editor, and with a solid grasp of what would fit in and what wouldn't, make the right decisions quickly and then applaud when you ended up doing a good job within your limitations.

His grammatical sensibilities were excellent, he had an eagle's eye for detail and his language skills were better than those of anybody working under him. On top of all this, he had enormous stamina – both mental and physical – and was fearless even in the most discouraging of situations. On the rarest of rare occasions I have seen Ram a little flustered, but even then he never lost perspective or made heat-of-the-moment errors of judgement.

He may not have been willing to delegate all too easily, but when he did, he uncannily not only found the right person but also seemed to know how to guide that person to produce his finest. And he always gave talent its due. Apart from all this, he was a mentor to many of us. Even when he knew a particular story had gone past its shelf-life or an editorial had lost context, he would find the time to edit these pieces and send them back to us so we could learn.

Sir Harold Evans, Editor of *The Sunday Times* (London) from 1967 to 1981, in his book, an essential guide to the best of English-language journalism, lists some of the top qualities of an editor:

1. A well-balanced and orderly mind
2. A cool head and not losing it when the going gets tough
3. Quickness of thought coupled with accuracy
4. Keenness, conscientiousness and ruthlessness – rightly used
5. Well-informed common sense that translates into sound judgement
6. The ability to see things from the reader's point of view
7. Familiarity with the major laws of the land concerning libel, copyright issues
8. Team spirit.

Ram has every one of these qualities and more. I have seen some of the most celebrated editors fall short in at least two or three of these categories. But not Ram. He is the quintessential "Great Editor."

On top of all this, Ram was outstanding when it came to spotting and then grooming young talent. One of the things I will always be grateful to him for is his recommendation of my name for Adjunct Professor (Sports Writing) in the Asian College of Journalism in Chennai, more than thirteen years ago. There were times when I would drop by at his room in the office or go up to him when he was left alone for a moment at a party – believe me, this was a rare occasion – when I would bring up a student's name and say that he/she was a fine young talent. In less than twenty-four hours Ram would have asked that person to see him and, most probably, assured him/her there was a place reserved for him in the Sports department of *The Hindu*.

I often go to great trouble to keep Ram's mobile number to myself. But I have not seen any other person as important as he is in society, someone whose time is very, very limited for most things, hand out his personal mobile number to Asian College of Journalism students. That is how accessible Ram is; that is how much he enjoys interacting with talented members of the younger generation.

But then, being a great editor is not just about nurturing talent. What

I have found exceptional in Ram is the manner in which he pulled average staff members up to the level he desired on a "Big News Day" in the news room, when some of our best hands happened to be off work.

Ram could be a supremely confident Editor-in-Chief and at the same time be compassionately aware of the limitations of lesser mortals who worked for him. There was a time, eleven or twelve years ago, when a huge sports scoop literally landed, by ordinary post from Sri Lanka, on Ram's lap. It was late in the evening and he called me to say that there was a big story coming up the next day. It was a letter and a 14,000-word document with graphs and statistical tables – something that required special attention and a rare ability to turn a large document into a readable 1,200-word story for the sports page, and a much shorter 300-word capsule for the front page.

Ram passed it to me and told me exactly what he had in mind. It happened to be a socially busy day for him and by the time he was through briefing me, his lovely wife Mariam had come into the news editor's room. They were already very late for a party. As suggested by him, I wrote the 1,200-word story for the sports page, but in one of those blink-of-an-eye, poor decision-making moments, I asked a colleague – who we later found out was not up to the job – to do the front page piece. When the copy landed on my desk two hours later, I literally shivered. We were on a deadline and there was only one place where that copy belonged – in the waste-bin! Ram, who came back to see if everything had gone along fine, took one look at the copy and did what he knew best. He rolled up his sleeves and churned out a 300-word gem for the front page in less than half an hour. It went under the byline 'Special Correspondent'. Little did the readers know that Ram had written it. What is more, on the way out he congratulated me on the good sports page story I had written, instead of taking me to task for delegating the front page work to the wrong person. If this didn't do to convince me about his skills as a writer and an editor – not to forget his compassion – then nothing else would.

I must say that for me, during my thirty-five years there, there was no more caring human being in the office. Hierarchy means nothing to Ram. He would be just as concerned if an attender at the office talked about a medical emergency in the family as he may be expected to be if someone from his own family did the same. He is an incomparable humanist and indefatigable champion of the underprivileged, the deprived and the plain unfortunate ones. The phrase "man with a golden heart" has been beaten to death. But employed here, it comes urgently alive and encapsulates the very essence of Ram's being.

He was also surprisingly tolerant and supportive of journalists who got into discussions outside their areas of specialization. And if he saw anything of value in their suggestions, he immediately acted on them. Once, during a morning editorial meeting, there was a discussion on an editorial on the death penalty. After Ram and the writer of the editorial had spoken to each other, I chose to butt in and refer to a masterly essay written by George Orwell from Burma, titled "A Hanging," which I had read as a student almost forty years ago. A senior colleague of ours, Nirupama Subramanian, also happened to have read it many years ago and she spent all day trying to convince Ram to acquire the reprint right for the Orwell piece and run it in the Op-Ed page. Ram phoned London, got our correspondent there to do what was needed, and then personally wrote a brilliant introduction for that exceptional piece of Orwellian magic.

It was no different when a sports-loving journalist from some other section of the paper had a good suggestion for the sports pages of *The Hindu* or *Sportstar*. When he was the Editor-in-Chief, Ram followed almost all the major sports, mostly on television – his job rarely gave him the opportunity to step out and watch the games at the grounds – and you could be sure that you rarely needed to bring him up to date during the evening news meeting on the latest developments in sports. As a former Ranji Trophy player – he played just one game for what was then Madras – Ram knows almost everything any expert might know about cricket. But he is hardly an ignoramus when it comes to tennis or football or motor racing, or any other major sport for that matter. Right in the middle of some of the most tense and serious editorial meetings on a busy news day, he would tap into his mobile or iPad and, with a pleasant smile, bring us up to date with the score at a Test match or One Day International. This had a huge psychological bonus as well, and he knew it – it eased the stress.

He is a big fan of the former Australian player and gifted cricket writer, Jack Fingleton – he also wrote on politics for the Australian newspapers – who contributed to the pages of *The Hindu* and *Sport & Pastime* for four decades. But as a professional, it was not only Fingleton's copy that Ram read fully – front page or back page or the edit page. He read almost every single word before making his decisions. He might have set impossible goals for himself, but he saw to it that he did not make unreasonable demands on those who were less gifted.

Some of the most memorable moments I spent with Ram were as a sports editorial writer. He is so good at it (the present tense is used advisedly as Ram is still writing sports columns, among other things) – both in his knowledge and love of sport, and his ability to write about it – that you sometimes don't know where to hide. Ram's coverage of the India–West

Indies Test series in India in 1974–75 is among the finest examples of sports journalism that I have come across. He has watched the last three football World Cup finals at the stadiums, and has written at least two memorable edits on his return.

His intellectual curiosity, critical thinking and knowledge of his turf are unmatched. We tend to think that good writing deserves good editors. You turn this around and it still holds good. But I don't think Ram got quite as many good writers as he deserved. Back in 1984, when I was working in Upstate New York (Albany) as a sports journalist for *The Albany Times Union*, my editor there, Harry Rosenfeld – who was City Editor at the *Washington Post* when Bob Woodward and Carl Bernstein broke the Watergate story – used to tell me that I was a "good writer" who should "learn to cut out the mayonnaise." I finally seemed to have learnt to do that from Ram on my return to *The Hindu* and Chennai.

Teaching younger journalists how to do their jobs well is one of the greatest qualities a good editor can possess. "The work of a good editor, like the work of a good teacher, is reflected in the work of others," said William Shawn, Editor of *The New Yorker* from 1952 to 1987. I am happy to say that some of my own best work was possible because Narasimhan Ram was my teacher. And I am proud, too, of the fact that some of my finest years as a sports writer were spent working for one of India's greatest editors.

NOTE

1 Nirmal Shekar wrote this in November 2015. He died on 1 February 2017. – *Editor*

Contributors

VENKATESH ATHREYA is former Professor and Head, Department of Economics, Bharathidasan University, Tiruchirapalli.

WAYNE BARRETT (July 1945 – January 2017) was senior editor of *The Village Voice*, New York and Fellow, The Nation Institute, New York.

C.P. CHANDRASEKHAR is Professor, Centre for Economic Studies and Planning, Jawaharlal Nehru University, New Delhi.

JOHN CHERIAN is Consultant/Chief of Bureau, *Frontline*, New Delhi.

NOAM CHOMSKY is Laureate Professor of Linguistics, Agnese Nelms Haury Chair, University of Arizona.

P. JACOB is Senior Managing Editor, *The Hindu*, Chennai.

T. JAYARAMAN is Professor, School of Habitat Studies, Tata Institute of Social Sciences, Mumbai.

KUMARI JAYAWARDENA is Secretary, Social Scientists' Association, Sri Lanka.

PRAKASH KARAT is a Member of the Polit Bureau, Communist Party of India (Marxist).

C.T. KURIEN is former Head of the Department of Economics, Madras Christian College and former Director, Madras Institute of Development Studies, Chennai.

PARVATHI MENON is former Regional Editor (Bengaluru) and former London Correspondent, *The Hindu*.

PRABHAKARA S. MOTNAHALLI is former North East India Correspondent and South Africa Correspondent, *The Hindu*.

SURESH NAMBATH is National Editor, *The Hindu*, Chennai.

PRABHAT PATNAIK is Professor Emeritus, Centre for Economic Studies and Planning, Jawaharlal Nehru University, New Delhi.

V.K. RAMACHANDRAN is former Professor, Economic Analysis Unit, Indian Statistical Institute, Bengaluru.

ALAN RUSBRIDGER is Principal, Lady Margaret Hall, Oxford and former Editor, *The Guardian*.

NIRMAL SHEKAR (September 1955 – January 2017) was Sports Editor, *The Hindu*, Chennai.

MADHURA SWAMINATHAN is Professor and Head, Economic Analysis Unit, Indian Statistical Institute, Bengaluru.

M.S. SWAMINATHAN is Founder Chairperson, M.S. Swaminathan Research Foundation, Chennai.

ROMILA THAPAR is Professor Emerita, Centre for Historical Studies, Jawaharlal Nehru University, New Delhi.